The Virgin Martyrs

A Hagiographical and Mystagogical Interpretation

Rev. Michael J. K. Fuller

HillenbrandBooks

Chicago / Mundelein, Illinois

Imprimatur
Francis Cardinal George, OMI, PHD
Archbishop of Chicago

Nihil Obstat
Reverend Lawrence Hennessey, MA, STD
Reverend Joseph Henchey, CSS, STD
censores deputati

THE VIRGIN MARTYRS: A HAGIOGRAPHICAL AND MYSTAGOGICAL INTERPRETATION © 2011 Archdiocese of Chicago: Liturgy Training Publications, 3949 South Racine Avenue, Chicago IL 60609; 1-800-933-1800, fax 1-800-933-7094, e-mail orders@ltp.org. All rights reserved. See our website at www.LTP.org.

Hillenbrand Books is an imprint of Liturgy Training Publications (LTP) and the Liturgical Institute at the University of Saint Mary of the Lake (USML). The imprint is focused on contemporary and classical theological thought concerning the liturgy of the Catholic Church. Available at bookstores everywhere, or through LTP by calling 1-800-933-1800 or visiting www.ltp.org. Further information about the **Hillenbrand Books** publishing program is available from the University of Saint Mary of the Lake/Mundelein Seminary, 1000 East Maple Avenue, Mundelein, IL 60060 (847-837-4542), on the Web at www.usml.edu/liturgicalinstitute, or e-mail litinst@usml.edu.

Cover image of St. Maria Goretti icon by Fr. William Hart McNichols © St. Andrei Rublev Icons.

Printed in the United States of America.

Library of Congress Control Number: PCN: 2011935276

ISBN: 9781595250223

HVM

Contents

Preface

In my first assignment as a priest I was stationed at Saint Bridget's in Loves Park, just outside of Rockford, Illinois. My first day there I made the mistake of mentioning something about Saint Bridget; I do not remember what it was I said, but it was quickly pointed out to me that I had the wrong Saint Bridget in mind. I was quietly, but strongly, told that this parish was named after the *real* Saint Bridget, Saint Bridgid of Ireland, and not that other one, from Sweden. Truth be told, I didn't even know that there was a Saint Bridget, let alone two. I had only looked up Bridget the night before, trying to show some connection, some respect for the parish, and I guess I hadn't turned the page to find out that there was another one. (Just for your knowledge: it turns out that, if you discount the spelling differences, there are two additional Saint Bridgets. One is a third Bridgid, this one a ninth-century Irish woman who followed her brother, Saint Andrew of Fiesole, to Italy and became a hermit. Legend has it that when Andrew was dying, angels came to this Bridgid and carried her to her brother's death bed.[1] The fourth Bridget is a fifth-century British saint who is said to be a princess who was martyred along with another British princess, Saint Maura. Both of these Bridgets are based mostly on local *cults* and there is very little evidence about them.)[2]

This little episode in my early priesthood actually began what would eventually become this project. As I began to preach daily, I also began to learn about the saints; each day, when there was a memorial or feast, I would look up the saint to learn what I could. And this became, for me, a real process of conversion.

Before, I really had not known much (if anything at all) about the saints. Their stories were never told to me as a kid, and in seminary, outside of the great theologian saints like Augustine, Ambrose, and Jerome, I'd had very little interest in them. But as I read about

---

1. Herbert Thurston and Donald Attwater, *Butler's Lives of the Saints*, vol. 3 (Allen, Tex.: Christian Classics, 1995), 382.

2. Ibid., 88.

them on their feast days, I began to see that their lives were teaching me how to grow closer to the Lord. Very subtly, unknowingly, their stories would pop up into my head at the most curious moments, providing a key, an insight, a way into a particular issue or problem that I was thinking about.

The stories of the saints began to connect me more and more to the Gospel. In fact, the people of Saint Bridget used to accuse me of making up these stories — forcing them to fit to the Gospel of the day, in order for me to have a story to tell. At first, after the daily Mass, someone would come up to me and say, "Father, that was very nice, but all that stuff you said about the saint, is any of that true?"

After a while, though, they stopped asking. It occurred to me that they had stopped not out of frustration but simply because the question of whether all those incredible stories were historically accurate simply did not matter as much. What was happening to me was also happening to them: we began to see the connections these stories had with the Gospel, with Christ, and we began to take their lessons to heart. In this way, the saints were acting as *mystagogues*, men and women leading us deeper into the mystery of Christ.

Later on, as I began my advanced studies in order to teach at Mundelein Seminary, I slowly came to realize that my experiences in the parish pointed to a need: we needed a method of reading, a way of placing into context these stories about the saints. I realized that I didn't have the tools or the vocabulary necessary to approach these narratives. In fact, I didn't even know whether any of the stories existed outside of the brief accounts found in *Butler's Lives of the Saints,* where the editors would give a short summary of the legend and then add the phrase, "but these accounts are highly suspect" or "hardly credible." However, these stories have been told and retold by preachers, parents, men and women, and held in esteem by the Church for over fifteen centuries. There must be more to them then examples of simpler times, of a more "pious attitude." There had to be a way of interpretation that would aid in the mystagogical role the stories of the saints play in the life of the faithful.

The problem is made even more difficult in how the lives of the saints are read today. Hagiography, I found out, was a hot topic indeed — but not among theologians. Rather, hagiography has become a new area of interest and specialization among historians and literary scholars. Within the Church, perhaps the greatest amount of work being done on hagiography is the continued work of the Bollandists, who, since the seventeenth century, have been applying modern historical methods to the texts of hagiography in a form of source criticism designed to get as close as possible to the original sources of these narratives. Of course their work is of great importance. In the end, however, no real historical biography, as we understand the term today, could ever be produced. This is due to the fact that most of these stories originated from the oral tradition and were not compiled or written down for decades, if not centuries, after the fact, and, as the Bollandists and others have shown, each new telling comes with a whole new set of presuppositions and intentions.

In my mind, the Bollandists were attempting to answer the basic question posed by both the Reformation and the cultural and intellectual movements of the Renaissance. The Renaissance's return to the classical and mythical texts showed a good deal of similarity with the lives of the saints (a concept that the late Allison Goddard Elliott explored in her book *Roads to Paradise: Reading the Lives of the Early Saints*).[3] But in comparison to the classic texts of mythology, the short summaries and legends of the lives of the saints, familiar to almost everyone in the Middle Ages, actually seemed somewhat flat and simplistic.

The Reformers, of course, had their own reasons to scoff at the notion of these "semi-divine beings" whom the Catholics appeared to worship (not appreciating the nuances of veneration). And so the Bollandists took these criticisms seriously and tried to systematically get to the bottom of things, looking for the sources and taking the historicity of the texts as a key scholarly pursuit. The results of centuries of their work are both phenomenal and quite valuable.

Within the rest of the Church, however, there has been a gradual downward slide in terms of interest in the saints. Because of the incredible, or some would say incredulous, aspects of these legends — the unbelievable, over-the-top number of miracles, the supernatural fortitude of the protagonist, the sequence of impossible occurrences and actions — a gradual dismissal of these texts occurred

---

3. Allison Goddard Elliott, *Roads to Paradise: Reading the Lives of Early Saints* (Hanover, N.H.: University Press of New England, 1994).

over the centuries,[4] culminating in the familiar phrase of the pre-Vatican II era: "You lie like a Second Nocturn," referring to the second reading of Matins, which usually told the story of the saint for that day. This growing historical awareness led the fathers of the Second Vatican Council to include in their instructions for reform of the Divine Office the command that "[t]he accounts of martyrdom or the lives of the saints are to accord with the facts of history."[5]

With the resultant so-called debunking of Saint Christopher and others caused by this reform, there was a perceptible decline in interest in the lives of the saints. This is a generalization, to be sure, but whole generations of Catholics have grown up without ever hearing these stories that were told for over a millennium, which brings us back to the need for a method that would help recover these stories.

In fact, a great deal of interest in the lives of the saints has been developing among younger Catholics and converts. People are seeking a greater connection to Catholic identity, and are discovering in the lives of the saints a great source of inspiration. These stories can lead us to a deeper relationship with the saints and with Christ, but in order for that to happen, we need to *relearn* how to understand their purpose, their function, something that many of us never really understood ourselves.

With all this in mind, I decided I needed a control group. I needed to narrow the number of saints down to a workable level, and so I choose the classification of saints known as the virgin martyrs. Why the virgin martyrs? Out of all the saints, they baffled me the most. The virgin martyrs always left me with questions, questions that seemed to coincide precisely along the lines I have been just drawing out:

- What is the purpose of their stories?
- Did people actually believe all those things, like lightning striking Saint Catherine's wheel that was meant to torture her, and instead shattering it into a million pieces, with the shrapnel killing thousands of pagans who gathered to watch her suffer? Or that Saint Cecilia spent three days bleeding out into a boiling tub of

---

4. See Sherry L. Reames, *The Legenda Aurea: A Reexamination of its Paradoxical History* (Madison: University of Wisconsin Press, 1985).

5. *Sacrosanctum concilium*, 92.

water, all the while preaching to onlookers and organizing her affairs so that her home could become a church?
• What do we do with such texts?

There are several ways in which people have read the legends of the virgin martyrs. The first way I would call the modern method. This method basically entails simply ignoring them — in other words, not reading them. This is the mentality of *"You lie like a Second Nocturn."* Here the virgin-martyr stories, along with all the other fanciful narratives belonging to other saints, are simply dismissed as tales of incredulity and sanctimonious claptrap. To readers of this ilk, these stories have no value except to remind us of the "Dark Ages" and how we live in more enlightened times.

Another way of reading these narratives I call the modern-traditional way. This we have come to know as the traditional way of reading led by preachers and priests. Here, the virgin martyrs are understood as *Martyrs of Purity*, an understanding that begins with the Church Fathers and culminates in Pope Pius XII's canonization of Maria Goretti. This understanding, always a part of the teaching of the Church, became even more predominant after the Reforms of Trent which re-categorized the virgin martyrs as *Virgins who were martyred*, instead of the original classification of *Martyrs who were virgins*.

But most of the interest in the virgin martyrs has come from secular academia; from, as I said, history and literary scholars who read the texts as historical and cultural artifacts that can reveal insights into the patristic and Middle Ages. These scholars read the virgin martyrs and other female saints in a variety of ways.

TYPE-A SCHOLARS

These are scholars who see in these texts evidence of misogyny, of rape, pornography, and male fetishes. As the medieval French scholar R. Howard Bloch has written, these stories teach that "the only good virgin — that is, the only true virgin — is a dead virgin."[6] In fact, this school of thought seems to be dominated by scholars of medieval French literature. As suggested be such titles as: *Ravishing Maidens:*

---

6. R. H. Bloch, "Chaucer's Maiden Head: 'The Physician's Tale' and the Poetics of Virginity," *Representations* 28 (1989): 120.

Writing Rape in Medieval French Literature and Law by Kathryn Gravdal of Columbia College,[7] and Simon Gaunt of Kings College, who, in *Gender and Genre in Medieval French Literature* argues that these stories are really just thinly disguised pornography.[8] Others outside of medieval French scholars, however, have also argued in this vain, such as University of Zurich professor Elizabeth Bronfen, who wrote *Over Her Dead Body: Death, Femininity, and the Aesthetic*, saying that these stories, written by men, reveal a subculture of fetishes and voyeurism.[9]

TYPE-B SCHOLARS

Here, scholars see in the virgin-martyr narratives stories of *radical resistance*. This way of reading can be seen in such authors as Katherine Lewis, of the University of Huddersfield, who has noted in several works that the virgin-martyr legends such as Katherine of Alexandria were extremely popular with both men and women, as seen in the number of books depicting her life that were mentioned in wills and other ownership documents.[10] From this Lewis concludes that these stories must have also spoken to female, and not just to male, readers. In these stories, she argues, female readers saw a strong woman who resisted male overtures of power and who had control over their own lives.

This is a reading of the legends that is supported by Jocelyn Wogan-Browne of Fordham, among others, who points out that many of these texts were written for houses of women religious. In these stories, Browne says, the women were edified by the women saints defying male authority and refusing to be treated as objects of desire and possession, instead of as a person in her own right.[11] This type of reading, however, seems a bit anachronistic and belies belief; if this

---

7. Kathryn Gravdal, *Ravishing Maidens: Writing Rape in Medieval French Literature and Law* (Philadelphia: University of Pennsylvania Press, 1991).

8. Simon Gaunt, *Gender and Genre in Medieval French Literature* (Cambridge: Cambridge University Press, 1995).

9. Elisabeth Bronfen, *Over Her Dead Body: Death, Femininity, and the Aesthetic* (Manchester: Manchester University Press, 1982).

10. Katherine J. Lewis, *The Cult of Katherine of Alexandria in Late Medieval England* (Woodbridge, Suffolk: Boydell Press, 2000).

11. Jocelyn Wogan-Browne, *Saints' Lives and Women's Literary Culture c. 1150–1300: Virginity and Its Authorizations* (New York: Oxford University Press, 2001).

were true, it would seem that such a strong and domineering male hierarchy as the clergy of those times were supposed to be, would hardly support the reading of such volatile materials.

TYPE-C SCHOLARS

In this third way of reading, scholars read these stories as archeological treasures whose secrets offer textual evidence of cultural shifts. Writers such as Jane Tibbetts Schulenburg (*Forgetful of their Sex*) [12] and Karen Winstead (*Virgin Martyrs*) [13] look at how these stories have subtly changed over the centuries, revealing nuances and developments in understanding female sanctity, and therefore reveal cultural attitudes about women in general.

The end result, however, of all these various ways of reading, whether it is modern rejectionist, historical or literary textual archeology, radical stances of independence, or even the modern traditional stance of martyrs for purity, the end result of all of these methods is that all of them actually impoverish our understanding of the virgin martyrs. In short, these various methods of reading, although more or less valid, end up reducing the saints to being one-dimensional figures. None of these interpretations seem strong enough to support the one central fact that these stories were told and retold for over 1,500 years; they were not simply preached, but read, written, and shared by lay men and women of every culture and every class. These stories must have been understood as having more than one-dimensional character plots; something else must have been seen in them. Whatever that was, it seems lost to those of us on this side of the Enlightenment.

AN ALTERNATIVE, MYSTAGOGICAL WAY

R. R. Reno, in an article from *First Things*, wrote about the status of biblical scholarship today. Although I am not qualified to comment on his opinion, one thing he wrote did seem to me to be applicable to

---

12. Jane Tibbetts Schulenburg, *Forgetful of Their Sex: Female Sanctity and Society, ca. 500–1100* (Chicago: University of Chicago Press, 1998).

13. Karen Winstead, *Virgin Martyrs: Legends of Sainthood in Late Medieval England* (Ithaca, N.Y.: Cornell University Press, 1997).

the current study of hagiography. At one point, Reno tries to summa-
rize James Kugel's conclusions:

> Whether or not one is convinced by this or that conclusion of modern
> biblical scholarship, as a tradition of reading it cannot be incorporated
> into living religious communities. There is a spiritual parting of the
> ways [Kugel] suggests, that separates ancient from modern traditions of
> interpretation. The old ways of reading involve "learning *from* the Bible,"
> while modern critical approaches end up learning *about* it. Ancient
> interpretation teaches us to live inside Scripture, modern reading keeps
> its distance.[14]

This same difference, I would argue, exists even more so between the
modern and medieval approaches to hagiography. The conclusion,
then, is that we need a way to recover, or more appropriately, discover
the purpose in reading hagiography. We need a way to read these
texts so that we can actually *learn* from them; so that we can actually
live by them as Christian disciples, so that they actually lead us even
deeper into the mystery of Christ.

What I have done in this book was to develop such a method,
such a way of reading. It is important to note that I am not trying to
recover how the ancients actually read these texts; rather, I was looking for a way for us to read these texts today. A way of recapturing
their hold on our Christian imagination so that they could edify
those of us who are living in the modern, and postmodern world.
Ironically, I found such a method in the ancients: the method of the
four senses of Scripture.

As far as I can tell, the *four senses of Scripture* has never been
applied to the reading of hagiography. But, as I hope to have shown in
this work, they can be applied in a very fruitful way. Initially, when
we read the stories of the virgin martyrs, and hear about the amazing
events — the unbelievable interventions of God and his angels, the
incredibe razor-sharp responses of these young girls to men of authority and power, the astonishing accounts of how they survive tremen-
dously horrific acts of torture — when we read all these things, our
first response is an incredulous: "WHAT?"

---

14. R. R. Reno, "The Bible Inside and Out," *First Things* (April, 2008): 14.

That response, I contend, points directly to the fact that these stories are meant to be probed deeper; they are meant to be read on different levels, on, what the Fathers would call, a spiritual level. The *four senses* allow us to approach these narratives at multiple levels of meaning—literal, historical, allegorical, moral, eschatological—all of which can stimulate our imaginations and cause us to look at our world in new ways.

Adapting Alan of Lille's image,[15] the historical sense, the structure and events of the virgin-martyr stories act as leafy boughs of the branches of the vine that is Christ; the allegorical and anagogical senses are the bright flowers that bloom with the fragrant scent, compelling us to recall Christ and our heavenly destiny; and the fruit that is brought forth from those flowers is the fruit of conversion, of the moral change, gleaned from and inspired by these stories. Highly poetic, yes, but nonetheless a true picture of what can happen.

By adopting the method of the *four senses of Scripture* to the hagiographic texts of the virgin martyrs, I believe that we have found a way to read them so that they are freed from one-dimensional understandings that diminish them to studies of sexuality and female gender roles. The layers of interpretation permitted by the *four senses* allow us to read these stories once more, in such a way that they, in Augustine's terms, delight us, teach us, and move us into action.[16]

Of course, this way of reading can be applied to other hagiographic texts, not just to my control group of the virgin martyrs. This is something that I have experienced in both preaching and in teaching others about the saints; the method of the *four senses* provides a key, not the only key, but a key that unlocks the immense complexity, the profound Christian teachings, and the beauty of holiness, that the lives of the saints can still offer us, even in this day and age.

This study, then, provides one possible answer to the question of how to read the ancient stories that have sprung up around the names of the early Christian saints in a way that might be inspiring to the contemporary Church. By focusing on the virgin martyrs, arguably the most difficult and controversial of the old stories, it is hoped

---

15. Alan of Lille, "Elucid. in Cant.," in Henri De Lubac, *Medieval Exegesis,* vol. 2, trans. Mark Sebanc (Grand Rapids, Mich.: Eerdmans, 1998), 133.

16. Augustine, *De doctrina christiana,* book IV.

that the method being proposed will demonstrate both its usefulness for recapturing the Christian imagination these stories once stimulated, and allow for a means to read and preach these stories in ways that will be helpful and edifying to the people of God.

*   *   *   *   *

As is true in any writing endeavor, this book would not have been possible without the assistance of so many people. In particular, I am grateful to Bishop Thomas Doran, Bishop of Rockford, who has generously allowed me to teach at Mundelein Seminary, and to Kevin Thornton of Hillenbrand Books. Also, I am grateful to the faculty, staff, and students of Mundelein Seminary, past and present, for their constant support, encouragement, and help, with a special note of thanks to Father Larry Hennessey.

Finally, I wish to dedicate this work to my mother, Kathleen A Fuller, 1940–2007.

Chapter 1

Recasting an Old Tool

The saints show forth every virtue in superhuman fashion . . . they make virtue attractive and ever invite Christians to seek it. Their life is indeed the concrete manifestation of the spirit of the Gospel; and, in that it makes this a sublime reality for us, legend, like all poetry, can claim a higher degree of truth than history.

Hippolyte Delehaye[1]

For over fifteen hundred years the virgin martyrs have been put forward by the Church as glorious witnesses to Christ, but today they are hardly mentioned at all. In fact, at worst, they seem to have lost their significance, or at the very least, they appear to be artifacts from an age now long gone.

Yet the stories of the virgin martyrs inspired countless works of art in the Middle Ages, Renaissance, Baroque, and Romantic periods, and many pieces of literature as well. The Anglo-Saxon poet Cynewulf's *Juliana* (c.750) is a poem about the virgin martyr Juliana, who was martyred during the Diocletian persecution; Chaucer's *Second Nun's Story* in his *Canterbury Tales* (c.1380s) is almost a word-for-word rendition of the tale of the virgin martyr Cecilia from the *Golden Legend* (c.1260), the medieval bestseller written by Jacobus de Voragine, and the Elizabethan playwright Philip Massinger's *The Virgin Martyr* (1622) is based on the legend of Saint Dorothea, just to name a few of the more obvious examples. Despite this long and illustrious past of inspiring works of art, the stories of the virgin martyrs are hardly even known today. So what is it that we are missing in our

---

1. Hippolyte Delehaye, *The Legends of the Saints. With a Memoir of the Author* (New York: Fordham University Press, 1962), 181.

neglect of these stories? Can we learn to be enriched by these stories once more?

HISTORY AND STORY

Today, a person reads the life of a saint and immediately categorizes it in terms he or she knows, as either biography or history. Since, by definition, a saint is someone who once lived, and who now is in heaven, it is natural to place what we know in terms of either of these two genres. This understanding, however, is really a product of both the Renaissance and the Reformation. With the cultural and intellectual changes that occurred in the Renaissance and the Reformation, history and biography began to be more and more clearly defined, leaving the stories of the saints to be ridiculed and dismissed as foolishness.

The most common source for the lives of the saints was called a *legenda*; the term suggests exactly what it was. *Legenda* is a gerundive of the Latin word for reading and refers to a collection of "readings"; it became a term synonymous with the anthologies of lives of the saints.[2] In fact, the historical changes in meaning of the word *legenda* track the changes in attitudes towards the lives of the saints through the Renaissance to the Modernist period of the eighteenth and early nineteenth centuries.

The humanism that arose in the Renaissance, tied to its idea of returning to the sources, made the popular versions of the stories, the *legenda*, seem to be exactly what they were, abridgements of early sources. Although artists and scholars at that time preferred the earlier, more extensive versions of the stories, they still recognized the value of a story. The word *legenda* maintained its basic meaning, but with an understanding that lent itself to the idea of literature, and not biography. The Reformers, however, saw in these lives of the saints tales of overly pious gullibility that distracted from Christ and led people into superstition and idolatry.[3] With such attacks, the term

2. This is because of the huge popularity of the *Legenda aurea*.

3. For a very detailed description of the Renaissance and Reformation attacks on the lives of the saints see Sherry L. Reames, *The Legenda Aurea: A Reexamination of its Paradoxical History* (Madison: University of Wisconsin Press, 1985). Reames's study focuses on the *Golden Legend* of Jacobus de Voragine. The fate of the *Golden Legend* can be seen as a description of the fate of the stories about the saints during the Renaissance and Reformation because the *Golden Legend* was synonymous with these stories.

legend began to take on its more familiar meaning, that of fiction
(a tale or fable). [4] This definition is later emphasized by scholars and
writers of the Enlightenment who attack "the total disregard of truth
and probability" that can be found in the lives of the saints, to quote
Edward Gibbon. [5] Here, the term legend becomes completely associated with the notions of fable. A similar change is seen in the use of
the word hagiography, which instead of simply meaning "writings on
the saints" became an adjective for unreliable, a meaning which has
continued to this day. [6]

    The lack of historical accuracy, the unsubstantiated dialogues,
and the improbable events of the narratives all contribute to the down-
fall of these stories. At one point in writing his massive *The History of
the Decline and Fall of the Roman Empire*, Edward Gibbon came to the
time of the Christian martyrs, which gave him a problem. His explanation of the problem is worth citing:

> In this general view of the persecution, which was first authorized by
> the edicts of Diocletian, I have purposely refrained from describing the
> particular sufferings and deaths of the Christian martyrs. It would have
> been an easy task, from the histories of Eusebius, from the declamations
> of Lactantius, and from the most ancient acts, to collect a long series of
> horrid and disgustful pictures, and to fill many pages with racks and
> scourges, with iron hooks, and red hot beds, and with all the variety of
> tortures which fire and steel, savage beasts and more savage execution-
> ers, could inflict on the human body. These melancholy scenes might be
> enlivened by a crowd of visions and miracles destined either to delay the
> death, to celebrate the triumph, or to discover the relics, of those canon-
> ized saints who suffered for the name of Christ. But I cannot determine
> what I ought to transcribe, till I am satisfied how much I ought to
> believe. [7]

We have inherited the same problem: what should we include in our
writings on the saints, what parts of their stories should we believe,

---

4. George V. O'Neill, "Preface," in *The Golden Legend by William Caxton* (Cambridge: Cambridge University Press, 1914), vii.

5. Edward Gibbon, *The History of the Decline and Fall of the Roman Empire*, ed. David Womersley (New York: Penguin, 1994), 1:539.

6. Thomas J. Heffernan, *Sacred Biography: Saints and Their Biographers in the Middle Ages* (New York: Oxford University Press, 1988), 55.

7. Gibbon, *The Decline and Fall of the Roman Empire*, 1:576–77.

and what part should we dismiss as fable? When hearing or reading the stories of the virgin martyrs, what is true, and what is fable? What is actually history, and what has been made up? This is such a strong question that the Church addressed it in the reforms of the Second Vatican Council.[8]

The *legenda* of the saints which were reduced to the modern concept of legends, was just one form of hagiographic writing that was used;[9] but, as the famous student of hagiography,[10] Hippolyte Delehaye, stresses,

> It is a serious mistake, and a very common one, to think that when a saint's story is declared to be legendary all is lost, that the discovery brings the saint into disrepute. Christian saints are not like Turnus or Dido. Saints have a real existence, outside written documents. Their memory is perpetuated and lives on in the very life of the Church.[11]

There is a difference, therefore, between the story of an early saint and the actual saint; a distinction that would seem to be self-evident, but has caused some confusion. "[Most] of the difficulties met in the study of hagiographical texts," Delehaye continues, "arise from the forget-

---

8. See *Sacrosanctum concilium*, 92. See also, Sacred Congregation for Divine Worship, *General Instructions to the Liturgy of the Hours*, 3.8 (no. 167). Cf. Paul VI, *Laudis canticum*.

9. The other forms of hagiography can be classified as 1) a *passion*, or *act* which were often eyewitness accounts of the martyrdom of a saint or saints. Examples would be *The Martyrdom of St. Polycarp*, and the *Acts of Perpetua and Felicity*. 2) *Vitae* or *lives* which were inspirational writings on the life of a saint written by either someone who claimed to know the saint or a near contemporary who has listened to witnesses, or even by someone centuries afterwards, examples would be Athanasius's *Life of Saint Antony*, or Jerome's *Life of Saint Paul, the Hermit*. 3) *Legenda* or legends, which were readings about a saint; these were an author's version of the story, usually based on the earlier sources. The greatest example is the *Golden Legend* by Jacobus de Voragine. Before the thirteenth century, a book containing the passions of the martyrs was referred to as a *passionary*, whereas those that reported the lives of the confessors was a *lengendary* a term that was transformed after the arrival of the *Golden Legend*. See Delehaye, *The Legends of the Saints*, 8.

10. The lines between hagiography, which are the writings on the saints, and the study of those writings have become quite blurred in the past century. Originally a hagiographer was someone who wrote a hagiographic text or in some way promoted the cults of the saints. This is how Hippolyte Delehaye saw himself and his other Bollandists. Today a hagiographer is often associated with a person who studies hagiographical writings. See Hippolyte Delehaye, *The Work of the Bollandists through the Centuries* (Princeton, N.J.: Princeton University Press, 1922). See also John Kitchen, *Saints' Lives and the Rhetoric of Gender: Male and Female in Merovingian Hagiography* (New York: Oxford University Press, 1998), 10.

11. Delehaye, *The Legends of the Saints*, xvii.

fulness of an elementary rule: the rule of not confusing the poet with the historian."[12]

This difference is a crucial point in understanding how the stories of the virgin martyrs can be still useful today. Unfortunately, most people, even scholars, continue to confuse the poet and the historian. For the past thirty years or so, the study of hagiography has been a type of textual archeology, where the stories of the saints are compared, contrasted, and analyzed to uncover the deeper, underlying currents of social history.[13] To this end, some very valuable work has been done in the area of gender studies and the study of medieval life. As such, these texts are not being considered biography or history, but as literary works in themselves, a step in the right direction. However, as John Kitchen has noted, when dealing with hagiographic texts the same questions of methodology keep coming up:

> Always the same issues arise: what to do with the swarming topoi, how miracles are to be understood, where the "historical kernels" are, and how they can be verified. These issues, to a varying extent, seem to concern all researchers, historian and literary critic alike. Yet for all the attention paid to methodology and the application of scientific, historical, or critical tools, no one has yet found any modern approach that can adequately handle the totality that is hagiographic literature.[14]

Although at times unfair, and even a bit cruel (as when he says that historians are "on the whole the most inept group of scholars ever to deal with the religious significance of the literature"),[15] Kitchen's main point deserves notice. How should scholars approach hagiographic texts? The answer, it seems, would be in a variety of ways: as historical documents;

---

12. Ibid., xviii.

13. In the case of the virgin martyrs and the virgin saints, this form of study has been prolific. Some examples: Anne Clark Bartlett, *Male Authors, Female Readers: Representation and Subjectivity in Middle English Devotional Literature* (Ithaca, N.Y.: Cornell University Press, 1995); Sarah Beckwith, *Christ's Body: Identity, Culture, and Society in Late Medieval Writings* (New York: Routledge, 1993); Kate Cooper, *The Virgin and the Bride: Idealized Womanhood in Late Antiquity* (Cambridge, Mass.: Harvard University Press, 1996); Katherine J. Lewis, "Model Girls? Virgin-Martyrs and the Training of Young Women in Late Medieval England," in Katherine J. Lewis, Noel M. James, and Kim M. Phillips, eds., *Young Medieval Women* (Phoenix Mill: Sutton Publishing, 1999); Karen A. Winstead, *Virgin Martyrs: Legends of Sainthood in Late Medieval England* (Ithaca, N.Y.: Cornell University Press, 1997).

14. Kitchen, *Saints' Lives and the Rhetoric of Gender*, 8.

15. Ibid., 11.

as sources for social history and cultural studies—the textual archeology discussed above; as sources for the theological tradition, as Marie Anne Mayeski proposes;[16] and as religious literature.

It is within this last category, hagiography as a religious literary genre, unique to itself, that a methodology of reading the narratives of the virgin martyrs can easily be developed that would reawaken the Christian imagination and open these stories to new and exciting interpretations. By reading these stories as a specific genre of literature, the poetry of each will come to the foreground and the questions of history, although important, become secondary to the impact the story can have.

A Methodology of Reading

Considering the narratives of the virgin martyrs as a form of literature raises the question of how such literature should be interpreted; in other words, what are the specific rules that pertain to the reading of a hagiographic genre? Augustine begins his *De doctrina christiana* with a similar question. "There are," he writes, "some rules for dealing with the scriptures, which I consider can be not inappropriately passed on to students, enabling them to make progress not only by reading others who have opened up the hidden secrets of the divine literature, but also by themselves opening them up to yet others again."[17] Augustine's students, of course, would be many of those who, down the centuries, wrote the stories of the virgin martyrs. As such, Augustine's insights into the reading and interpreting of scripture should also be applicable to the stories of the saints, which, after all, have a similar purpose of inspiration and edification.

Augustine begins his discussion by noting that "there are two things which all treatment of the scriptures is aiming at: a way to discover what needs to be understood, and a way to put it across to others."[18] This is accomplished by the use of signs and things, through which "we may proceed from temporal and bodily things to grasp

---

16. Marie Anne Mayeski, "New Voices in the Tradition: Medieval Hagiography Revisited," *Theological Studies* 63 (2002): 690–710.

17. Augustine, *De doctrina christiana*, Prologue I, trans. Edmund Hill, 101.

18. Ibid., I.1, 106.

those that are eternal and spiritual."[19] He was, of course, discussing
the correct use of physical things, which should be used for their
proper end—heaven, but the point can be carried over to the use of
stories as well. We take something that is known, such as the details
of a story, and through the use of the imagination, seek out what is
unknown—the moral of the story, the symbolism and hidden meanings of certain details, the possibilities presented—and we are somehow changed. D. W. Robertson, who at one time translated the *De
doctrina* and will be discussed further, once borrowed a phrase from
William Godwin, a nineteenth century political philosopher and novelist; it is a phrase that describes the impact that poetry, and therefore,
by extension, stories, can have. They can "awaken the imagination,
astound the fancy, or hurry away the soul."[20]

Of course in his treatise, Saint Augustine is discussing the
proper ways to study Sacred Scripture. But what he says about the
reading of Sacred Scriptures is also applicable to the interpretation of
the lives of the saints.

> So if it seems to you that you have understood the divine scriptures, or
> any part of them, in such a way that by this understanding you do not
> build up this twin love of God and neighbor, then you have not under-
> stood them.[21]

Saint Augustine's entire point is that all efforts at understanding should
lead to the building up of charity. The word he used was *aedificet*, that
is, edification. By implication, then, the reading of the lives of the
saints can and should be useful for the edification, the building up,
of charity. The lives of the saints can stimulate the imagination and
encourage the faithful.

Augustine's purpose of edification, of reading Scripture for
the ultimate goal of building charity, should not, however, be understood as supporting superstition or the "dumbing down" of the study
of Sacred Scripture. In other words, the building up of charity should

19. Ibid., I.4, 108.

20. D. W. Robertson, "Translator's Introduction," in *On Christian Doctrine* (Upper Saddle
River, N.J.: Prentice Hall, 1958), xv. The original context for this quote was a critique of Chaucer,
whose poem "Troilus" Godwin believed did none of these things. See W. Godwin, "Shakespeare
and Chaucer Compared," in N. Drake, ed., *Memorials of Shakespeare* (London, 1828), 262–63.

21. Augustine, *De doctrina christiana*, I.36, trans. Edmund Hill, 124.

not be seen as simply an emotional response to the Scriptures, nor is it denying the usefulness of reason or a scientific approach to studying them. The very nature of Christian charity makes it an intensely rigorous intellectual activity where one has to rethink and reprogram every aspect of how one understands the world—love your enemy is by definition a paradox. Charity is also a demanding moral challenge. Augustine is saying that the ultimate purpose of such study has to be the building up of the theological virtues, of *faith, hope,* and especially *charity.* Study of the Sacred Scriptures, therefore, cannot be simply for the sake of knowledge; it has to be more. This also holds true for the reading of the lives of the saints.

With the definition of edification as the building up of charity, we come to an understanding of the purpose the genre of hagiography can serve. The stories are vehicles that can build the virtue of charity in the reader by teaching, entertaining, and motivating him. But if the reader has lost the ability to read these stories in such a way, then the story itself loses its purpose and is reduced to a simple piece of literature. Luckily there is a long tradition of teaching reading and interpretation referred to as the *four senses of Scripture* that can be applied to recover the edifying and inspirational components of these stories.

The *Four Senses*

In his landmark study, *Medieval Exegesis,* Henri de Lubac shows how the *"four senses"* were used by medieval theologians as a method to teach the reading of the Bible. This method goes as far back as the third century to Origen, the great Alexandrian exegete, and made its way into the teaching of the Church to such an extent that it was considered part of the Tradition of the Church, or even part of revelation itself.[22] There was even a mnemonic device for students to learn the *four senses*:

The letter teaches what's been done;

Allegory—your belief;

---

22. See Henri de Lubac, *Medieval Exegesis*, vol. 1, trans. Mark Sebanc (Grand Rapids, Mich.: Eerdmans, 1998), 1–14.

Moral—what you ought to do;

Anagogy—where you will get relief.[23]

Although there is no evidence of these four senses being applied to the interpretation of the legends of the saints, it is not hard to see that all reading would have been colored by the method of the *four senses*; it would not have been possible not to be affected by such a method for it was in the air that they breathed.[24]

The use of the *four senses*, as mentioned, can be traced all the way back to the third century theologian named Origen who wrote that there are many layers of meaning within Scripture. In his homilies, he consistently used a threefold system to understand the sacred texts.[25] In the second homily on the book of *Genesis*, among other places, Origen identified these three senses of Scripture as historical, mystical, and moral.[26] The first sense is the historical; it is historical in the sense that it tells you what has happened. It is, then, the literal meaning of the words and events of the text. The second sense, according to Origen, is the mystical, or the allegorical sense, by which various elements of Scripture are read symbolically or metaphorically. Here a person, object, or experience described in one part of Scripture points to another. For example, the parting of the Red Sea in the Old Testament becomes a "type" of baptism when interpreted allegorically through the New Testament. And the third sense of Scripture for Origen was the moral or tropological sense, in which one reads a passage in terms of a lesson on how he or she should behave.

---

23. Edward Synan, "The Four 'Senses' and Four Exegetes," in Jane Dammen McAuliffe, Barry D. Walfish, and Joseph W. Goering, eds., *With Reverence for the Word: Medieval Scriptural Exegesis in Judaism, Christianity, and Islam* (Oxford: Oxford University Press, 2003), 225. This was a verse common in the Latin Middle Ages used to teach the use of the four senses of Scripture: Littera gesta docet, quid credas allegoria, Moralis quid agas, quo tendas anagogia. It is usually attributed to Nicholas of Lyra (c.1270–1349), but Henri de Lubac assigns it to the Dominican Augustine of Dacia (d. 1282). De Lubac, *Medieval Exegesis*, 1:1.

24. See James W. Earl, "Typology and Iconographic Style in Early Medieval Hagiography," in Hugh T. Keenan, *ed., Typology and English Medieval Literature* (New York: AMS Press, 1992), 105. See also Harry Caplan, *Of Eloquence: Studies in Ancient and Mediaeval Rhetoric*, ed. Anne King and Helen North (Ithaca, N.Y.: Cornell University Press, 1970), 95–96.

25. See De Lubac, *Medieval Exegesis*, 1:145–46.

26. Origen, *Homilies on Genesis*, 2.6, trans. Ronald E. Heine, vol. 71, *Fathers of the Church* (Washington, D.C.: The Catholic University of America Press, 1982), 85. See also De Lubac, *Medieval Exegesis*, 1:145.

As time went on, Origen's original three senses were expanded
and rephrased and used by many. As Henri de Lubac has demonstrated, these senses of Scripture had a profound effect which helped
shape the theology of the Middle Ages.[27] In the fourteenth of his
hugely popular *Conferences*, the fifth-century monk, John Cassian,
added to Origen's threefold senses of literal, allegorical, and moral, a
fourth sense called the anagogical. Even though Origen never speci-
fies this fourth sense, it can easily be construed from his writings.[28]
The anagogical is the eschatological sense; it is the reading of Scripture in a way that teaches one what to hope for in the second coming
of Christ and the end of the world.

As Beryl Smalley has noted in her classic work, *The Study of
the Bible in the Middle Ages*, "Cassian distinguished four scriptural
senses, one literal or historical and three spiritual; he gave an example
which caught the fancy of the middle ages and became classical."[29]
This example, found in the fourteenth conference, helps demonstrate
how the *four senses* were understood by demonstrating how the word
"Jerusalem" had four different meanings, depending upon which sense
was being used. It is worth citing in full:

> The four figures that have been mentioned converge in such a way that,
> if we want, one and the same Jerusalem can be understood in a fourfold
> manner. According to history, it is the city of the Jews. According to
> allegory, it is the Church of Christ. According to anagogy, it is the
> heavenly city of God "which is the mother of us all." According to
> tropology, it is the soul of the human being, which under this name is
> either frequently reproached or praised by the Lord.[30]

27. By saying this, I do not mean to imply a fixed structure to the *four senses*. Each theologian
(which is the same thing as a biblical scholar in the Middle Ages) worked up his own way of
describing and using the "senses of Scripture." For example, Hugh of St. Victor, in book VI.2 of
his *Didascalicon* had only the three senses found in Origen (see Jerome Taylor, *Hugh of St. Victor:
Didascalicon; a Medieval Guide to the Arts, Records of Civilization: Sources and Studies, No. 64* [New
York: Columbia University Press, 1961], 135). Gregory the Great also only had three senses, the
historical, typical, and moral, but included under the typical sense was Cassian's allegorical and
anagogical senses. See Beryl Smalley, *The Study of the Bible in the Middle Ages* (Notre Dame, Ind.:
University of Notre Dame Press, 1978), 32–35.

28. De Lubac, *Medieval Exegesis*, 1:143–54. De Lubac argues that the fourth sense, anagogy,
is derived by others (including Cassian) from various works of Origen, the principle one being
the fourth book of *De principiis*, IV.2.4.

29. Smalley, *The Study of the Bible in the Middle Ages*, 28.

30. John Cassion, *Collationes*, XIV.4, in Boniface Ramsey, O.P., trans., *The Conferences, vol.
57, Ancient Christian Writers* (New York: Paulist Press, 1997), 510.

Since these *four senses of Scripture* had a tremendous effect on the medieval imagination, it is reasonable to employ them in the reading of the virgin martyrs and to hagiographic texts in general. The narratives of the virgin martyrs, and all the saints, were used by preachers and laity alike as sources of inspiration, catechesis, and moral development. Our problem today, however, is the same as Edward Gibbon's; we have difficulty in discerning poetic truth from historic. The use of the *four senses* as a tool for reading restores the main function these narratives were employed to perform, to edify the people of God.

The Saints and Preaching

Research into medieval ownership of various books that contain the stories of the virgin martyrs shows a wide range of readers, and speaks of the popularity of these stories.[31] This is also attested to by the advice given to preachers by Bishop Maurice of Sully (1120–96), the successor to Peter Lombard as bishop of Paris, and who oversaw the bulk of the construction of the Cathedral of Notre Dame. Maurice points out the role that the stories of the saints can play in the teaching and strengthening of the faith in his book of model sermons entitled *Exsecutis superioribus sermonibus*:

> More particularly regarding [the] feast days [of the saints], it is not solely by the authority of the Scriptures or by the reasons of divine precepts that we must inform the people entrusted to us by God for their instruction, so that they might obtain the supreme and eternal good. In proclaiming the life and virtues of the saints within and beyond the Church, it is necessary for us to encourage the people carefully. Some people, in effect, are more easily led to act by way of examples rather than reason.[32]

Encouragement, instruction, obtaining the eternal good, all point to an understanding of edification and inspiration that the lives of the

---

31. Karen A. Winstead, *Chaste Passions: Medieval English Virgin Martyr Legends* (Ithaca, N.Y.: Cornell University Press, 2000), 1. See also Katherine J. Lewis, *The Cult of St Katherine of Alexandria in Late Medieval England* (Woodbridge, Suffolk: Boydell Press, 2000). Lewis demonstrates how one virgin martyr, Katherine of Alexandria, was one of the most popular saints in medieval England, citing the numerous versions of her life that have survived, how often she is mentioned in wills, and in the many guilds that were formed under her name.

32. Quoted in George Ferzoco, "The Context of Medieval Sermon Collections on Saints," in Carolyn Muessig, ed., *Preacher, Sermon and Audience in the Middle Ages* (Boston: Brill, 2002), 281.

saints can provide; these stories were a handy tool for the preacher to use, as becomes evident in the large number of model sermons that were produced.

At around the time of Maurice, there began "an explosion of sermon literature."[33] From the twelfth to the fifteenth centuries, there was a huge increase in the number of books that were compilations of model sermons, many of which were sermons on the lives of saints. As George Ferzoco notes, the sermons on the saints found in these books were dependent on many aspects of the saint's story; and so at some point or another, the preacher would have to stop and tell the story, or at least part of the story. The result of this was, Ferzoco theorizes, the need for concise, yet detailed sources for these stories. This led to the development of collections of saints' lives called *legenda*, which became synonymous with the lives of the saints.[34]

What is important to note about this development, however, is how the stories of the saints began to be a source of inspiration for both the preacher and the congregant. The preacher can be inspired to talk about moral or doctrinal issues by using an episode from a saint's life, and the people can be inspired to change their lives, or act with greater charity, or understand a teaching of the Church by such a story. It is no coincidence, then, that the rise in collections of both saints' lives, and sermons on the saints, coincided in Europe with the flood-tide of the mendicant orders, bent on preaching.

The *Golden Legend*

The greatest of the *legenda*, and arguably the major access to the stories of the early saints for medieval audiences, was the *Legenda aurea* of Jacobus de Voragine (the very book of saints read by Ignatius of Loyola during his recovery and conversion). Most of the stories of the early saints known today have, more than likely, come to us through this book. Written in the 1260s, under Jacobus's original title of *Legenda sanctorum* (*Readings on the Saints*), it came to be called the *Legenda aurea*, the *Golden Legend*, one of the most popular books in

---

33. Ibid., 280.
34. Ibid., 287–88.

medieval times.[35] In his English translation of the work (1483), William Caxton explains the change in title:

> I have submised myself to translate into English the legend of the saints which is called Legenda Aurea in Latin, that is to say the Golden Legend. For in likewise as gold is most noble above all other metals, in likewise is this Legend holden most noble above all other works.[36]

The *Golden Legend* was so popular that it outpaced other books on the saints by a margin of about forty to one; it was the "best seller" of the Middle Ages.[37] For the three centuries following its first publication, it was printed and reprinted, and translated into various languages throughout Europe. In the fifteenth century, Robert Seybolt reports, the *Golden Legend* "led the Bible" in the number of copies printed.[38] Its popularity soon spread from its original audience of preachers to educated laity with the means to afford it.

The book's title, author, and even its very existence might not have been known by the general population, who were more than likely illiterate; however, because it was a tool used by so many preachers, they surely knew the stories it contained. Barbara Fleith, in her detailed study of the history of the *Golden Legend*, discovered that Jacobus wrote it specifically to aid preachers and that it quickly became required reading for all those studying to be preachers at Dominican houses and universities. Other university students, for both religious orders and the secular clergy, used the *Golden Legend* for their preparation as preachers as well.[39]

---

35. The date of publication is hard to determine with any accuracy. In the introduction to his translation of the *Golden Legend*, William Granger Ryan places it in the 1260s; but many scholars believe it to have been written after 1249, and before 1265. There exists a complete copy of the work dated 1265. Ernest Cushing Richardson follows early scholars and places the date of publishing at 1255; see *Materials for a Life of Jacopo da Varagine* (New York: H. W. Wilson, 1935), 51ff. The most extensive research into the *Golden Legend*, to date, has been Barbara Fleith, who places the date of composition between 1252–60, although she clearly favors a date close to 1260 as possible, *Studien Zur Überlieferungsgeschichte der Lateinischen Legenda Aurea* (Bruxelles: Société des Bollandistes, 1991), 16.

36. William Caxton, "Introduction," in George V. O'Neill, ed., *The Golden Legend* (Cambridge: Cambridge University Press, 1914), 16.

37. Reames, *The Legenda Aurea*, 198. See also Fleith, *Studien*, for a detailed and exhaustive study on the numerous medieval manuscripts of the *Golden Legend* found throughout Europe.

38. Robert Francis Seybolt, "The *Legenda Aurea*, Bible, and *Historia Scholastica*," *Speculum* 21 (1946): 342.

39. Fleith, *Studien*, 429–30.

In turn, once these students were ordained, they would take the *Golden Legend* with them to their parishes and assignments as a resource for preaching. Eventually, the audience of the *Golden Legend* grew to be not only preachers using it as a source for sermons, and, of course, those who heard them preach, but also those among the laity who could read and afford copies, with whom it became a source for private, devotional reading.[40] Various printers and translators, William Caxton among them, would add and subtract certain saints in their editions of the *Golden Legend* depending on local and personal preferences, which made for a variety of stories attributed to Jacobus that he actually did not write. Today, the *Golden Legend* and its variations across nations and centuries is used by medieval scholars to study cultural and societal attitudes, by art historians to decipher paintings and other artworks depicting the saints, and even by dramatists looking into medieval plays, many of which were drawn from the stories of this widely used book.[41]

Carlo Del Corno argues that the *Legend* implanted a profound image of holiness in the consciousness of the western mind. In every aspect of the *Legend*, Del Corno points out, there can be found the central theme of Christian spirituality: the choice between life or death, good or evil, God or Satan.[42] Although this is a broad, sweeping statement, it does further emphasize the edifying aspect of hagiographic narratives. The *Golden Legend*'s portrayal of miracles and angelic appearances should not, therefore, be understood as representing a medieval superstition; rather, it should be seen as representing the Christian imagination and understanding of God acting in this world. The *Golden Legend* also shows an ideal of holiness that has Christ always as its reference point.[43] In fact, throughout the *Golden*

40. Renate Blumenfeld-Kosinski, "Review of *de la Sainteté à l'Hagiographie*," *Speculum* 78, no. 3 (2003): 880.

41. William Granger Ryan, "Introduction," in *The Golden Legend: Readings on the Saints* (Princeton, N.J.: Princeton University Press, 1993), xv.

42. Carlo Del Corno, "La 'Legenda Aurea' e la Narrativa dei Predicatori," in Giovanni Farris, Benedetto Tino Delfino, eds., *Jacopo Da Varagine: Atti del I Convegno di Studi, Varazze, 13–14 Aprile 1985* (Cogoleto [Ge.]: Edizioni SMA, 1987), 27–49.

43. Cf. Reames, *The Legenda Aurea: A Reexamination of Its Paradoxical History*. Reames argues that Jacobus's *Legenda* devalued many of the balances and nuances of earlier original *passions* and *vitae* which he used as source material. In so doing, she believes Jacobus represented the ideal of sanctity in a very narrow way. This narrow interpretation was, in fact, representative of the understanding of the hierarchy and clergy of his times. In the second half of the thirteenth

Legend one is constantly bombarded with imagery, Scripture quotes, and other signs and symbols that are meant to remind the reader of the story of Christ. Simply put, in the *Golden Legend*, we come to recognize the saints as those who retell the story of Christ in their very lives, and in hearing that story once more, we are inspired.

Saint Lucy

One important reason, then, to tell the stories of the saints is that the story of one saint often inspires another to become a saint, to grow in holiness. Such a pattern of inspiration is a common occurrence. In his *Confessions*, Augustine tells us how he still resisted giving himself fully to Christ: "I had already found the pearl of great value, and I ought to have sold all that I had and bought it. But I still held back."[44] He went to his friend, the elderly Bishop Simplicianus, the spiritual father of Ambrose, who encouraged Augustine by telling the story of Victorinus, a widely acclaimed man of learning who was awarded a statue of himself in the Roman forum. This great man in Roman society was, naturally, a worshiper of idols, but after carefully studying the Sacred Scriptures, and through conversations with Christians like Simplicianus (done in secret for Victorinus feared the loss of his reputation), he came to be a Christian. At first, he did not proclaim his faith publicly; but one day he came to fear that if he continued to deny Christ through his silence, Christ might deny him. And so he publicly made a profession of faith and was seized by "arms of love," the Church.[45]

A little later, another friend, Ponticianus, told Augustine the story of Antony, the Egyptian monk who fled to the desert and embraced a life of asceticism and prayer that has inspired every monk

---

century, a narrowing of the ideal of sanctity was emerging which defined holiness almost exclusively in terms of solitary and contemplative virtues (199). Cf. Barbara Fleith, "The Patristic Sources of the *Legenda Aurea*: A Research Report," in Irena Backus, ed., *The Reception of the Church Fathers in the West* (Leiden: Brill, 1997), 247–50. Fleith is basically sympathetic to Reames's claim, but notes that her assumption of Jacobus's sources is hardly conclusive. In fact, it seems that Jacobus relied more on earlier *legenda* which were already abbreviations of the earlier and longer sources, than previously thought. However, there are many examples in which Jacobus does enrich these texts with material from other sources, including from the earlier *passions* and *vitae*. "Few texts," Fleith concludes, "are copied absolutely word for word from a single source" (282).

44. Augustine, *Confessiones*, VIII.1, in R. S. Pine-Coffin, trans., *Confessions* (Baltimore: Penguin Books, 1961), 158.

45. Augustine, *Confessiones*, VIII.2, 159–61.

since. Ponticianus went on to tell of the countless others who followed
Antony's lead and have been living holy lives in monasteries that filled
the desert. These stories finally led Augustine into a feeling of despair
and anxiety that prompted him to say to his friend Alypius,

> What is the matter with us? What is the meaning of this story? These
> men have not had our schooling, yet they stand up and storm the gates
> of heaven while we, for all our learning, lie here groveling in this world
> of flesh and blood! Is it because they have led the way that we are
> ashamed to follow? Is it not worse to hold back?[46]

The rest of the story is well known. Augustine is propelled into the
garden where he hears a voice that says "Take and read!" He picked
up the text of Saint Paul; and once and for all, let down his resistance
and called on Saint Ambrose to baptize him.

Saint Ignatius of Loyola, many centuries later, was brought
both to a deeper faith and to his vocation, in large part, due to his
reading of the stories of the saints found in the *Golden Legend*. As his
autobiography relates, through his reading of the Lord's life (Rudolph
Saxony's *Life of Christ*) and the lives of the saints, Ignatius began to
wonder, "What if I should do what Saint Francis did, and what Saint
Dominic did?"[47] And of course, after years of deep study and prayer,
Ignatius and his companions followed these saints in holiness and
eventually founded the Society of Jesus.

The pattern of sanctity influencing sanctity is also found in
the narratives of the virgin martyrs, giving us one way in which these
hagiographic texts are meant to function. In the *Golden Legend*, we are
told how Lucy, a young girl of noble birth, heard the legend of Saint
Agatha.[48] This inspired her to take her mother on a pilgrimage to the
church of Saint Agatha where the famous virgin and martyr was buried. When they reached the Church, mother and daughter went in

46. Ibid., VIII.8, 170.

47. Ignatius of Loyola, *Autobiography*, in George E. Ganss, trans., *Ignatius of Loyola: The Spiritual Exercises and Selected Works, Classics of Western Spirituality* (New York: Paulist Press, 1991), 70.

48. The story of Saint Lucy can be found in Jacobus de Voragine, *Legenda aurea*, in Giovanni Paolo Maggioni, ed., *Millennio Medievale 6* (Tavarnuzze: SISMEL : Edizioni del Galluzzo, 1998), 1:49–52. Unless otherwise noted, all English translations of the *Legenda aurea* will come from *The Golden Legend: Readings on the Saints*, 2. vols., trans. William Granger Ryan (Princeton, NJ: Princeton University Press, 1993). In that text, Lucy's story can be found in volume 1: 27–29.

and heard the Gospel being proclaimed. The passage was from the Gospel of Saint Mark which reported the healing of the woman who suffered from bleeding for twelve years and went up to touch the hem of Jesus' cloak.[49]

Now it just so happened that Lucy's mother suffered from a similar illness. Upon hearing this particular Gospel, Lucy decided that they should stay there at the tomb of Saint Agatha and spend the night in vigil, seeking the intercession of the holy virgin martyr. Lucy's mother readily agreed, and so the two spent the night in prayer. At one point, Lucy must have fallen asleep because she met the holy Agatha in a dream. "My dear sister in Christ," Agatha addressed Lucy, "why do you pray to me for something you yourself can grant? Indeed, your mother is already cured of her affliction." After hearing this, Lucy woke up and told her mother that she was healed.

The rest of Lucy's story becomes in its own right an instrument of edification and encouragement for those who hear it. Lucy convinced her mother to allow her to renounce her engagement and to dedicate her life to Christ as a virgin, just as Agatha did before her. Mother and daughter then promptly sold Lucy's entire dowry in order to give the money to the poor. The intended groom, "being a stupid fellow," is at first tricked into helping Lucy by one of Lucy's servants who told the young man that they were selling everything in order to buy a bigger house as a wedding gift to him. Naturally thinking this was a step in the right direction, the young man enthusiastically aided Lucy in the selling of her dowry. When the truth finally dawned on him (presumably when he saw the profits being given away), the one-time suitor, as is typical in the legends of the virgin martyrs, became enraged and turned Lucy into the authorities, denouncing her as a Christian.

The story now turns to the familiar contest between the Roman authorities, in this case the consul Paschasius, and the stubborn virgin who refuses to offer sacrifice to the idols. Lucy responds to Paschasius's command to sacrifice by saying, "The sacrifice that is pleasing to God is to visit the poor and help them in their need. And since I have nothing left to offer, I offer myself to the Lord." Paschasius snaps back that Lucy should tell that foolishness to others, but he

---

49. Mk 5:25–34. All scriptural quotations are from the *Jerusalem Bible* unless otherwise noted.

abides by the decrees of his masters, and so should she. Lucy cleverly argues that just as Paschasius does not want to offend his masters, she does not want to offend God: "You want to please them; I wish to please Christ. Do then what you think will be of benefit to you, and I shall do what I think is good for me."

At this point, frustrated by this young girl's courage, Paschasius sentences Lucy to what was essentially gang rape; she is to live as a prostitute in a house of ill repute. Before the sentence could be carried out, however, God intervenes, making it impossible for anyone physically to move her. Not even a team of a thousand oxen could budge the saint from the ground she occupied. After failing in that endeavor, Paschasius orders Lucy to be tortured. The maiden is first doused in urine, thinking that this would break any magic spell that kept her from being moved. When that did not work, she was drenched in oil and set on fire; but the flames did not scathe her at all, and she went on, unharmed. Out of frustration and embarrassed that this young girl was making a mockery of them, one of Paschasius's friends plunged a dagger into Lucy's throat. "But, far from losing the power of speech," she prophesied that peace had come to the Church of Christ. That very day, she said, would see the emperor Diocletian driven from his throne. She then told the city of Syracuse, where she was suffering death, that she would be an intercessor for them as the holy Agnes was for Catania. A priest brought her communion, which she received and then died. This ordeal occurred in the year 310. Lucy was laid to rest, and a church was built over her grave in her honor, just as it was with the saint who inspired her, Saint Agatha.

Imagination and Edification

One story of saintly holiness, therefore, can lead others to sainthood; in fact, this seems to be the primary reason they have been told and retold over the two millennia of Christianity. After hearing the story of Lucy, it is easy to see how this can happen. Two aspects of her story stand out which are quite common in all the legends of the saints but which take on important dimensions when trying to understand the intent of the authors in writing the virgin-martyr narratives. The first aspect is the great dialogues between the saint and her antagonists. The second is all the miraculous events that happen within the story and those that are reported after the saint's death. Indeed, both of these aspects are common attributes of these narratives of the virgin martyrs.

Both the great dialogues and the various miracles contribute to the effect of hearing a story like Lucy's which can hardly go unnoticed. The mental picture produced by the narrative inspires, entertains, and strikes a chord with human nature. Here is a young, teenage girl, someone with no legal or moral standing within the Roman society, standing up to and verbally out-maneuvering adult, male authority. For every intimidation, every threat, every logical argument, the little girl has a valid, logical, and unflinching response. Paschasius tells her that everyone is under the command of another, including himself. Lucy responds, "Yes, that is true, but the one who commands me is of higher authority than those that command you." At one point in the interrogation, after his attempts of logical persuasion have failed, Paschasius threatens her by saying, "The sting of the whip will silence your lip!" But here too, the saint responds, "The words of God cannot be stilled!"

Paschaisius tries another tack: "So you are God?" Unfazed, Lucy is clear in her response: "No, I am the handmaid of the Lord, who said to his disciples that they would be brought before kings and governors, but they should not fear what to say, for the Holy Spirit will speak through them." "So the Holy Spirit is in you," the consul asks; and Lucy responds, "Yes, all those who live chaste lives are temples of the Holy Spirit."

Even more desperate now, Paschasius resorts to threats; "I shall have you taken to a brothel where your body will be defiled and you will loose the Holy Spirit." But Lucy is undaunted, she fears nothing. "The body is not defiled," she responds, "unless the mind consents. If you ravish me against my will, my chastity will be doubled, and the crown will be mine." And then, seizing the upper hand, the young girl turns the consul's attempts of intimidation on end. "You will never be able to force my will. As for my body, here it is, ready for every torture. What are you waiting for? Son of the devil, begin! Carry out your cruel designs!"

The reversal of roles, the comedy of phrases, the twists and turns of the dialogue all combine to both amuse us and to make us think. In such a way, the dialogue between the virgin martyr and the prosecutor, along with the other elements of the story, fulfill many of the aspects of what Saint Augustine finds necessary for eloquence. Quoting Cicero, Augustine writes,

> An eloquent man once said, you see, and what he said was true, that to be eloquent you should speak "so as to teach, to delight, to sway." Then he added, "Teaching your audience is a matter of necessity, delighting them a matter of being agreeable, swaying them a matter of victory."[50]

These three attributes of eloquence, employed in the story of Saint Lucy, provide a way of categorizing the various facets of the story and the purpose those facets serve. At various points the narrative serves to teach doctrinal and spiritual truth. For example, Lucy's insistence that her body cannot be defiled, nor could she loose her virginity without her willing it, teaches the theological understanding of virginity. As will be discussed, Augustine and others have consistently taught that virginity and purity are first and foremost spiritual attributes, above and beyond any physical considerations.[51]

Other parts of the narrative serve to delight the listener. One example is the reversal of authority, when Lucy, the little girl, dominates over Paschasius, the Roman consul, we cannot fail to be delighted and amused (unless, for some reason, we side with Paschasius). Lucy's quick wit and defiant nature, refusing to surrender what seems like a hopeless cause, also serves to delight, as well as to sway. The actions of these saints contradict what would seem to be normal, self-preserving behavior, and the audience is left to ponder the actions of Lucy and the other martyrs, thinking, "How can they go into that trial, into that arena, knowing that they will die, and yet show no sign of fear? What kind of courage, what kind of confidence do they possess?"[52]

The same holds true for the parts of the narrative that relate the miracles. To modern ears, the miraculous aspects of Lucy's tale may be a bit distracting; but these too are meant to teach, to delight, and to sway. The miracle stories not only help to demonstrate the holiness of a particular saint, but along with the dialogues and other aspects

---

50. Augustine, *De doctrina christiana*, IV.27, in John E. Rotelle, ed., Edmund Hill, trans., vol. I/11, *Teaching Christianity, The Works of Saint Augustine: A Translation for the 21st Century* (New York: New City Press, 1996), 215.

51. See Justin Martyr, *Second Apology*, XII, 44–45.

52. Justin Martyr discusses how the courage of the martyrs led him, in part, to Christ. See Justin Martyr, *Second Apology*, XII.

of the story, they teach God's faithfulness to His people. As is the case in any piece of literature, the audience is delighted when good triumphs over evil; and the miraculous provides the climax of the story where justice is restored. The miracles also sway the reader. The incredible signs and the astonishing events of the story are meant to foster an increase in the virtues of faith, hope, and especially charity in the listener, a fact reinforced in the very telling of the legend. The reader or listener of Lucy's story, standing alongside the audience found within the story, who witness Lucy's determination, and who see the miracles that happen, can develop a great devotion to both the saint and to her groom, Christ.

Application

The popularity of the virgin-martyr stories, such as Saint Lucy's, make them a wonderful "test" group for reading hagiography through the *four senses of Scripture*. The very fact that they were once regarded as very significant saints, as attested to even today by their inclusion in the Roman Canon, tied to the fact that today they are hardly known to most of the faithful, allows for the opportunity to recapture their stories in such a way that they can be both useful and edifying to present-day readers.

In the following chapters, then, the narratives of the virgin martyrs will be read through the various levels of interpretation found in the *four senses*. In order to manage the number of virgin martyrs, and to control for variations found in different texts by different authors, only those virgin martyrs mentioned in the *Golden Legend* will be examined (with the one exception of Maria Goretti). The *Golden Legend*, and its huge impact on the medieval Church, makes it a natural source for the lives of the virgin martyrs.[53]

---

53. The *Golden Legend* of Jacobus has many features that make it appropriate as a source for our narratives. In addition to its widespread usage, the *Golden Legend* offers us 1) The consistency which comes from looking at a single author, which brackets the interesting but not germane historical questions of difference between authors, origins of composition, time of writing, selections of saints in each, etc.; 2) Even though the *Golden Legend* is an abridgment of earlier legends, *vitae*, and other sources, it, nonetheless, offers more complete narratives than its modern equivalents, such as *Butler's Lives of the Saints*; and 3) because the actual number of virgin martyr saints is impossible to pinpoint, the use of the *Golden Legend* offers a limiting factor. Even here, however, there are some problems, as subsequent editors and translators added their own favorite or local saints to the original manuscript of Jacobus. To keep the confusion to a minimum, we

Again, although the *four senses of Scripture* have never been applied to the narratives of the virgin martyrs in the *Golden Legend* or any other source for the stories, there is some precedence to their being used outside of reading Sacred Scripture. In his famous letter to Congrande della Scala, to whom he apparently dedicates his third book *Paradiso*, Dante Alighieri explains that the whole *Divine Comedy* should be read through the *four senses*:

> In order to render comprehensible the things I am going to say, it must be understood that there is not just a single sense of this work; on the contrary, it may be said to be polysemous, that is, of many senses; for the first sense comes through the letter, another comes by that which is signified by the letter. And the first is designated the literal, the second however, allegorical or moral or anagogical.[54]

He goes on to explain how such a process would work. On the literal level, the *Divine Comedy* is simply about the status of the soul after death. On the spiritual levels, though, the subject is man, and how justice rewards or punishes according to what he has done through his own free will.[55]

What at first seems like another precedent for the application of the *four senses* outside of Sacred Scriptures began in the 1950s with D. W. Robertson, who, with the help of others, developed what would later be called "exegetical criticism." In truth, it quickly became known as "Robertsonianism" and was a highly controversial literary

---

will be limiting our study to those narratives of the virgin martyrs found in the critical edition of Dr. Th. Graesse, *Legenda aurea* (Osnabruck: Otto Zeller Verlag, 1969). This has been translated into English by William Granger Ryan. Details of the lives of the virgin martyrs mentioned in this document can be found under the saint's name in Ryan's translation unless otherwise noted. In the last twenty years there has been a renewed interest in the *Golden Legend* and in Jacobus de Voragine, which has been highlighted by several international conferences and a new, revised critical edition of the text by Giovanni Paolo Maggioni, 2a ed., 2 vols., *Millennio Medievale 6* (Tavarnuzze: SISMEL: Edizioni del Galluzzo, 1998).

54. "Per rendere ben comprensibili le cose che si diranno occorre sapere che il senso di quest'opera non è unico, anzi può essere definito polisemo, ossia di più significati: infatti un primo significato è quello che viene prodotto per mezzo della lettera, un altro è quello che viene prodotto per mezzo delle cose significate dalla lettera. E il primo è chiamato letterale, ma il secondo allegorico o morale o anagogico." Dante Alighieri, *Epistola a Congrande*, no. 7, ed. Enzo Cecchini, *Biblioteca Del Medioevo Latino* (Firenze: Giunti, 1995), 9. Cf. Dante Alighieri, II *Convivio*, II.1 where Dante uses the *four senses* to defend some of his poetry.

55. Dante Alighieri, *Epistola a Congrande*, numbers 8, 10.

theory.[56] Robertson saw his approach more as "historical criticism," which he defined as a "kind of literary analysis which seeks to reconstruct the intellectual attitudes and the cultural ideals of a period in order to reach a fuller understanding of its literature."[57] The way to do such an analysis, he argued, was to understand how medieval literature followed the teachings set out by Saint Augustine in *De doctrina christiana* and the use of the "spiritual senses" (the *allegorical, tropological,* and *anagogical senses*) — especially the allegorical — that were found in the medieval "glosses" on Sacred Scripture. His argument was that medieval literature was produced in a world dominated intellectually by the Church; and that to truly understand its literature, one needed to be fluent with the symbols, allegories, and typologies that were used — all of which, he argued, came from the Church.

Although rightly criticized for painting all of medieval culture with just one brush — that all medieval literature was theologically ordered — implying that all of Europe was a single, monolithic culture and stayed that way over several centuries — Robertson's approach is quite different from the method being proposed in this study.[58] And this difference is important to note. Robertson's goal was to understand a piece of literature "as it was initially presented."[59] In other words, Robertson wanted to return medieval literature to its original context, a context, he argued, that was saturated with Christian symbols and theology. As such, he turned to the medieval *Gloss* on Scripture as the primary source for an allegorical reading of medieval texts. In applying the *four senses* to the narratives of the saints, as is being proposed here, what is sought is not an attempt to find the original context of the hagiographic texts; rather, what is being sought is a way that these texts can be read in today's context. Asked another way,

---

56. See Alan T. Gaylord, "Reflections on D. W. Robertson, Jr., and 'Exegetical Criticism,'" *The Chaucer Review* 40, no. 3 (2006): 311–12.

57. D. W. Robertson, *Essays in Medieval Culture* (Princeton, NJ: Princeton University Press, 1980), 3.

58. Despite the criticism against Robertson, it is interesting to note that Julia Reinhard Lupton has argued something similar. Lupton presents the case that hagiography and the omnipresent lives of the saints, along with many of the Christian "types" or motifs such as martyrdom, trials, and suffering, had a structural effect on the secular literature of the Renaissance. Whether her arguments are convincing is beyond the expertise of this author, but it is an interesting hypothesis. See Julia Reinhard Lupton, *Afterlives of the Saints: Hagiography, Typology, and Renaissance Literature* (Stanford, Ca.: Stanford University Press, 1996).

59. Robertson, *Essays in Medieval Culture*, 84.

what meaning can these stories have for us today, in the modern and postmodern world?

Felice Lifshitz has argued that the concept of hagiography as a specific genre is an ideological construct originating in the late nineteenth and early twentieth centuries. As such, it is a tool that "had no function in the ninth, tenth, and eleventh centuries, and thus as a conceptual category did not exist. [And it] should not be anachronistically applied to [the] analysis [of those texts]."[60] This is perfectly true: the writers, preachers, and laity alike had no need for such a construction; to them, the writings on the saints served their purpose, whether that was edification, or instruction, or whatever. With the rise of historical consciousness that is present today, however, such a construction seems not only quite useful but quite necessary. Historical consciousness has allowed for an analysis of these stories which has revealed wonderful and useful insights into medieval culture and history, but the results of such a consciousness have come at a cost; it has reduced these stories to mere artifacts, and not as sources of inspiration and spiritual growth. In short, it has marginalized these stories, a conclusion supported by the Pontifical Biblical Commission:

> Historical-critical exegesis adopted, more or less overtly, the thesis of the one single meaning: A text cannot have at the same time more than one meaning. All the effort of historical-critical exegesis goes into defining "the" precise sense of this or that biblical text seen within the circumstances in which it was produced.
>
> But this thesis has now run aground on the conclusions of theories of language and of philosophical hermeneutics, both of which affirm that written texts are open to a plurality of meaning.[61]

Today, most of the scholarship being applied to hagiographic texts revolves around this *specific form* of the historical-critical method. This work is best seen in the Bollandists, the society to which Delahaye belonged. The Bollandists seek to establish critical editions of hagiographic texts, tracing the history and development of the various

---

60. Felice Lifshitz, "Beyond Positivism and Genre: 'Hagiographical Texts' as Historical Narrative," *Viator* 25 (1994): 113.

61. Pontificia Commissione Biblica, *L'interprétation de la Bible dans l'Eglise* (Vatican City: Libreria Editice Vaticana, 1993), section II B, translation in Origins 23, no. 29 (January 6, 1994): 511.

manuscripts, and analyzing the literary pieces internal to these texts in order to discover authorship, sources, and influences. In addition to the Bollandists, other scholars apply a variety of techniques, such as narrative, form, or reader-response criticisms, sociological, anthropological, literary, and historical techniques, all in an attempt to glean economic, cultural, gender, and other insights into past generations.[62] All this is quite good, and quite useful. As the Pontifical Biblical Commission states quite clearly, "The historical-critical method is the indispensible method for the scientific study of the meaning of ancient texts."[63]

The application of the *four senses* to these stories, however, is meant to stimulate our understanding even further, and in a particular way, allowing the meaning of these texts to become even more multivalent. In no way, then, does such an application deny the fruits of the historical-critical method. Simply because we interpret the Transfiguration of Christ allegorically, as a sign of the Resurrection, does not deny the historical reality of the actual event. Rather, an application of the *four senses* allows the narratives of the saints to move beyond "cultural artifacts" to be examined, categorized, and filed away as archeological evidence. The literal and spiritual senses open readers to deeper dimensions of insight which edify them, that can teach them Christian truths, and help them take delight in such truths; ultimately, the *four senses* can sway the reader of these hagiographic texts to greater and greater charity. In such ways, the application of the *four senses of Scripture* to these narratives restores them to their rightful place within the tradition of the Church.[64]

In reading the lives of these virgin martyr saints through the *four senses*, these stories can take on new meanings. Rather than being laughed at, or dismissed as foolish, or even as being seen as promoting a harmful attitude about women and sexuality, these stories can be read as strengthening and encouraging the theological virtues, and inspiring the reader to holiness. It can no longer simply be a question

---

62. Ibid., Preface, vii–ix.

63. *Origins* 23, no. 29 (January 6, 1994): 500.

64. See Pontificia Commissione Biblica, *L'interprétation de la Bible dans l'Eglise*, II A: "Reason alone cannot fully comprehend the account of these events given in the Bible. Particular presuppositions, such as the faith lived in ecclesial community and the light of the Spirit, control its interpretation. As the reader matures in the life of the Spirit, so there grows also his or her capacity to understand the realities of which the Bible speaks." *Origins* 23, no. 29 (January 6, 1994): 511.

of imitating their "good works" or their "dedication to purity," but something far more edifying—something far more transformative; it is a matter of becoming more and more like Christ. But, in order to see how a recasting of the old senses of scripture can be beneficial to the reading of the hagiographic texts of the virgin martyrs, we need to first see how these texts have been read, or to be more precise, the various ways they have been read through the centuries, beginning with today.

Chapter 2

Virgin or Martyr?
Reading in Context

You have heard, O parents, in what virtues you ought to raise and with what discipline you ought to instruct your daughters, so that you may have ones by whose merits your own sins may be forgiven. A virgin is a gift of God, a protection for her family, a priesthood of chastity.

Saint Ambrose[1]

Growing up in the generation after Vatican II, one heard all sorts of stories dealing with the "old days," stories about how nuns used to be tough, and how the days in Catholic schools had a ritual all their own. Among these stories was the sense of a universal theological curriculum. Indeed, everyone learned the same basic catechism; but in addition, the same prayers were memorized, and the same stories of the saints were told. This is not the case today. Gone are the days, it seems, when Sister would tell her classroom the stories of the heavenly saints and the glorious lives of the martyrs.

One group, in particular, seems to have gone out of favor. In a perceptive article in her book *The Cloister Walk*, Kathleen Norris describes how we have lost an appreciation for the virgin martyrs. Over the centuries the stories have been watered down to the point where their original vitality and heroism have been reduced to pious clichés. To the modern ear the stories of the virgin martyrs are voices from a past best forgotten, a time when women were subject to men;

---

1. Ambrose, *De virginibus*, I.32, in Boniface Ramsey, trans., *Ambrose, Early Church Fathers* (New York: Routledge, 1997), 82.

any reference to that time is seen as "setting women back."[2] To many contemporary scholars and laity, the promotion of the virgin martyrs as saints seems to send the message that the Church values virginity in women even to the point that they should prefer death to being raped.[3]

SAINT MARIA GORETTI

Norris provides a case in point, the story of Saint Maria Goretti, a modern virgin martyr.[4] Born in 1890 in a small village in Italy, her father, a farmer, entered into a partnership with a man named Serenelli. Serenelli and his son Alessandro moved into a room at the Goretti house and helped in the fields. Maria's father died of malaria when she was ten years old; in order to make ends meet, her mother maintained the partnership with Serenelli and his son.

"On a hot afternoon in July 1902, Mary [sic] was sitting at the top of the stairs in the cottage, mending a shirt."[5] Alessandro saw her and beckoned her into his room, as he had done many times before. Just as she always did, Maria refused his lustful advances. This time, however, Alessandro grabbed her and pulled her into his room. She struggled and tried to yell for help, but he pinned her down. She told him that she would rather die than allow him to commit such a terrible sin; he grew furious, tore her dress, and started to stab her with a long knife.

After stabbing her fourteen times, Alessandro came to his senses and ran off. A while later, Maria was found bleeding to death and taken to the hospital, but there was little the doctors could do. She remained conscious for a few hours, repeatedly forgiving her attacker. After receiving viaticum, she died. A little while later, Alessandro was found; he eventually was sentenced to thirty years in prison. At first, he was a wild and angry man; he even attacked the priest who came to visit him in prison. Later he would admit that in the years before he attacked Maria, he spent his free time reading novels and magazines that stimulated his fantasies of sex and power.

---

2. Kathleen Norris, *The Cloister Walk* (New York: Riverhead Books, 1996), 186.

3. See Norris, *The Cloister Walk*, 186–205.

4. Norris, *The Cloister Walk*, 186–205.

5. Herbert Thurston and Donald Attwater, *Butler's Lives of the Saints*, vol. 3 (Allen, Tex.: Christian Classics, 1995), 28.

After eight years in prison, he had a dream that Maria came to him, presented him with a bouquet of lilies, and forgave him. After that dream, Alessandro changed and became a new man. He was released after serving twenty-seven years, three years early due to good behavior; he eventually worked up the courage and went to Maria's mother and asked for forgiveness.[6] Maria was canonized a virgin martyr by Pope Pius XII on June 24, 1950. At her beatification three years earlier, the Pope described her as a modern-day Saint Agnes and called down "woe on all those who would corrupt the young."[7]

MARTYRS OF CHASTITY

It may appear odd that Maria Goretti is considered a martyr; usually a martyr is one who dies because she refuses to deny her faith. In the case of Maria, the issue of faith seems a little distant from the immediate events of the story. Her faith can be deduced by her understanding of the sinfulness of Alessandro's actions, and by her desire for the salvation of his soul; but technically, this is not a defense of faith. In naming Maria a martyr as well as a virgin, the Church was following an understanding established by Saint Thomas Aquinas. Aquinas stated that the motive behind martyrdom was not limited to a direct confession of the faith, but also "to any other virtue . . . that has Christ for its end."[8] As such, Maria's desire for the salvation of her attacker, and her willingness to die rather than allow him to sin in such a manner, can be understood as martyrdom. Indeed, since the canonization of Maria Goretti, the Church has beatified four others as virgin martyrs. Three are from Italy: Pierina Morosini (1931–57), Antonia Mesina (1919–35), and Teresa Bracco (1929–44). One is from Poland: Karolina Kózkówna (1898–1914). All four of these virgin martyrs have stories that parallel Maria Goretti's.

---

6. For an account of these events given by Alessandro, see Pietro DiDonato, *The Penitent* (New York: Hawthorn, 1962).

7. Pius XII, *Allocution on Maria Goretti*, April 28, 1947, *Acta Apostolicae Sedis* 39: 352–58, in Godfrey Poage, C.P., *trans., In Garments All Red*, 9–16.

8. Thomas Aquinas, *S. T.,* suppl. 96,6, ad. 9, vol. V, trans. Fathers of the English Dominican Province (Chicago: Benzinger Brothers, 1992), 2979. Another example of this application can be seen in the case of Maximilian Kolbe who was canonized on October 10, 1982, and named a *martyr of charity*. See *Acta Apostolicae Sedis* 74 (1982): 1219–24.

Blessed Pierina Morosini, for example, was a young lady who already, at the age of sixteen, took a leadership role as a catechist in her home parish located in Fiobbio, a district in the municipality of Albino, Italy. She worked as a seamstress in the local cotton mill where her co-workers had the impression that she "worked in profound union with God."[9] Pierina desired to be a religious missionary, but the circumstances of her family and their need prevented that; instead, on the advice of her spiritual director, she made private vows of chastity, obedience, and poverty and developed her own religious rule of life. At the age of twenty-six, Pierina was attacked by a young man and thrown into a hedge. On the ground, she picked up a rock to defend herself, but her attacker got control of it and used it to strike her repeatedly in the head. With her skull crushed in, he raped her. She was later found in a coma by her brother; she died two days later.

The reporting surrounding Pierina's death seems to validate Kathleen Norris's argument that the story of Saint Maria Goretti has been exploited by the Church and others to promote the virtue of chastity to the point of implying that a young girl is better off dead than raped.[10] In her life, Blessed Pierina made only one trip outside of her home region, and that was to Rome in 1947, where she attended the beatification of Maria Goretti. "When some of her friends questioned Maria's choice of death, Pierina remarked that she would do the same."[11]

A similar situation can be seen in the story of the virgin-martyr Blessed Teresa Bracco, who died in 1944 at the hands of a Nazi officer who was trying to rape her. As described by her family and friends, at the age of nine, Blessed Teresa saw a picture of the then Venerable Dominic Savio in a Salesian magazine. Under the picture was the caption "Death rather than sin," one of the four promises Dominic Savio was said to have made before his first communion, and which

9. An account of these details can be found in *L'Obsservatore Romano* (English Edition), October 5, 1987, 20. The Beatification of Pierina Morosini by John Paul II, along with two others, occurred on October 4, 1987. One of the other two was the virgin martyr Antonia Mesina, who was killed in a rape attempt in 1935.

10. Norris, *The Cloister Walk*, 223–36. This can also be seen in an article in *Lay Witness* magazine, which states that Maria Goretti "chose death when there was no other way to defend her virginal purity." See James Likoudis, "Patroness of Purity—St. Maria Goretti, Virgin and Martyr," *Lay Witness* 4, no. 4 (2002).

11. *L'Obsservatore Romano* (English Edition), October 5, 1987, 20.

became a motto for him. Blessed Teresa cut out this picture along with its caption and hung it over her bed. Eleven years later, several Nazi officers came to Teresa'a village and seized three young women, one being Teresa. One of the officers took her off to a deserted place in the woods and attempted to rape her. She struggled greatly causing the officer to choke her in fury; he then shot her twice and crushed part of her skull by kicking her in the head. [12]

In his homily at her beatification, Pope John Paul II reinforces the interpretation of the virgin martyrs as defenders of chastity, as well as Teresa's attachment to Dominic Savio's motto.

> [In] Teresa Bracco it is the virtue of chastity that shines out, and she was its champion and witness to the point of martyrdom. She was 20 years old when, during the Second World War, she chose to die rather than yield to a soldier who was threatening her virginity. That courageous stance was the logical consequence of a firm desire to remain faithful to Christ, in accordance with the intention she had several times expressed. When she learned what had happened to other young women in that time of turmoil and violence, she exclaimed without hesitation: "I would rather die than be violated!" [13]

Both cases, that of Blessed Pierina Morosini and of Blessed Teresa Bracco, echo the themes promoted in some of the popularized biographies of Maria Goretti. Typical of these "biographies" were John Carr's *Saint Maria Goretti: Martyr for Purity* and Alfred MacConastair's *The Lily of the Marshes: The Story of Maria Goretti*; [14] the lily, of course, is the traditional symbol of purity and goodness. In these biographies, this teenage girl is presented to the people of Christ as a model of chastity to be followed and called upon in times of temptation. Bishop Denis Moynihan's forward to Carr's book expresses the ideal this way:

> This life in English of the little Italian girl who died in defence of her purity in our own century should get a warm welcome from Catholics in these lands. In its pages we see, not merely a pious child, but one who practised in a notable way all the virtues which are the basis of a happy

---

12. *L'Obsservatore Romano* (English Edition), May 27, 1998, 2.

13. *Acta Apostolicae Sedis* 90, no. 12 (1998): 1010.

14. John Carr, *Saint Maria Goretti: Martyr for Purity* (Dublin: Clonmore and Reynolds, 1950); Alfred MacConastair, *Lily of the Marshes: The Story of Maria Goretti* (New York: Macmillan, 1951).

Christian home and the pledge of happy Christian unions later on . . . I should like to see this little book in the hands of every young girl of to-day, of every Child of Mary, and of every mother who is at all alive to the responsibilities of Christian motherhood and has any desire to be true to them.[15]

The Church of the 1950s, facing a rapidly changing world, saw in the witness of Maria a way to promote traditional values. Pius XII himself mentioned this at her canonization noting that, "Radical transforma-tions have upset the life of our young girls and women."[16] The story of Maria Goretti, therefore, was needed more than ever. Pope Pius XII went on to say that in Maria the "personal and supernatural val-ues" shine out, and these, in turn, help strengthen them in modern girls and women. "Those who have at heart the welfare of human society . . . must resolutely demand that the public morality protect the honor and dignity of woman."[17]

This is a theme that has been consistently held by Pius XII's suc-cessors. In his homily on the centenary of Maria Goretti's death, Pope John Paul II explicitly recalls Pius XII's words:

In the homily for her canonization, Pope Pius XII of venerable memory pointed to Maria Goretti as "the sweet little martyr of purity" because she did not break God's commandment in spite of being threatened by death. What a shining example for young people! The non-committal mindset of much of our society and culture today sometimes has a struggle to understand the beauty and value of chastity.[18]

With such statements, it would appear that the Church is defining the sanctity of the virgin martyrs as solely revolving around the virtue of chastity. Kathleen Young characterizes this interpretation in very strong language: "Young women who 'gave' their lives because of a spiritual commitment to the preservation of the hymen are held up as

---

15. Carr, *Saint Maria Goretti: Martyr for Purity*, 7–8.

16. Allocution of Pope Pius XII printed in Poage, *In Garments All Red*, 14.

17. Ibid.

18. John Paul II, "To the Bishop of Albano for the Centenary of the Death of St. Maria Goretti," Vatican: July 6, 2002. See also the homily of Pope Paul VI during his visit to the Sanctuary of Nettuno, Sept. 14, 1969.

role models. Virginity is viewed as a spiritual commitment more important than the young Catholic woman's life."[19]

A DEEPER CONTEXT

This, of course, was never the official teaching of the Church; rather the importance of virginity to the Church lies in its eschatological grounding—the focus on eternal life. It was never seen as a "spiritual commitment to the preservation of the hymen." It has to be understood that Pope Pius XII and others in the Church, including Pope John Paul II, were working within a different conception of the world. To them, the radically transforming world was one in which they saw an exponential increase of all that is debased and sinful. The great increase in novels, films, and newspapers dedicated to secular things was seen as promoting corrupt, indecent lifestyles and ideas. Maria Goretti and her remarkable stance against sin, then, stood as a great symbol against what was perceived as an ever increasingly sinful world. Her story, and her virginity, became a vehicle for fighting the onslaught of secular attitudes towards sexuality.

Open any book published in the last two centuries which mentions a virgin martyr, and one will see this emphasis. In the nineteenth century, Saint Agnes was invoked as the secondary patroness of the Arch-Sodality of Mary. Commonly referred to as the "Children of Mary," this sodality was established to help young girls throughout the world grow in virtue. Saint Agnes was seen by the founder as the perfect guide for girls who had to face a world that was hostile to purity and goodness.[20] In his popular *Lives of the Fathers, Martyrs and other Principal Saints*, Alban Butler stressed a similar theme, observing that marriage is good in itself, but those who choose voluntary chastity are practicing the more perfect virtue. "The tradition of the

---

19. Kathleen Z. Young, "The Imperishable Virginity of Saint Maria Goretti," in Pauline Bart and Eilen Geil Moran, eds., *Violence against Women: The Bloody Footprints* (Newbury Park, Ca.: Sage, 1993), 105.

20. See Right Rev. Abbot Smith, *Life of Saint Agnes, Virgin and Martyr* (London: Burns, Oates and Washbourne, 1906), 126–28. See also Margaret Visser, *The Geometry of Love: Space, Time, Mystery, and Meaning in an Ordinary Church* (New York: North Point Press, 2000). Visser recalls being a member of this sodality as a young girl growing up in Rhodesia of the 1950s (see 139–41).

Church," he writes, "has always been unanimous on this point; and among the Romans, Greeks, Syrians, and Barbarians, many holy virgins joyfully preferred torments and death to the violation of their integrity."[21] When writing about the life of Saint Lucy he added this commentary:

> There are few Lucies now-a-days among Christian ladies because sensuality, pride, and vanity are instilled into their minds by the false maxims and pernicious example of those with whom they first converse. Alas! Unless a constant watchfulness and restraint produce and strengthen good habits, the inclinations of our souls lean of their own accord toward corruption.[22]

Butler was correct that the Fathers of the Church taught that virginity was the "more perfect way." From all of this, though, it would seem that the primary focus, the key purpose in promoting the stories of saints like Maria Goretti does revolve, as the critics argue, around virginity. The importance of virginity, however, lies far beyond just the preservation of sexual purity.

THE IMPORTANCE OF VIRGINITY

In many of their works, the Church Fathers wrote of holy men and women whom they considered to be a tremendous gift to the Church. In their lives and even in their deaths, these holy ones witness to the Church's faith in Christ. First among these are the martyrs, who imitate Christ to the highest degree possible. Following them are the virgins, who witnessed to Christ in their chaste celibacy. And after them, are those who were married, who, as Saint Paul noted in his Letter to the Ephesians, echo the great mystery of Christ's love for his Church.[23] After the peace of Constantine and the apparent end to martyrdom, Saint Jerome reorders this schema by placing virginity

---

21. Alban Butler, *Lives of the Fathers, Martyrs and Other Principal Saints Compiled from Original Monuments and Other Authentic Records*, vol. 1 (London: Joseph Booker, 1833), 89.

22. Ibid., 2:1036.

23. Eph 5:21–32. The division of martyrs, virgins, and married is based on Mt 13:8, and comes from Cyprian, *De habitu virginum*, XXI. It is also found in Augustine's *De virginitate*, no. 46.

as the highest witness, followed by widows, and then those who are married.[24]

Many of the Church Fathers had a similar understanding. Several took the Parable of the Sower and read into its last line the various vocations within the Church. As Jesus explains the parable, *"And the one who received the seed in rich soil is the man who hears the word and understands it; he is the one who yields a harvest and produces now a hundredfold, now sixty, now thirty* (Mt 13:23)." And so Cyprian of Carthage, writing when the persecutions were still a threat, teaches the virgins that:

> The first fruits, that of the hundred-fold, belong to the martyrs; the second, sixty-fold, is yours [O Virgins]. Just as with the martyrs there is no thought of the flesh and of the world, and no slight and trivial and dainty struggle, so also in you, whose reward is second in the order of grace, let the power of endurance be next to theirs.[25]

Saint Augustine, in his own treatise on virginity, *De virginitate*, brings up this traditional interpretation of the hundredfold and basically accepts it. Martyrdom, the hundred-fold, is above virginity, and marriage, the thirty-fold, is below virginity in terms of the reward. However, he does think this schema is a little too simplistic:

> Or, as seems more probable to me, because God in his kindness grants many gifts, and some are greater and better than others, so that the apostle can say *aspire to the better gifts* [1 Cor 12:31], should we conclude that there are too many for them to be divided in three kinds?[26]

It is important to understand exactly what the Fathers are saying in all of this. It is not the person who receives the glory; the gift itself is the glory, and it is the gift which gives glory to God. Saint Augustine continues:

---

24. Jerome, *Epistle* XLVIII.2. In that same letter, it should be noted, Jerome defends himself against the charge of being anti-marriage.

25. Cyprian, *De habitu virginum*, XXI, in Roy J. Deferrari, ed., Sister Angela Elizabeth Keenan, S.N.D., trans., *Treatises, vol.* 51, *Fathers of the Church* (Washington, D.C.: The Catholic University of America, 1958), 49.

26. Augustine, *De virginitate*, no. 46, in John E. Rotelle, ed., Ray Kearney, trans., *Marriage and Virginity: The Excellence of Marriage, Holy Virginity, the Excellence of Widowhood, Adulterous Marriages, Continence*, vol. I/9, *The Works of Saint Augustine: A Translation for the 21st Century* (Hyde Park, N.Y.: New City Press, 1999), 98–99.

There are, therefore, many gifts, and some are more splendid and more perfect than others; each person has his own gifts. Sometimes one person receives fewer gifts but greater ones, and another receives lesser gifts but more of them.[27]

The gift of virginity, of course, was "practiced" by both men and women, but it seems to have been associated almost exclusively with women.[28] This may be due to the fact that virginity can be "verified" more easily in women than in men, or it could also be that holiness in men was construed mainly through their office in the church, as bishop, priest, or deacon. Regardless, the importance of virginity itself, whether practiced by men or women, was taught and promoted by Saint Paul (e.g., 1 Cor 7) and the Church Fathers, for example, Saints Jerome, Augustine, and especially Ambrose, who all wrote on virginity and promoted virginity as an acceptable and even virtuous alternative to marriage (sometimes to the point that they sounded almost totally against marriage). Three major images were developed in this spiritual theology of virginity: first, virginity implied the achievement of the virtue of purity; second, virgins were understood as being the brides of Christ; and third, virginity was seen as the new martyrdom. And, as will be seen in the succeeding chapters, all three of these ideas are explicitly expressed in the stories of the virgin martyrs.

VIRGINITY AND PURITY

In the classical world of pagan Rome, virginity had a special role in the religion of the empire. The Vestal Virgins were the keepers of the sacred fire which burned at the center of the city in the Forum Romanum. From the finest patrician families, they were selected between the ages of three to ten; they were expected to serve chastely for thirty years, after which they could leave the priesthood and marry, or continue on as they were. Their virginity was equated with purity, and was seen as a way of guarding the purity of the city, keeping it intact

---

27. Ibid.

28. The idea that virginity was associated with both men and women has become something of a controversy. John Bugge argues that in the early Church virginity was seen as an ideal stance for both men and women. See John Bugge, *Virginitas* (The Hague: Martinus Nijhoff, 1975). This has been argued against by several writers who see virginity as being always in the realm of female holiness. See especially, Maud Burnett McInerney, *Eloquent Virgins from Thecla to Joan of Arc* (New York: Palgrave Macmillan, 2003).

and complete.[29] The purity of the Vestal Virgins was seen as so crucial to the survival of the city that any infidelity on their part was punishable by being buried alive.[30]

The virgin in the Church, however, was seen differently; she was the contemporary equivalent of the martyr who provided a witness for the faith. As Cyprian described virgins:

> They are the flower of the tree that is the Church, the beauty and adornment of spiritual grace, the image of God reflecting the holiness of the Lord; the more illustrious part of Christ's flock.[31]

Their chastity was not a way of keeping the Church pure; rather, it was a reflection of the faith and purity of the entire Church. The virgins were also witnesses to the Church herself, as an inspiration to the faithful, and also to the world.

Contrary to both modern and classical thought, the Church Fathers emphasized that it was far more important to understand virginity *as a spiritual condition*; the physical condition of being a virgin was secondary. As Ambrose points out, "It is more tolerable to have a virgin mind than virgin flesh. Both would be good if it were possible. If it is not possible, let us at least be chaste for God and not for man."[32] In Roman religious belief, a sure sign that one of the Vestal Virgins had lost her purity was if the sacred flame she was entrusted to protect went out. This was a serious issue, as the fate of the entire city was governed by the protection of that fire.[33] In the minds of the Christian Fathers, however, much more important than physical purity was a purity of heart, an inner purity. Jerome warns the virgin Eustochium that "virginity may be lost even by a thought."[34] A few lines later, he also points out that physical virginity is not enough for salvation.

---

29. See Aulus Gellius, *Attic Nights*, 1.12.1–3, and Dionysius of Halicarnassus, *Roman Antiquities* 2.67, in Jo-Ann Shelton, ed., *As the Romans Did: A Sourcebook in Roman Social History* (New York: Oxford University Press, 1998), 427–28.

30. Johann Joachim Eschenburg, *Manual of Classical Literature*, 2nd ed., trans. N. W. Fiske (Philadelphia: Edward C. Biddle, 1847), 236.

31. Cyprian, *De habitu virginum*, III, in *Treatises*, vol. 51, *Fathers of the Church* (Washington, D.C.: The Catholic University of America, 1958), 33.

32. Ambrose, *De virginibus*, II.24, 97.

33. Dionysius of Halicarnassus, *Roman Antiquities*, 2.67.

34. Jerome, *Epistle* XXII.5, in W. H. Freemantle, trans., vol. 6, *Nicene and Post–Nicene Fathers, Second Series* (Buffalo: The Christian Literature Publishing Company, 1893), 24.

In at least one version of the story of Saint Lucy, this point is highlighted. The virgin martyr yells at her would-be rapist and persecutor, "You will never be able to force my will. As for my body, here it is, ready for every torture." Her purity rested upon her ultimate desire to remain true to Christ; her body did not cause her any concern. The teaching of Augustine is that the body is not corrupted unless the mind consents,[35] an opinion that echoes the words of Lucy when she says, "The body is not defiled unless the mind consents. If you have me ravished against my will, my chastity will be doubled and the crown will be mine."[36]

In the first book of the *City of God*, Augustine makes it very clear that virtues, such as chastity, belong to the soul and are not lost when the body is forced into an immoral act. As long as the will is strong in its intention to maintain the virtue, whatever happens to the body, the person is still virtuous. If this were not so, then virtues such as chastity would simply become attributes of the body in the same way beauty, strength, and health are used to describe the body. Virtues must be something more important than a mere description of the body.[37]

By making the connection of purity with the inner life of the soul, the early Fathers, like Jerome, were especially insistent that a virgin should work very hard to avoid the major stumbling block to her spiritual development—pride. In the same letter he wrote to Eustochium, Jerome warns, "My purpose is to show you that [in this life of virginity] you are fleeing from Sodom and that you should take warning by Lot's wife [and not look back]. . . . I would have you draw from your monastic vow not pride but fear."[38] And later in this letter he repeats this idea. "You must also be careful to avoid the snare of a passion for vainglory . . . this is a defect which few are without."[39] So the virgin must fight against vainglory, the desire to be seen and admired

---

35. Augustine, *De civitate Dei*, I.16.

36. Jacobus de Voragine, *Legenda aurea* IV, Maggioni critical edition, in William Granger Ryan, trans., vol. 1, *The Golden Legend* (Princeton, N.J., Princeton University Press, 1993), 28. Please note that the narrative of Saint Lucy actually came after Saint Augustine and that Jacobus, a great reader of Augustine, is clearly following Augustine's line of thought in the words he has given Saint Lucy.

37. Augustine, *De civitate Dei*, I.18.

38. Jerome, *Epistle* XXII.2–3, 23.

39. Ibid., XXII.27, 33.

by others, to have others praise her for what she has done. Vainglory is especially a problem because it leads directly to pride, a tendency too often found in the virgin and the clergy. This pride can easily arise from the idea that virgins are the "the more illustrious part of Christ's flock," as Cyprian described them.[40]

All this indicates that the life of virginity is a life of asceticism, one that requires a determined and constant dying to self. In this way virginity becomes a new form of martyrdom. The virgin must always remember that even though her way of life is described as the superior way, one that produces fruit a hundredfold, she is in no way exalted over others. "The fruit which is [a] hundredfold and that which is sixtyfold both spring from one seed, and that seed is chastity."[41]

A New Martyrdom

There are other selfish vices beside pride that the virgin must die to as well. In his *Banquet of Ten Virgins*, Methodius has the virgin, Thekla, who in some accounts is also a martyr, describe the glories won by those who succeed in this life of self-denial and virginity. "The virgin who first overcomes the devil and destroys his *seven heads*, wins *seven diadems* of virtue." This battle embraces the seven great contests of the virtue of chastity. The seven heads of the devil are the seven vices of luxury and incontinence, weakness and cowardice, folly and disbelief, "and all the other fruits of wickedness."[42] Although Methodius does not spell out all the vices (luxury and incontinence, for example, form one vice that receives one diadem, weakness and cowardice is another) the discipline of dying to self is clearly stated: "But if, with the help of Christ, you tear [these vices] out by the roots, you will receive the divine heads, adorned with the diadems taken from the Dragon." The "Divine Heads" is a poetic image that refers to the virtues, as opposed to the vices which "flourish by nature around the heads [of the dragon, i.e., Satan]."[43]

---

40. Cyprian, *De habitu virginum*, III.

41. Jerome, *Epistle* XXII.15, 27.

42. Methodius, *The Symposium: A Treatise on Chastity*, VIII.13, trans. Herbert Musurillo (Westminster, Md.: Newman Press, 1958), 119.

43. Ibid., 120.

The self-mastery needed in the virtuous life, which is exemplified *par excellence* in the virgin, is the redirecting of desires for something greater, for the next world. Methodius describes this through the character of Thekla:

> But those who are nimble and light of wing [those who have not fallen into their passions], soaring up into the supramundane regions above this life, see from afar things that no mortal has gazed upon, the very meadows of immortality bearing a profusion of flowers of incredible loveliness. [44]

And, like those in the heavenly meadow, those who live the noble life of virginity experience the freedom of God's children, the freedom that was meant to be lived in the Garden, before the fall.

THE FREEDOM OF THE BRIDES OF CHRIST

Virginity also carried with it freedoms from certain social norms. In the classical pagan world, for example, the Vestal Virgin, as noted, held a position of honor and respect; she was free from the authority of her father; she could own property and enter into legal agreements; she could testify without taking an oath; and she had the attendance of a *lictor*, a personal guard, whenever she went out. She could also spare condemned prisoners from the penalty of death if she looked on them while they were on the way to their execution. [45]

The freedom of the Christian virgin, however, was far different. For one thing, the Christian virgin was not tied to a specific temple. It is true that most lived in their homes with their families, in a special room or wing of the house isolated from the rest, and by the fourth century, many lived together in community in a house of one of their own who was well off, as we see in the women who were associated with Jerome during his stay in Rome. [46] They were also free to travel, unlike many women of the time. Most notable of Jerome's circle were the ascetic Paula and her virgin daughter Eustochium;

---

44. Ibid., VIII.2, 106.

45. Eschenburg, *Manual of Classical Literature*, 236.

46. Susanna Elm, *Virgins of God: The Making of Asceticism in Late Antiquity* (New York: Oxford University Press, 1994), 34–39. See also Jo Ann McNamara, *Sisters in Arms: Catholic Nuns through Two Millennia* (Cambridge, Mass.: Harvard University Press, 1996), 12.

together they followed Jerome to Bethlehem, where they established a monastery of virgins and lived a life of study and asceticism.[47] Many virgins, coming from the noble and wealthy class, went on pilgrimages, not only to the Holy Land, but even to spiritual sites where noted holy men and women were reported to live, like the deserts in Egypt. We have a firsthand account of such travels in the journals that one ascetic, Egeria, wrote for the benefit of her fellow virgins back home.[48]

There were other freedoms enjoyed by virgins as well, which Ambrose describes in his *De virginibus* and other writings to promote the life of consecrated virginity. In much of his language, and that of other Fathers too, the ideas advanced to promote the life of virginity might sound as if they were arguing against marriage entirely. The truth is that the Fathers did promote marriage; however, they were more excited about the "greater gift" of virginity. Although they praised marriage, the Fathers found it necessary to promote virginity all the more because of its rarity and level of difficulty. Everyone knew and understood marriage, even though the Fathers did preach how Christian marriage should be lived out; but virginity was different, a special vocation. Ambrose himself describes the difference between marriage and virginity as something akin to comparing apples and oranges:

> I am not discouraging marriage, then, if I enumerate the benefits of virginity. [The] latter, to be sure, is the work of a few, while the former is of all. Virginity cannot exist unless there is the possibility of being born. I am comparing good things to good things.[49]

Earlier in his treatise he writes, "By no means am I advising against marriage, but I am expatiating upon the benefits of virginity."[50] However, Ambrose does see the life of virginity as a better way, as is apparent in the end of his thought, "I am comparing good things to good things, so that what is superior may be that much more apparent."[51]

---

47. Jamesetta Kelly, O.P., *Life and Times as Revealed in the Writings of St. Jerome Exclusive of His Letters* (Washington, D.C.: The Catholic University of America Press, 1944), 136–38.

48. "*Egeria, Itinerarium,*" in George E. Gingras, trans., *Diary of a Pilgrim*, vol. 38, Ancient Christian Writers (New York: Newman Press, 1970).

49. Ambrose, *De virginibus*, I.35, 83.

50. Ibid., I.24, 79.

51. Ibid.

Jerome, and, as will be seen, Gregory of Nyssa, have a slightly different take on the differences of virginity and marriage. While both see marriage as a good thing, they agree that it is a good thing only in terms that follow the sin of Adam and Eve. "The command to increase and multiply," Jerome writes to the virgin Eustochium, "first finds fulfillment after the expulsion from paradise, after the nakedness and the fig-leaves which speak of sexual passion." And a little later, "In paradise Eve was a virgin, and it was only after the coats of skins that she began her married life." Again, like all the Fathers, he was defending a way of life few understood; he was also writing to encourage a young woman who was already living a life of virginity. He does so by showing all the possible benefits, especially the notion that, like Eve before the fall, "Now paradise is your home too. Keep therefore your birthright."[52]

Many pastors of the fourth and later centuries wrote about the life of consecrated virginity in terms that stressed how it frees a woman from the anxieties and passions that come with marriage. Freedom from these anxieties and passions is a key element in Ambrose's attempt to recruit more women to a life dedicated to Christ in virginity. Ambrose writes: "The chains of wedlock are golden. But they are chains all the same."[53] A life of virginity, of course, would free one of such worldly concerns.

Ambrose continues by showing how virginity is a way to avoid the "heavy burdens" of marriage and the obligation to please a husband. "With marriage comes lamentation," he writes. From the pains of childbirth and the trials of nursing, to the "heavy service and the slavery that binds them to their husbands," Ambrose tries to win women over to the freedoms of living a life dedicated to Christ in continence.[54]

Jerome, in a letter designed to persuade a woman named Furia not to marry again, writes, "What troubles matrimony involves you have learned in the marriage state itself. [But now] you have expelled the indigestible and unwholesome food; you have relieved a heaving stomach. Why will you again swallow what has disagreed

---

52. Jerome, *Epistle* XXII.19, 29.

53. Ambrose, *De virginitate*, 33, in James Shiel, trans., *Given to Love* (Chicago: Scepter, 1963), 89.

54. Ambrose, *De virginibus*, I.27, 80.

with you? . . . Even brute beasts and flying birds do not fall into the same snare twice."[55]

In this way, both Jerome and Ambrose are following a tried and true tactic used by many of the earlier Fathers, especially Cyprian of Carthage. "Do you wish to know from what misery the virtue of continence is free, what advantage it possesses?" he writes towards the end of his *De habitu virginum.* "You do not fear the sorrows of women and their groans; you have no fear about the birth of children, nor is your husband your master, but your Master and Head is Christ."[56] It is very important, again, to realize that in such writings, the Fathers were writing in defense of virginity against very strong opposition. The emphasis of such freedoms from "the chains of marriage" was also an attempt to recruit more young women to follow such a way of life.

Freedom from the anxieties of life is also central to Peter Brown's reading of Gregory of Nyssa's *On Virginity.*[57] This freedom, however, is far more existential than the comparatively trivial social issues that were used by Ambrose and Jerome. Unlike his virgin sister Macrina and his bishop—brother Basil, who saw a life of continence as a way of working for the poor, for Gregory, virginity was a way to escape the anxiety of time, which is interesting, given the fact that Gregory was himself married. The fate of his marriage to Theosebeia, however, is disputed. Some say that after her death, Gregory lived a celibate life, while others contend that upon Gregory's ordination to the priesthood, Theosebeia retired to the monastery of her sister-in-law, Macrina. In either case, it seems that at some point in his life

---

55. Jerome, *Epistle* LIV.4, 103.

56. Cyprian, *De habitu virginum,* XXII, 50. Several contemporary writers, such as Joyce Salisbury and Jocelyn Wogan-Browne, have examined the idea of freedom found in the theological teachings on virginity and have found that in some cases the virgins pushed for even more freedom, specifically the freedom from subordination and patriarchal control. One example the authors use to support this is the case of virgins distinguishing themselves in Carthage by not wearing the veil. This interpretation, however, seems anachronistic. As we read in Tertullian's response in *On the Veiling of Virgins,* the assertion not to wear the veil is read in spiritual terms as pride and vanity, not in male-female gender conflicts, although they certainly can be read into the text from a twenty-first century perspective. For the alternative theory, see Joyce E. Salisbury, *Church Fathers, Independent Virgins* (New York: Verso, 1991). See also, Jocelyn Wogan-Browne, *Saints' Lives and Women's Literary Culture c. 1150–1300: Virginity and Its Authorizations* (New York: Oxford University Press, 2001).

57. Peter Brown, *The Body and Society: Men, Women, and Sexual Renunciation in Early Christianity* (New York: Columbia University Press, 1988), 291–304. See also John Milbank, *The Word Made Strange: Theology, Language, Culture* (Cambridge, MA: Blackwell, 1997), 195–96.

Gregory adopted celibacy for himself.[58] For Gregory, the human soul existed in a sea of anxiety. We feel comfortable and at home in this material world; but at the same time, we are constantly yearning for something else, for something more. We are restless and try to fill that unease, which leads us to a life dominated by passions and anxieties. The greatest of these anxieties is the fear of death itself. The goal of the ascetic life, therefore, is to train one's heart to be able to overcome this great fear.

Marriage, according to Gregory's understanding, was "a consolation" for the fact that after the invention of evil by Adam, we are going to die.[59] He doesn't condemn marriage, but tries to defend the asceticism involved in the life of continence by showing that it frees one from the cares of the world.[60] Along with Saint Paul, Gregory did not think you could love the Lord with your whole heart and still be attached to the world in marriage.[61] To return to the life of paradise, to be one with God, it made sense to him that one would have to imitate life before the Fall, which meant before marriage.

Gregory's obsession with escaping the anxieties of this world allowed him to see the passions and the fear of death as conspiring to enslave the soul. Social custom teaches that the accumulation of wealth and of children will protect a person from the annihilation that comes from death, but Gregory sees the falsehood of this convention.

The radical stance of the virgin is one of independence, of freedom from the conspiracies of the world attempting to escape the certainty of death. The virgin knows differently; by renouncing the standard path of society, she escapes the tyranny of a false idea and is free to see the ultimate truth of life, which is the gift of eternal life that comes to us through the gift of the Son of God.

---

58. Burns, *Butler's Lives of the Saints*, 1:65. Theosebeia is mentioned by Gregory of Nazianzus in a letter to Gregory of Nyssa consoling him upon Theosebeia's death. See *Letter* 197, in J.- P. Migne, ed., *Patrologia graeca*, vol. XXXVII.321C–24 (Paris: 1862). Some, however, have read that letter believing that Theosebeia was Gregory of Nyssa's sister. See Anthony Meredith, *Gregory of Nyssa, The Early Church Fathers* (New York: Routledge, 1999), 2–3.

59. Gregory of Nyssa, *De virginibus*, XII.

60. Ibid., VII.

61. Ibid., IX.

THE VIRGINITY OF THE VIRGIN MARTYRS

Given all of this, it should become clear that in promoting the virgin martyrs as *martyrs of purity* there is a lot more being said than a simple defense for sexual chastity. In using the virgin martyrs to defend and promote virginity, one must always keep in mind the eschatological context in which virginity is defined. In the words of Saint Augustine, "[Virginity] belongs with the angels, and [when lived out] in corruptible flesh, it is a foretaste of eternal incorruptibility."[62] This is a thought that echoes Saint Cyprian's address to virgins, "What we shall be, already you have begun to be . . . while you remain chaste and virgins, you are equal to the angels of God."[63] The rhetoric against the "chains of wedlock" was motivational, helping others to see that this earthly life is but temporary, and that our true home is in heaven.

Of course, such an eschatological context is quite consistent with how the Church has understood the virtue of chastity. Whether practiced by the celibate, who freely chooses not to marry for the sake of the kingdom or by the single person, who refrains from sexual activity, or the married person who remains faithful to his or her spouse, chastity is the virtue which is part of the vocation of a disciple. The purity sought in chastity "increases the human person's dignity and enables him to love truly, disinterestedly, unselfishly and with respect for others."[64] It is a sharing in the one, pure, holiness of God, following Christ's teaching in the Beatitudes, where he said "Blessed are the pure of heart, for they shall see the face of God (Mt 5:8)."

Given this theological understanding, it is clear why virginity was promoted so strongly by the Church from a very early age. The eschatological witness of these holy women provided an impulse to holiness in the Church; people saw them and desired to work toward the perfection of charity in their own lives, whether they were married or single. By preaching on the freedoms that come with being a Bride of Christ, and combining those with the appeal of heroic asceticism and the desire for spiritual purity, the Fathers of the Church provided

---

62. Augustine, *De virginitate*, XIII, 74.

63. Cyprian, *De habitu virginum*, XXII, 50.

64. Sacred Congregation for the Doctrine of the Faith, *Persona humana*, December 29, 1975, nos. 11–12, See also, *Lumen* gentium, no. 42, and Aquinas, *S. T.*, II. 151, 2.

a highly eschatological argument for virginity, one that lent itself very easily to the lives of the virgin martyrs. Indeed, Ambrose, the most avid promoter of virginity, used the stories of Agnes, an unnamed virgin martyr of Antioch, and Thekla in his most famous treatise *De virginibus*.

In turn, the teaching of the Church Fathers on virginity would become a crucial component in how the stories of the virgin martyrs were told and retold. However, the focus on virginity and chastity is only half of the story, as can be deduced by the title *virgin and martyr*. Despite the emphasis on the virginity of these saints, the Church has always seen something more in the lives of the virgin martyrs.

THE COMMON OF VIRGINS

By naming Maria Goretti and those that followed virgin martyrs, the Church was instinctively following an understanding of holiness that linked these women with the great female saints of the early Church. This linkage, though, reveals a subtle shift in the Church's perception of the holiness in all of these women. Originally, the early virgin martyrs, such as Lucy, Agnes, and Agatha, were understood as first, *martyrs*, and second, as *virgins*. But in the descriptions of Maria Goretti and the others that came after her, it would seem that the emphasis had changed; now the predominant attribute seems to be *virginity*, a virginity that was cherished to the point of becoming *martyrs*.

This subtle transformation appears to be the result of a shift reflected in the very liturgy of the Church. In the Roman Rite before the Second Vatican Council, virgin martyrs were placed under the *Common of Virgins*, which, in turn, had two subcategories: one for a virgin martyr (*pro virgine et martyre*) and another for other virgins (*pro virgine tantum*).[65] In the pre-Trent liturgy, however, it was exactly the opposite. In the liturgy of the early Middle Ages, the virgin martyrs of the second through the fourth centuries were remembered much more in connection with their status as martyrs than their status as

---

65. See any of the Tridentine Sacramentaries, e.g., *Missale Romanum Ex Decreto Ss. Concilii Tridentini Restitutum S. Pii V Pontificis Maximi Jussu Editum, Clementis VIII, Urbani VIII. Et Leonis XIII. Auctoritate Recognitum.* (Rome: Sumptibus et typis Societatis S. Joannis Evang. Desclée, Lefebure et soc., 1907).

virgins. Their virginity was mentioned, but not always, and not to the same degree in which they were remembered for their martyrdom.

In the three earliest liturgical books (seventh to ninth centuries), the prayers that are attached to five of the early virgin martyrs—Agatha, Agnes, Anastasia, Cecilia, and Lucy, the five still mentioned in the Roman Canon today—the descriptive title martyr outnumbers that of virgin by a factor of almost three to one.[66] Although in some versions of the ninth-century *Gregorian Sacramentary*, there is a *Common of Virgins*, only one of the prayers found in it deals solely with virginity; all the rest use the term martyr almost exclusively—reflecting the experience that almost all the women saints venerated by the Church were martyrs.[67]

In the reform of the sanctoral calendar initiated by the Council of Trent, the association between the virgin martyrs and the *Common of Virgins* is strengthened. In the Tridentine Sacramentary of Pope Pius V, we see the results of a systematic reform not only of the liturgy, but also the classification of saints within the liturgy. Here the virgin martyrs are clearly placed under the *Common of Virgins*, and the distinction of *pro virgine et martyre* and *pro virgine tantum* is firmly established. This change may help to explain why Pope Pius XII and others during the last two centuries have interpreted the lives of the virgin martyrs in ways that emphasized their chastity.

In the Tridentine calendar, the martyrdom of a virgin is read under the rubric of her virginity; in other words, she is described first in terms of her virginity. A possible unintended consequence of this may have been that the primacy of her virginity was read as a catalyst

---

66. The first is the *Veronese Sacramentary* (often called the Leonine) originating in the seventh century, in Charles Lett Feltoe, ed., *Sacramentarium Leonianum* (Cambridge: Cambridge University Press, 1896). The second is the *Gelasian Sacramentary* from the eight century, in H. A. Wilson, ed., *The Gelasian Sacramentary. Liber Sacramentorum Romanae Ecclesiae* (Oxford: Clarendon Press, 1894). The third is the *Gregorian Sacramentary* from the ninth century, in Jean Deshusses, ed., *Le Sacrementaire Grégorien, Ses Principales Formes d'après les plus Anciens Manuscrits. Ed. Comparative* (Fribourg: Éditions Universitaires, 1971).

67. *Le Sacrementaire Grégorien, Ses Principales Formes d'après les plus Anciens Manuscrits. Ed. Comparative.* For an understanding of the history of the sanctoral calendar see Aimè Georges Martimort, *The Church at Prayer: An Introduction to the Liturgy*, vol. 4 (Collegeville, Minn.: Liturgical Press, 1985), 118–27. See also Kevin Donovan, "The Sanctoral Calendar," in Cheslyn Jones, Geoffrey Wainwright, Edward Yarnold, and Paul Bradshaw, eds., *The Study of the Liturgy* (New York: Oxford University Press, 1993), 472–84.

for martyrdom. In other words, the virgin martyrs seemed to have gone from being witnesses to Christ by their deaths (martyrs for the faith) to being witnesses to the virtue of chastity (martyrs for purity). This, of course, cannot really be verified; but along with the major changes in society and culture that have come about in the nineteenth and twentieth centuries, it could be seen as one factor in the re-reading of the virgin-martyr saints.

VIRGINITY AND MARTYRDOM

Despite this apparent shift in emphasis, the virgin martyrs have always held and continue to hold a unique place within the pantheon of saints. The stories of the virgin martyrs that come down to us through the *passiones, vitae, hymns,* and *legenda*[68] all begin with a threat to the saint's virginity by a would-be suitor, but quickly move into the context of martyrdom. The saint is turned in by her suitor, not for her refusal to marry, although that certainly causes him to desire revenge, but because she is a Christian, the only charge the state would accept. It is her Christianity, then, that leads to her being tortured and finally executed.

This sequence holds true even in the case of Maria Goretti and the other modern virgin-martyrs. They were not turned into the state for being Christian; instead they were horrendously killed for their adamant refusal to cooperate in any way with the evil, the sinfulness, of another person. In this way, like the early virgin martyrs, their virginity was not the cause of their martyrdom, as is commonly held, but a catalyst to their strong, steadfast resistance to evil which was the cause of their deaths. As attested to by none other than her attacker, Maria Goretti did not see herself as sinning; rather she knew that the sin was Alessandro's, and her one desire was to prevent *him* from sinning.[69]

It is in this way that these women can be seen as combining the two great ways of giving glory to God and to witnessing to the

---

68. *Passiones* (or Acts of the martyrs), *Vitae*, hymns, and *legenda* are all types of hagiographic texts that have developed through the tradition of the Church.

69. In 1929, Alessandro testified in the process of Maria Goretti's beatification where he stressed that "Maria's appeals had been for the safety of his soul and that she had urged him not to commit such a grave sin." Burns, *Butler's Lives of the Saints*, 7:42. Cf. DiDonato, *The Penitent.*

Church, the Body of Christ—they were both martyrs (witnesses to Christ) and virgins (models of single-hearted charity). And it is in this combination of martyrdom and virginity that the virgin martyrs still present a great gift to the Church, in and through their stories. The early stories of the virgin martyrs may not have all the credibility of historical accuracy that their modern counterparts do, nor do they try to pretend they do, but all of them, early and modern, are told as a way to inspire the Christian faithful, pointing to something far more than simple sexual purity.

Problems in Understanding the Virgin Martyrs

At a time when women's studies, gender roles, and sexuality are all university courses, when there is an increasing awareness of violence and its effects on both the victim and the perpetrator, and when sexual scandal occurs in the very ranks of the teaching authority of the Church, reading the narratives of the virgin martyrs through the *single lens* of sexual purity causes many people to be either disdainful or dismissive of the Church's teaching role. As a result, the stories of the virgin martyrs have not been told as much; they have become pious clichés of a time when misogyny, enslavement, and sex were not spoken of, and when silence and passivity were considered the appropriate demeanor of young women.

The result is that these stories are now read in a very different context, with very different conclusions being drawn. They are no longer stories told to reflect the deep and old tradition of the Church with its emphasis on growing in holiness. Now, the stories of the virgin martyrs are picked over by scholars as sources for social and gender history, and by members of the Church who favor the use of these saints to counteract a society they believe to be overly sexually charged.

The problem, however, is that for a great number of the faithful, the greater context of both virginity and martyrdom has been lost. The results of this lost is that the stories of the virgin martyrs simply do not make sense; often they are understood as the Church teaching that it is better for a young girl to be dead than to be raped, a ghastly thought that invokes righteous anger. Rightly or wrongly, the virgin martyrs have become both irrelevant and objects of ridicule. These stories should be neither. And so the question becomes, is there another way to read these stories, another way to understand them? Is there a way to hear their stories once more in a way that captures the imagination and the hope of the Christian heart? In the next four chapters, we will recast the use of the *four senses* of Scripture to do just that.

Chapter 3

Disciples of the Lord: A "Literal" Reading of the Virgin Martyrs

We are afflicted in every way, but not constrained; perplexed, but not driven to despair; persecuted, but not abandoned; struck down, but not destroyed; always carrying about in the body the dying of Jesus, so that the life of Jesus may also be manifested in our body. For we who live are constantly being given up to death for the sake of Jesus, so that the life of Jesus may be manifested in our mortal flesh.

Saint Paul[1]

The letter teaches what's been done . . .

Augustine of Dacia

According to the tradition of the *four senses of Scripture*, any reading of a text has to begin on the level of belief. As seen in the teaching of Origen, "One must believe, first of all, that the things happened as they are recounted."[2] This is the *literal sense* of a text. In both biblical reading and in hagiography, however, this leads to a problem. Many of the narratives found in the Bible, and in writings about the saints are, from an historical perspective, unbelievable. Historical and scientific research, in fact, reveals great holes in these texts which question a person's ability to believe them "as they are recounted." But the literal

---

1. 2 Cor 4:8–10.

2. Henri de Lubac, *History and Spirit: The Understanding of Scripture According to Origen*, trans. Anne Englund Nash (San Francisco: Ignatius Press, 2007), 105.

sense allows for such problems. As the Pontifical Biblical Commission attests, "When it is a question of a story, the literal sense does not necessarily imply belief that the facts recounted actually took place, for a story need not belong to the genre of history but be instead a work of imaginative fiction."[3] In such cases, the literal sense is determined by "the direction of thought expressed by the text."[4] In other words, when reading these accounts, the literal sense is achieved by suspending disbelief and following the flow of events and interpreting them as they are given meaning within the context of the story itself. This can be more easily understood by looking at a particular example, such as the narrative of Saint Agnes, virgin and martyr.

SAINT AGNES

Just as the vestal virgins maintained the sacred fire in the heart of the city, on the outside of Rome's wall, there was another temple built for the protection and health of the city. This temple was dedicated to the goddess Fortuna. She too was a virgin, who, as *Turrigera* or Tower Wearer—because of her headdress—stood at the gates of Rome just outside the *Porta Collina*. As her name Fortuna suggests, she was the Roman equivalent of the Greek goddess Tyche, the goddess of fortune. With these two temples, then, one to Vesta and the other to Fortuna, the city of Rome was seen as being well protected. "Virginity at the heart of the city, virginity at her walls: together they represented and preserved the city's integrity."[5]

With such a high regard for virginity, it is ironic that the Romans perceived a threat to their city precisely in the form of young women who dedicated themselves to such a life. Yet, according to the story of Saint Agnes, that is precisely what happened. Agnes lived on the road that leads to the temple of Fortuna, the road named *Nomentana*. She was a young, beautiful girl who decided on a virginal lifestyle as a sign of her dedication to Christ; she would become one of

---

3. Pontificia Commissione Biblica, *L'interprétation de la Bible dans l'Eglise*, IIB, trans. *Origins* 23, no. 29 (January 6, 1994): 512.

4. Ibid.

5. Margaret Visser, *The Geometry of Love: Space, Time, Mystery, and Meaning in an Ordinary Church* (New York: North Point Press, 2000), 239.

the most celebrated saints of the church.[6] She has been written about by saints, bishops, and scholars. Ambrose began his treatise on virginity, *De virginibus* (written in 377), discussing her, as well as writing a hymn to her. The great Christian poet Prudentius (348–c.413) includes her in his collections of poems in honor of the martyrs.[7] Gregory the Great, Augustine, and Jerome all mention her, and Thomas Aquinas wore her relic around his neck, which he used to cure a brother Dominican who was struck with fever.[8] Other saints down through the centuries, such as Martin of Tours, Bridget, Gertrude, the Venerable Bede, and Thérèse of Lisieux, have had a special devotion to her.[9]

Of the actual existence of Saint Agnes, virgin and martyr, there is no real doubt of both her martyrdom and the development of her cult in early sources.[10] Believed to be martyred sometime around the year 303, we have Ambrose and Prudentius writing about her at the end of the fourth century, eighty years after her death. There is also the testimony of Pope Damasus. During his reign as pontiff (366–84), Damasus paid particular attention to the tombs of the martyrs, having restored many of the shrines and having short epitaphs that he himself wrote caved into marble and placed over their tombs.[11]

6. See Rev. Thomas Shearman, C.S.S.R., *The Veneration of Saint Agnes, V.M.: "Mary's Waiting Maid"* (New York: Benzinger Brothers, 1908).

7. Prudentius, *The Poems of Prudentius*, trans. Sister M. Clement Eagan, vol. 43, *Fathers of the Church* (Washington D.C.: The Catholic University of America Press, 1962), 274–80.

8. Gregory the Great, *Homily 9*, trans. Dom David Hurst (Kalamazoo, Mich.: Cistercian Publications, 1990), 65; Ambrose, *De virginibus*, I.5, trans. Boniface Ramsey, O.P., *Ambrose, Early Church Fathers* (New York: Routledge, 1997), 74; Augustine, *Sermon 273*, in John E. Rotelle, ed., Edmund Hill, trans., vol. III/8, *The Works of Saint Augustine: A Translation for the 21st Century* (Hyde Park, N.Y.: New City Press, 1994), 19–20; and Jerome, *Epistle* CXXX.5, *in W. H. Freemantle, trans., vol. 6, Nicene and Post-Nicene Fathers, Second Series* (Buffalo: The Christian Literature Publishing Company, 1893), 262. For the story of Aquinas see Shearman, *The Veneration of Saint Agnes, V.M.: "Mary's Waiting Maid,"* 7–8.

9. Right Rev. Abbot Smith, *Life of Saint Agnes, Virgin and Martyr* (London: Burns, Oates and Washbourne, 1906), 118–22. Cf. Shearman, *The Veneration of Saint Agnes*, 3–19. Saint Thérèse de Lisieux had a sister by the name of Agnes and wrote a poem in memory of the saint called "The Responses of Saint Agnes," found in Thérèse de Lisieux, *The Poetry of Thérèse of Lisieux*, trans. Donald Kinney (Washington, D.C.: Institute of Carmelite Studies, 1996), 136–38.

10. Paul Burns, *Butler's Lives of the Saints*, vol. 1 (Collegeville, Minn.: Liturgical Press, 1998), 146.

11. Right Rev. Abbot Smith, C.R.L., *Life of Saint Agnes, Virgin and Martyr* (London: Burns, Oates and Washbourne, 1906), 6. See also Visser, *The Geometry of Love*, 211.

At Rome in 1728, during renovations of the Church of Saint Agnes Outside the Wall, which was built over Agnes's tomb, a stone was uncovered in which had been carved the words Pope Damasus had ordered inscribed over Agnes's grave. The inscription shows a familiarity with aspects of the story we will come to know:

> Tradition attests that our pious ancestors have related how, at the dreadful sound of the trumpet signal, (announcing an outburst of persecution) Agnes, still a child, was at once prepared to leave the embrace of her guardian. Valiantly and willingly she would trample underfoot the cruel threats and the rage of the tyrant, who would deliver her pure body to the flames. With the strength of a child she surmounted the intensity of fear. Stripped of her garment, her hair by miraculous profusion covered her as a new vesture, that human eyes might not gaze upon that temple of the Lord. O Thou, the object of my veneration, holy and glorious example of purity, illustrious martyr, I beseech thee, hear with favour the prayers of Damasus.[12]

An additional piece of evidence that supports the early development of Agnes's cult was discovered in 1901. During renovation at the same *Sant'Agnes fuori le Mura*, another tomb marker was found. Inscribed on this one was the name, Serena the Abbess. The marker was also dated, and reveals that Serena was an abbess of the earliest known convent in Rome which existed on the site before the year 514, the year Serena died at the age of eighty-five.[13] This convent must have been attached to what was the original church of Saint Agnes. Tradition says that the first church on the site was built by the daughter of the emperor Constantine, Constantina, shortly after Agnes's death at the beginning of the fourth century, although it must have been a different Constantina, and not the emperor's daughter, who built the basilica.[14] The dedication to Agnes, however, was not limited to the Church of the fourth century; it continued to flourish century after century as her story was told throughout the Church. "So ancient

12. Smith, *Life of Saint Agnes, Virgin and Martyr*, 115. Cf. Damasus, *Damasi Epigrammata, no.* 40, ed. Max Ihm (Lipsiae: in aedibvs B. G. Tevbneri, 1895), 43–44.

13. Smith, *Life of Saint Agnes, Virgin and Martyr*, note on 90. See also Visser, *The Geometry of Love*, 25.

14. Visser, *The Geometry of Love*, 191–95.

is the worship paid to Saint Agnes that next to the evangelists and Apostles there is no Saint whose effigy is older."[15]

The story of Saint Agnes comes to us mainly from a fifth-century Latin *Acts of St. Agnes*. Attributed to Ambrose, it actually was the work of an unknown author; it was also an expansion of an earlier story of Saint Agnes written in Greek.[16] A second anonymous *Acts of Saint Agnes*, also written in Greek, was discovered in the nineteenth century, but is simply a translation of the expanded Latin text.[17] The Latin *Acts* must have originated in the early half of the fifth century because it was quoted by Maximus of Turin sometime between the years 450 to 470 A.D.[18] Over the centuries, scholars have called into question many of the events and details depicted in these texts; but the story they contain, with all its miraculous details, has continued to be told throughout the church.[19]

In his *Golden Legend*, Jacobus de Voragine repeats the story of Saint Agnes almost word for word from the pseudo-Ambrosian text, telling us that at a very young age, Agnes decided to live a life of virginity dedicated to the Lord. Born into a Christian family, she lived with her devout parents on the outskirts of the city of Rome, on the Via Nomentana; and that "her face was beautiful, her faith more beautiful."[20]

The story goes on to tell us that on one occasion Procus, the son of Symphronius, the Prefect of Rome, caught sight of the beautiful Agnes and immediately fell in love.[21] Knowing that his father's

15. From Mrs. Jameson, *Sacred and Legendary Art*, 2nd ed. (London: 1850), 358, as quoted by both Shearman, *The Veneration of Saint Agnes, V.M.: "Mary's Waiting Maid,"* 123. Cf. Smith, *Life of Saint Agnes, Virgin and Martyr*, 124.

16. The Latin narrative can be found in *Acta Sactorum (AASS)*, January XXI.

17. See Pio Franchi de Cavalieri, *S. Agnese nella Tradizione e nella Leggenda* (Roma: 1899).

18. Maximus of Turin, *Sermon 56*, in *PL* 57:537A–642A. (See especially introductory note on 645.)

19. Parts of the Latin *Acts of St. Agnes* were used in the readings for her feast day in the Roman Breviary (January 21st) before the reforms of the Second Vatican Council. Parts of the *Acts* were also used in the veiling ceremony of nuns.

20. This narrative is derived from Jacobus de Voragine, *Legenda aurea*, Maggioni critical edition, vol. 1, 24:169–73, trans. William Granger Ryan (Princeton, N.J.: Princeton University Press, 1993), 101–4.

21. The names of both the father and the son are not found in Jacobus's account. The name of the prefect Symphronius is found in the fifth-century *Acts*, see *AASS*, Jan. XXI. The name of the son, Procus, enters into tradition from a poem by Saint Aldhelm. See Smith, *Life of Saint Agnes, Virgin and Martyr*, 35.

position made him a good catch for any woman, Procus immediately went up to Agnes and offered her great wealth if she would marry him. Upon her refusal, he began to beg Agnes to marry him, "offering her houses, riches, and luxury, as well as the power of being a member of the prefect's family, if she would agree."[22] Her continued refusal was something that probably never even entered his mind.

"Be gone from me," Agnes told him. "Go away you spark that lights the fire of sin, you fuel of wickedness, you food of death! I am already pledged to another lover!" When asked about this other lover, Agnes laid out a devastating list of qualities: "He is far nobler than any person, and has offered me wealth that cannot be measured. His virtue surpasses all. His mother was a virgin and his father knows no woman; he is served by angels and even the sun and the moon wonder at his beauty."

After hearing her adamant refusal, the young man went home and became so despondent that his father called for a doctor. The doctor soon learned the reason and told the father that the young man suffered from love sickness. Learning from his son the name of the cause for such misery, the father, Symphronius, went to Agnes to tell her of his son's devotion. She replied that she was sorry for him, but nothing could induce her to break her covenant with her betrothed. Symphronius then pressed for the name of this rival, but Agnes remained silent. He later learned from someone else that Agnes's betrothed was Christ, and that she was, in fact, a Christian.

The prefect decided to use this piece of knowledge as a bargaining chip to persuade Agnes to marry his son. If she continued to refuse his son, then she would have just two choices: either she would maintain her precious virginity in an acceptable way, by joining the Vestal Virgins and sacrifice to the goddess Vesta; or she would lose her virginity by being placed into a brothel. The choice was hers. Agnes responded strongly: "I will not sacrifice to your gods, and no one can sully my virtue because I have with me a guardian of my body, an angel of the Lord."

At this point the prefect, seeing his failure at trying to intimidate this thirteen-year-old girl, became so enraged that he ordered Agnes to be stripped of her clothing and paraded to the house of ill

---

22. Visser, *The Geometry of Love*, 96.

repute. But God protected his maiden; as soon as the clothes were ripped off of her, her hair grew and covered her body even more perfectly than her clothes did.

Once in the brothel, Agnes was indeed protected by an angel whose radiance stopped anyone from violating her.[23] Procus, seeing an opportunity to appease his lustful desires, went to the brothel with his friends. To show his disgust for her, and to teach Agnes a lesson for refusing his proposal, he told his friends to go in and have their fun with her. Barely inside the room, each of them quickly ran back out, terrified by the angel of light. Procus ridiculed them for being cowards and went in to show them his resolve; but as soon as he entered Agnes's room, he was struck down by the blinding light and fell over dead. Procus's father, upon hearing of his son's death, went to Agnes, fearing some magic power. Agnes told him that the others went unharmed because they were terrified of the miraculous light, but Procus, with evil in his heart, was killed not by the light, but by the one who had power over him, the devil. The evil in him had overwhelmed Procus. Symphronius then begged Agnes to have his son restored to life. She readily agreed to pray for him. With the words of her prayer barely finished, the young man rose back to life; from that day on, he preached the name of Christ.

News of the miracle, however, reached the crowd, causing great anxiety. They began shouting for her death, believing that Agnes was some kind of witch. Symphronius, grateful for the restoration of his son's life, wanted to let Agnes go free, but the crowd seemed set on her destruction. Instead of following his own wish, he assigned the case to his deputy, Aspasius, and hastily went away.

Aspasius, going right along with the crowd, ordered Agnes to be burned in the public square. Yet, when she was thrown into the blaze, the flames turned away from her and onto the crowd. Those closest to the fire were burned, while Agnes was untouched. Seeing her unharmed, Aspasius ordered a soldier to thrust his sword into her neck; and so, she died. Her family and fellow Christians buried her in

---

23. Prudentius does not include the brothel in his poem. Instead, he has Agnes being stripped and placed in the public square. The people averted their eyes out of respect for the maiden. Anyone who did dare to look at her with lustful eyes was blinded by a miraculous light, see Prudentius, *The Poems of Prudentius*, 276.

the catacombs underneath her parents' home, barely escaping the stones thrown at them by the pagans of the city.

Immediately after her death, Agnes's final resting place became a site of worship for the Christians. Her tomb, like many of those of her fellow martyrs, became a gathering place to celebrate the Eucharist. Two days after her death, her step-sister, Emerentiana, who was also a virgin pledged to Christ,[24] was stoned to death after berating the pagans who came to torment the Christians holding vigil at Agnes's grave. But, as she was dying, and the pagans were elated by their actions, an earthquake suddenly shook the whole city, killing many of those who mocked Emerentiana and the other Christians. After that, no one bothered those who gathered around the tomb of Saint Agnes.

Jacobus concludes the story of Agnes by stating that Constantina, the daughter of the emperor Constantine and another virgin, had a basilica built over the tomb after praying to Agnes and being cured of leprosy. There is some confusion here, however, in the fact that according to the Roman historian Ammianus Marcellinus, the daughter of Constantine, Constantina, was very cruel and was married. Added to this fact is that there appears to have been another Constantina, the sister of the emperor, who is thought to have been baptized and "apparently blameless," which makes people suspect that this sister was the one who dedicated the basilica to Saint Agnes.[25] Nevertheless, the tradition holds that this Constantina gathered many virgins around her, forming a company of virgins who took inspiration from Saint Agnes, although there is no evidence to connect these virgins with the sixth-century convent at the basilica of Saint Agnes headed by the Abbess Serena.

THE LITERAL SENSE

After reading the story of Saint Agnes, we are left with the question of what to do with it; how are we to understand what we have read? As mentioned, the first level of interpretation, according to the tradition of the *four senses of Scripture*, is the literal sense. The literal sense,

---

24. Actually, she was the foster sister of Agnes's. See Jacobus de Voragine, *Golden Legend*, 1:101.

25. Visser, *The Geometry of Love*, 96.

often called the historical sense, is the foundation of all the other senses; it gives the plain, simple facts of the story and was often associated with the teaching of grammar, of how words were put together to impart meaning.

When we read the story of Saint Agnes and the other saints, the inevitable question that comes to modern minds is, "Is any of this true? Did any of this actually happen?" Certainly on the surface of the narrative, the story of Saint Agnes explains how and why her cult grew and expanded to the universal Church; people found the story interesting and entertaining, just as they do today. The narrative captures the imagination and helps us to see Agnes as a saint, a holy one of God. Historically speaking, of course, most of it, if not all of it, is obviously constructed. All that can be said with any historical accuracy is that an actual young girl was martyred, and her name was either Agnes, or her story quickly supplied that name for her. Nonetheless, she existed and the tombstone found beneath the church dedicated to her honor testifies to the early existence of her cult. Somehow, in some way, she affected people to such a degree that they considered her a saint; and at some point, exactly when is impossible to discover, the story we have today begun to be told. Outside of these few facts, nothing else is historically known.

If that is the limit to our historical knowledge, then an obvious reading of these narratives as biography is out of the question. A literal reading, then, cannot be one of biography or history as we understand those genres today. But, as discussed earlier, the literal sense must be found within the circumstances of the story itself.

The format of story, common to both hagiography and fiction, conveys a literal, or clear, meaning in a particularly powerful and unique way. Paul Griffiths has seen the power of narrative as an indispensable component of Christian (and possibly all forms of) theology: "[Narrative discourse] has cognitive powers and transformative capabilities not available to religious communities in any other way."[26] This does not limit theology to the study of narratives, but as Christ has shown in his own use of parables, some dimensions of faith are better told in the form of a story, which can touch a reader or listener on multiple levels, not just the intellectual. The American novelist

---

26. Paul Griffiths, "The Limits of Narrative Theology," in Keith E. Yandell, ed., *Faith and Narrative* (Oxford: Oxford University Press, 2001), 232.

Walker Percy made a similar connection when he saw a strong relationship between the novel and Christianity; Christianity, he realized, actually produced the cultural and philosophical perception necessary to give birth to the novel as a unique art form:

> Here I can only give my own conviction. It is that there is a special kinship between the novel as an art form and Christianity as an ethos, Catholicism in particular. It is no accident, I think, that the novel is a creature of the Christian West and is virtually nonexistent in the Buddhist, Taoist, and Brahmin East, to say nothing of Marxist countries.
>
> It is the narrativity and commonplaceness of the novel which is unique. Something is happening in ordinary time to ordinary people, not to epic heroes in mythic time.[27]

Although there is a fundamental difference between a novel and hagiography, there is also a similarity, this same sense of "narrativity." One could even argue Percy's point further, and say that the legends of the saints with their wonderful plots and imagery were a key component in the development of literature.[28] On the surface, for example, Cervantes's grand novel *Don Quixote* seems to support a reasoned approach to life and the world, one that rejects the more fanciful elements found in the stories of chivalry. But it is not the "rational" Don Quixote that inspires and amuses us, it is the knight errant off on his foolish adventures that we remember and celebrate. At the end of the story we find ourselves lamenting with Sancho, desiring to take his master back to new adventures; we find ourselves asking how

---

27. Walker Percy, "Another Message in the Bottle," in Patrick H. Samway, ed., *Signposts in a Strange Land* (New York: Farrar, Straus, and Giroux, 1991), 365.

28. See Gordon Hall Gerould, Saints' Legends (Boston: Houghton Mifflin, 1916). In his preface Gerould writes: "In the pages that follow I have tried to write the history of saints' legends as one part of the survey of English literature to be presented by the series of which this volume is a member. My difficulties have been many. Although the lives of saints began to affect the vernacular literatures of Europe as soon as such literatures came into being, and although legends in the vulgar tongues were everywhere exceedingly popular until modern times, they have been little studied, at least in their relations to one another and to their historical backgrounds [emphasis added] (vii)." Gerould's penultimate chapter discusses the saints' lives in drama. See also Charles Altman, "Two Types of Opposition and the Structure of Latin Saints' Lives," *Medievalia et Humanistica* 6 (1975): 1–11. Altman has noted the influence of the lives of the saints in the development of the old French romances, specifically those referred to as the chanson de geste. "It would be a simple matter to show how these structural characteristics [of the general form of saints' vitae] become an important part in the organization of vernacular romance (8)."

much better the world would be if we all saw things as Don Quixote did—a world of honor and valor, of love and loyalty. In the end, Cervantes's apparent critique is not of fanciful tales, but of our inability to be inspired and live by them.[29]

There is also the novel *Pamela*, written by Samuel Richardson in 1740, one of the earliest of the modern novels in England, and the first example of what would later become known as a bestseller.[30] The original title, *Pamela, or Virtue Rewarded*, hints at the plot: a young heroine is pursued by a man who threatens her with abduction and even rape. Although it is no way a straight rehearsal of the virgin-martyr narratives, it does explore some of the same themes: a woman decides to preserve her virginity, her virtue, in the midst of threats from a male antagonist. These themes are furthered evidenced in another novel by Richardson, *Clarissa*. The Richardson scholar Margaret Anne Doody actually interprets the title character as a virgin martyr.[31]

Underlining all western literature, of course, whether it is the later novel or the earlier hagiographic text, is the one common narrative, the Christian Scriptures.[32] The life of virtue, common to *Don Quixote*, *Pamela*, and the *Golden Legend*, has its roots in the Gospels and the writings of Saint Paul. And even though many would say that the virgin-martyr saint is far more an epic heroine than an ordinary character, the affect of her story can be understood as reflecting ordinary desires, except in this case, those desires are brought to their Christian perfection. As in the novels of Jane Austin, the protagonists of the virgin martyrs are women who seek truth and goodness, and overall, love. And just as in the Austin novels, which revolve around the themes of love and marriage, so too do the virgin martyr narratives, albeit the mystical love and marriage with Christ.

---

29. See Michael Fuller, "To Edify the People of God: A New (Old) Method of Reading Medieval Hagiography," *Chicago Studies* 44, no. 3 (2005): 284–94.

30. Margaret A. Doody, "Introduction," in Samuel Richardson, *Pamela*, ed. Peter Sabor (New York: Penguin, 1981), 7.

31. Margaret Anne Moody, "Tyrannic Love and Virgin Martyr: Tragic Theme and Dramatic Reference in *Clarissa*," in Margaret Anne Moody, *A Natural Passion: A Study of the Novels of Samuel Richardson* (Oxford: Clarendon Press, 1974), 99–127.

32. G. R. Owst has written an extensive study on the influence of preaching in the development of literature including both the preaching on Sacred Scripture and the lives of the saints. See G. R. Owst, *Literature and the Pulpit in Medieval England* (New York: Barnes and Noble, 1961), 56–148.

PATTERN AND MEANING

Given all of this, in the case of a story, the literal sense involves looking for the obvious interpretation, the straightforward meaning of the
events being told. As Augustine of Dacia describes it, the letter, the
literal sense, "teaches what's been done."[33] What happens in the story?
Who are the characters? The reader needs to enter into the world created by the story, and interpret what is happening within that world.
As Hugh of St. Victor taught his students, the first step is to *learn*
the story.[34] In hagiography, the learning of a story, particularly a story
of a virgin martyr, is greatly aided by the fact that there are so many
similarities between them. In the *Golden Legend*, there are seventeen
specific narratives about virgin martyrs; and the basic structure of
each of these narratives is very similar and quite easy to discern.

In each story of the virgin martyr, the saint is typically
described as beautiful, from a noble family, and of marriageable age.
One notable exception is Apollonia, who was described as "well along
in years," but who was, we must assume, beautiful and noble when she
was younger.[35] Like Saint Agnes and Saint Lucy, each of the virgin
martyrs decides early on to dedicate herself to Christ by a promise of
virginity; invariably, at some point she will have to defend this deci-
sion against a suitor who arises in one form or another and who
desires the virgin saint. This defense is done in a variety of ways; but
somewhere, and in some way, each of the virgin saints will echo the
sentiment of Saint Agnes, "I am already pledged to another!"

This, of course, becomes the catalyst in most of the stories
that leads to the arrest and trial of the virgin martyr. The obstinacy of
the saint, in the eyes of her antagonist, begs the question of who this

---

33. Henri de Lubac, *Medieval Exegesis*, vol.1. trans. Mark Sebanc (Grand Rapids, Mich.:
Eerdmans, 1998), 1.

34. See Ibid., 87.

35. In later narratives written by later writers, Saint Apollonia is transformed into a young
woman, thereby falling into line with the other narratives of the virgin martyrs. Katherine J.
Lewis writes that this transformation of Apollonia "exemplifies the process by which the criteria
for female sanctity were narrowed and the saint's forthright defense of her faith came to be
embodied above all in her unsullied sexual status, *The Cult of St Katherine of Alexandria in Late
Medieval England* (Woodbridge, Suffolk: Boydell Press, 2000), 82." Barbara Fleith, in her study
on the actual manuscripts of the *Golden Legend*, believes that Apollonia was not included in the
original text written by Jacobus. Barbara Fleith, *Studien Zur Überlieferungsgeschichte der
Lateinischen Legenda Aurea* (Bruxelles: Société des Bollandistes, 1991), 36.

other suitor is and eventually leads to the revelation that she is a
Christian. Here the story takes a definite turn; bigger issues are at
work. What might have been provoked by a sense of revenge, a jilted
man denouncing the virgin as a Christian, has now become an issue
of the state. The concern is no longer the girl's virginity and refusal to
marry, but the atheistic and irreligious reasons for her virginity—her
Christianity. The saint's belief and behavior have threatened the very
nature of society; the gods of the Roman pantheon needed to be shown
due reverence by all citizens. Because of their refusal to participate in
the state cult, the Christians were deemed subversive and atheists,
crimes in the Roman system of law.[36] With such dire threats to society, the story now becomes a clash of wills between the virgin saint
and the officials of government.

  This highlights another shared aspect of the narratives of the
virgin martyrs. Each of the virgin martyrs displays an amazing combination of wit and wisdom. Lucy turns the tables on the consul by
using his own argument against him, "You do not want to dishonor
your gods, why then can you not understand why I do not want to dishonor my God?" Katherine not only holds her own against the world's
fifty wisest philosophers; but in the end, they all convert to Christianity! Naturally enough, the wit and wisdom displayed by the virgin
martyr combined with the fact that he has failed to intimidate a young,
frail girl, infuriates the Roman official, triggering his anger to the
point that he orders the saint to suffer some form of excruciating
torture. In many cases, like both Agnes and Lucy, there is a first
attempt to take her virginity away from her, usually by sending her to
a brothel; but after a miracle prevents this from happening, she is
physically and brutally tortured. In the *Golden Legend*, however, the
martyrs, male and female, survive all types of physical torture with
high spirits and no experience of pain.

  Somewhere in the course of the narrative there is also some
form of divine intervention, usually the appearance of an angel or
some other heavenly messenger, who heals and/or protects the saint.
In every case, the original mode of execution fails, and the second and

---

36. The refusal to offer sacrifice to the state gods also led to a variety of accusations against
the Christians. Minucius Felix, a third-century Christian, lists some of the accusations made
against the Christians in *Octacius* 8–9, trans. Gerald H. Rendall, *Tertullian and Minucius Felix,
Loeb Classical Library* (New York: Putnam's Sons, 1931), 333–38.

third attempts fail as well. Cecilia is burned in a boiling bath for a
night and a day without succumbing to death. Margaret survived
being hung on a rack, beaten with iron hooks, burned with torches,
and placed in a tub of boiling water; finally she was beheaded (as a
side, it should be noted that even before any of these gruesome events,
Margaret was first swallowed by a dragon, which explodes when she
makes the sign of the cross). Eventually, though, after the tortures
have either failed or have been prevented, an executioner steps in and
stabs the saint in the throat, which ultimately becomes the cause of
her death. Throughout the story, there are also reports of miracles;
these continue on after the saint's martyrdom as Jacobus discusses
how veneration of the virgin martyr grew after people witnessed such
extraordinary events.

Although there is this basic outline, different details and
events unique to each saint are expressed. Sometimes, for example,
the desire of the suitor for the virgin saint enters the story at the
beginning and becomes the initial catalyst for the saint's trial, as in
the case of Saint Agnes. In stories of other virgin martyrs, the suitor
may appear later, after debating with the virgin for some time, as
when the judge in charge of her case follows Euphemia into the jail,
desiring to have his way with her. In still other cases, the suitor is not
directly stated, but rather implied. We see this particularly in the story
of the great Katherine of Alexandria, when the Emperor himself
becomes the suitor. After debating her, the emperor becomes overwhelmed with admiration of her knowledge and beauty.

It is this pattern, this basic outline, shared by each and every
narrative of the virgin martyrs, which becomes the vehicle that carries
the meaning of the lives of these saints. The reporting of the story
through such a common outline does not mean that these narratives
are works of pure invention, as much as it denotes a particular work as
part of the genre of a virgin martyr.[37] In reading the story, and seeing
the familiar elements, the reader automatically recognizes the outline,

37. Interestingly, a recent article by Samantha J. E. Riches argues that the legend of Saint
George fits into the genre of the virgin martyr. Her argument is that the narrative of Saint
George contains all the elements of the narratives of the virgin martyrs outlined above. This, of
course, leaves open the question as to why only women are classified as virgin martyrs and not
men. See Samantha J. E. Riches, "St. George as a Male Virgin Martyr," in Samantha Riches and
Sarah Salih, eds., *Gender and Holiness: Men, Women and Saints in Late Medieval Europe* (New
York: Routledge, 2002), 65–85.

the bones of the story of a virgin martyr, and knows what it is he or she is reading. The differences and details of each story allow flesh to be added to the bones; and with each nuance, turn of phrase, allusion, description, and twist of the story, that flesh delights and entertains the reader.

The structure of the virgin-martyr stories conveys the deeper mystery of *what has been done for us*? As Origen points out, the literal sense involves a reading that understands that everything happens within the greater context of mystery, but a mystery that presupposes a real event.[38] The real event presupposed in these narratives is the reality of salvation history. The inclusions of miracles, the amazing fortitude of the saint, the angelic and divine interventions, all support the understanding that these stories are about a history that is larger than the individual virgin martyr. Jacobus himself points to this broader scope in the prologue to the *Golden Legend* where he places his legends of the saints within the context of the Church's liturgical year, a calendar that records the history of reconciliation between God and humanity from creation to its completion at the end of time. As a result, the historical sense of these narratives, the history that is being reported, is not the story of the historic virgin martyr *per se*; rather, it is the story of God acting in the world. Even more specifically, the history being reported through the structure of the narratives is the human response to God's actions.

In all stories, biblical, hagiographic, and those found in novels, the literal sense is the straight-forward, obvious meaning that is being conveyed to the reader. To use a metaphor by Origen and others, "[The] Word is incarnate in Scripture, which, like man, has a body and a soul. The body is the words of the sacred text, the 'letter,' and the literal meaning; the soul is the spiritual sense."[39] Just as in this life, without a body, there can be no place for the soul to dwell; consequently, the body provides the potential for the soul. In the same way, the literal sense allows for the possibility of the spiritual senses. In the case of the virgin martyrs, the body, the literal sense, can be seen in the virtues and strengths of their characters, the very familiar elements of discipleship.

---

38. De Lubac, *History and Spirit*, 106.

39. Beryl Smalley, *The Study of the Bible in the Middle Ages* (Notre Dame, IN: University of Notre Dame Press, 1978), 1. See also, De Lubac, *History and Spirit*, 105.

Put another way, in order for these narratives to convey the deeper meaning of salvation history, they first have to supply a body in which that deeper, spiritual meaning can exist. The bones of such a body are the elements of discipleship communicated in the unfolding of these narratives. The only way for these stories to make sense is if they articulate the primary and essential elements that allow us to "believe the events as they are recounted." These stories, therefore, first have to teach the reader how to be a disciple. It can be no coincidence that the basic outline of the narrative of a virgin martyr is the same outline given by Christ to his disciples when he was teaching them what they should do, and what they should expect to happen, when they follow him.

THE WAY OF DISCIPLESHIP

At the very beginning of their stories, the virgin martyrs are described as beautiful, young, and noble. Their virginity and their youth immediately raise images of innocence and purity, but all these terms can describe the disciple as well, as can be seen in the narrative of the New Testament. In the *Letter to the Philippians* Paul tells the disciples to be blameless and innocent children of God, shining out like lights in a darkened world. [40] In his first pastoral letter, John describes how charity distinguishes the children of God from the children of the devil; such a distinction is a consistent theme in the accounts of the virgin martyrs where the good saint is pitted against a whole onslaught of evil people. [41] Earlier in that same letter, John begins by affirming the nobility of the disciple, "Think of the love that the Father has lavished on us, by letting us be called God's children; and that is what we are." [42] In the Gospels, Jesus summarizes all these attributes with the word "blessed." A disciple is one who is blessed, who hears the word of the Lord and follows it. One who is blessed is one who receives the joy and the glory of the kingdom, as Jesus asserts in the Beatitudes, [43] and when he says, "Then the King will say to those on his right hand, 'Come, you whom my Father has blessed,

---

40. Phil 2:15.
41. 1 Jn 3:10.
42. 1 Jn 3:1.
43. Mt 5:3–12.

take for your heritage the kingdom prepared for you since the foundation of the world.'"[44]

That the stories of the virgin martyrs convey the meaning of discipleship is reinforced in the story of Saint Agnes when she is described as being even more beautiful in her faith. Christ continually teaches that the one thing necessary for discipleship is faith in him, a fact demonstrated by many of his parables which describe the faithful servant, and the many miracles he performed because, as he said, the person had faith. The beauty of Agnes's faith is reinforced by her very name: Agnes is the Greek word for chaste—a particularly strong form of faithfulness.

The dignity given to a disciple of Christ can be seen throughout the Gospels, but perhaps one particular episode can stand for the rest. At one point in his ministry, Christ sends his apostles out to preach to "the lost sheep of Israel." As he sends them on their way, he gives them authority over unclean spirits and the power to heal "all kinds of diseases and sickness."[45] Upon hearing these words, Saint John Chrysostom asks, "Do you perceive the unparalleled magnificence of their ministry? Do you comprehend the dignity of the apostles?"[46] A little later in his instructions to his disciples, Jesus says, "The disciple is not superior to his teacher, nor the slave to his master. It is enough," he says, "for the disciple that he should grow to be like his teacher, and the slave his master."[47] Here again, we see how the Fathers of the Church saw in these instructions the nobility given to those who follow Christ. Theodore of Mopsuestia explains that, "he who is made like his teacher by adoption can never go beyond his nature, but to be made like his teacher is the highest end he can reach."[48] It is the highest end because to be like Christ is to return to the original dignity given to humanity at the moment of creation, when man and woman were created in the *image* and *likeness of God*.[49]

---

44. Mt 25:34.

45. Mt 10:1–2.

46. John Chrysostom, *Homily* 32.4, in Manlio Simonetti, ed., *Matthew 1–13, New Testament vol.1a. Ancient Christian Commentary on Scripture* (Downers Grove, Ill.: InterVarsity Press, 2001), 195.

47. Mt 10:24–25.

48. Theodore of Mopsuestia, *Fragment* 53, in Simonetti, *Matthew 1–13*, 203.

49. Gn 1:26.

There is, in fact, a strong parallel between the instructions
Christ gives to the apostles and the structural outline of the narratives
of the virgin martyrs; the events of their stories follow Christ's
instructions with amazing closeness, showing how these stories depict
the story of every disciple. As Saint Augustine reminds us, when we
hear these instructions, and hear Christ's prediction that the apostles
will be "handed over" and "dragged before governors and kings" and
will be "hated by all,"[50] we know that the "Lord was referring, rather
not only to those about to depart this life, but also to the others,
including us, and those who will come after us in this life."[51] Through
the familiar structure of these stories, the life of discipleship depicted
by Christ to his apostles becomes apparent once more. "When Christ
has been prophesized by the words of the martyrs amid the tortures of
savage persecutors," Hilary of Poitiers proclaims, "the way will be
open for the Gentiles to believe in him, though they remain stubborn."[52] And although he was speaking of actual words spoken by the
martyrs, and not stories written about them, the idea still holds true.
We, the Gentiles, need to hear these stories over and over again if
only to break down our stubborn resistance to become better disciples.

THE SUITOR

The virgin martyr narratives, however, offer a few interesting twists to
the story of discipleship. Perhaps one of the most difficult aspects of
their stories and how they connect to the life of every disciple comes
with the introduction of the suitor into the life of the saint. Who is
the suitor that a disciple of Christ has to face? Again, in his instructions recorded in the Gospel of Matthew, Jesus tells his apostles to go
out to the lost sheep of Israel, but that they should not "turn [their]
steps to pagan territory, nor enter into any Samaritan town."[53] The
suitor Jesus warns his apostles about is the same suitor every disciple
faces, including the modern one. Saint Jerome writes in his commentary on this passage, "In line with this metaphor, we who call ourselves Christians are advised not to walk in the ways of the Gentiles

50. Mt 10:17–22.
51. Augustine, *Sermon* 64A.2 in Simonetti, *Matthew 1–13*, 201.
52. Hilary of Poitiers, *On Matthew*, 10.12, in Simonetti, *Matthew 1–13*.
53. Mt 10:5.

and heretics, for they have not only a separate religion, but also a separate way of life."[54] Hilary of Poitiers makes a very similar comment: the suitor the disciple has to resist is the "works and lifestyle of the unenlightened Gentiles."[55]

At first, this may seem to be on the level of *allegory*, where the "lost sheep" or the suitor, points to something else, Israel and the temptations of the world," respectively. But such an allegory is so intrinsic, so obvious within the context of what is being said, that is actually becomes part of the literal sense. There is no more basic meaning to the "lost sheep" ; and what is meant by the "suitor" in these stories is plainly seen by how they are described: what is to be avoided are the trappings of the world, the temptations that come and take us away from Christ. These are the very same things the suitor Procus uses to ensnare Agnes — jewels, wealth, and power. "Do not," Paul exhorts the Romans, "model yourselves on the behavior of the world around you, but let your behavior change, modeled by your new mind."[56] Even the specific pledge of virginity made by the saints becomes a bold statement of every disciple against this suitor. The world defines relationships in terms of sex and power, but the disciple defines such things in terms of charity. This is not to say that there isn't love in the world; rather, it is to adopt the language of Saint Paul who uses the expressions "world" and "flesh" to signify human passions and desires that are misdirected and running amok.

The suitor, then, that each disciple faces is worldly temptation. It is also his own sinfulness that has come about before his life of discipleship, from a lifetime of habitually giving into that temptation. As Paul confesses:

> The Law, of course, as we all know, is spiritual; but I am unspiritual;
> I have been sold as a slave to sin. I cannot understand my own behavior.
> I fail to carry out the things I want to do, and I find myself doing the
> very things I hate.[57]

N. T. Wright argues that the "I" Paul is referring to is Israel under the Torah, under the Law, and therefore before any conversion to

---

54. Jerome, *Commentary on Matthew*, 1.10.5–6, in Simonetti, *Matthew 1–13*, 194.

55. Hilary of Poitiers, *On Matthew*, 10.3, in Simonetti, *Matthew 1–13*.

56. Rom 12:2.

57. Rom 7:14–15.

Christ.[58] The "I" he references, then, is humanity still stuck in the realm of sin and death, still under the power of the worldly suitor.

Paul does not leave us in despair, however. He asks, "Who will rescue me from this body doomed to death? Thanks be to God through Jesus Christ our Lord!"[59] In this way, the virginity of Agnes and the others takes on a deeper meaning. Virginity is not simply a rejection of male-dominated social structures, or even an acceptance of defining oneself in terms of sexuality. Rather, the grace-filled Agnes, who can say to the suitor, "Go away you spark that lights the fire of sin," serves as a reminder of the disciple's faith that in Christ, we can resist the temptations of the world, the temptations that, if accepted, reduce a person's dignity rather than build it up.

TRIALS OF DISCIPLESHIP

If discerning the suitor in our own story of discipleship seems the most abstract aspect of a literal reading of the virgin-martyr stories, then the easiest to comprehend would be Christ's instructions to his disciples concerning the trials they shall face:

> You will be dragged before governors and kings for my sake, to bear witness before them and the pagans. But when they hand you over, do not worry about how to speak or what to say; what you are to say will be given to you when the time comes; because it is not you who will be speaking; the Spirit of your Father will be speaking in you.[60]

As we saw earlier, in her confrontation before the Roman consul, Lucy repeats Christ almost word for word:

> I am the handmaid of the Lord, who said to his disciples that they would be brought before kings and governors, but they should not fear what to say, for the Holy Spirit will speak through them." "So the Holy Spirit is in you," the consul asks, and Lucy responds, "Yes, all those who live chaste lives are temples of the Holy Spirit."

---

58. N. T. Wright, "The Letter to the Romans," in *The New Interpreter's Bible*, vol. 10 (Nashville: Abingdon Press, 2002), 565.

59. Rom 7:24–25.

60. Mt 10:18–20.

Naturally, in all of the accounts of the martyrs, and not just the virgin martyrs, these words of Christ hold a distinct importance along with the ones he says to his disciples later in the same instructions. "So if anyone declares himself for me in the presence of men, I will declare myself for him in the presence of my Father in heaven. But the one who disowns me in the presence of men, I will disown in the presence of my Father in heaven."[61]

Saint John Chrysostom explains these instructions as Christ's way of preparing his disciples for "a new sort of combat." In this new warfare, a war with the world, the powers and principalities, the disciples will "suffer wrong and willingly permit others to inflict punishment upon them." This is to show how the Gospel turns the world completely upside down. "[Victory] is in suffering evil for the sake of good."[62] All of this, of course, is to "accentuate [Christ's] unspeakable power."[63] It is the same confidence that the virgin martyrs exhibit in their trials and sufferings for the Lord. At every turn, the expectations and desires of the governors and kings are thwarted by the saint, who for all appearances is a weak, young girl.

All the plans of the consul's son, Procus, to persuade Agnes to abandon Christ by marrying him come to nothing. To every incentive he can think of, be it wealth, prestige, or actual power, Agnes responds by saying she already has it in Christ. Every attempt by the authorities to persuade her to do what was lawful and acceptable to society, to offer sacrifice to the gods like every other person, falls on deaf ears. Every move made to intimidate her, to make her fearful, has just the opposite effect. When they try to terrorize her into submission, she becomes even bolder. In all of this, Agnes represents the precise stance of a disciple who follows the Lord's command. As Chyrsostom puts it:

> Then, to press this reverse strategy to its limits, [Christ] tells them to exhibit the gentleness of sheep, even though they are going out among wolves, and not simply toward the wolves, but trustfully moving right into the midst of the wolves.[64]

---

61. Mt 10:32–33.

62. John Chrysostom, *Homily on the Gospel of Matthew*, 33.2, in Simonetti, *Matthew 1–13*, 199.

63. John Chrysostom, *Homily on the Gospel of Matthew*, 33.1, in Simonetti, *Matthew 1–13*, 200.

64. Ibid.

Agnes and the other virgin martyrs exemplify these instructions to the letter. They are told by Christ that he is sending them out like sheep among wolves; their virginity and their youth both represent the innocence Christ wanted them to have, for they are to be "as harmless as doves." At the same time, though, he commands them to be "cunning as serpents,"[65] which the virgin martyrs also exhibit to a high degree. Lucy's short but direct comments to the consul demonstrate not only this cunning, but also the Spirit's gift of supplying the words to say. Saint Margaret realizes that her persecutor knows at least something about Christ in his attempt to persuade her that her belief is foolish. She responds by cleverly pointing out that since he has read the Christian books, he should have not only read about Christ's suffering, but also his glory, since both are portrayed in the Gospels. "You should be ashamed," she then tells him, "to believe the one and yet deny the other!" In other words, you can't have it both ways — either what the texts say is all true, that Christ suffered and was raised, or neither happened. Through her words too, Saint Cecilia cunningly convinces her new husband and his brother of the truth that comes with faith in Christ.

By fulfilling each of Christ's instruction in regard to handling persecution, the virgin martyrs provide not only the inspiration for the modern disciple, but by doing so in such a delightful way, the reader's spirits are lifted. "Knowledge of things to come," Hilary points out, "is very edifying for acquiring tolerance, especially if our own will has been modeled by another's example."[66] Not only does Christ give the apostles and disciples these instructions to follow, he gives his own life as an example to imitate. In the stories, the virgin martyrs teach the way of discipleship by listening to his instructions, and following his example.

WHY NOT FLEE?

There does seem to be one instruction of Jesus that the virgin martyrs do not follow, the command to flee from town to town. Jesus says, "If they persecute you in one town, take refuge in the next; and if they

---

65. Mt 10:16.

66. Hilary of Poitiers, *On Matthew*, 10:15, in Simonetti, *Matthew 1–13*, 203.

persecute you in that, take refuge in another."[67] Many of the stories of martyrs found in the early *Acts* and *Passions*, and in the subsequent *Golden Legend*, do not seem to demonstrate any obedience to this teaching. One exception can be found in the fourth-century account of the martyrdom of three young women from Saloniki. The three, Agapê, Irenê, and Chionê, apparently fled after the Diocletian's first edict, dated February of the year 303, which ordered the burning of the Christian books.[68] "When the persecution was raging under the emperor Maximian [one of the tetrarchy, along with Diocletian], these women who adorned themselves with virtue . . . fled the persecutors, according to the commandment, and took refuge on a high mountain."[69] On the surface, this looks like a wise thing to do, and we wonder why other virgin martyrs do not follow such prudent actions as Christ commands.

One possible answer, it should be noted, comes from the fact that even though these three saints did flee, they still, eventually, received martyrdom by following what seems to be the higher command, to be true to Christ in front of men. In facing the exact same question, though, the Fathers of the Church reflected on the need for the disciples to preach so that others may hear the Word of God. Saint Cyril of Alexandria tells us that the command to flee persecution is not a command to be cowardly, rather, Christ "is telling them not to cast themselves into dangers and die at once, for that would be a loss to those who otherwise will benefit from their teaching."[70]

Two things should be mentioned in regard to this idea and its relation to the narratives of the virgin martyrs. First, as we saw with both Saint Agnes and Saint Lucy, the martyrdom of the saint essentially becomes the vehicle for her preaching. Within the story, the virgin martyrs survive such horrendous attacks unharmed and go on proclaiming Christ, winning over many in the crowds. Even when it comes to the end, these saintly women go on preaching: Saint Lucy lectures the crowd for three more days after having been stabbed in the neck; Cecilia is tortured by being boiled alive in her bathtub, but

67. Mt 10:23.

68. Herbert Musurillo, S.J., *The Acts of the Christian Martyrs* (Oxford: Clarendon Press, 1972), xlii.

69. Ibid., 281.

70. Cyril of Alexandria, *Fragment* 120, in Simonetti, *Matthew 1–13*, 203.

she goes on singing the praises of the Lord all the while. The virgin martyrs do not flee because the very witness they give in their stories accomplishes what Cyril points out as Christ's wish — that others may benefit from their teaching.

Second, it must be remembered that these are hagiographic stories, meaning just that, they are stories. It is precisely as a story that these readings help spread the Good News. As noted, stories can impart not just certain teachings, but can carry emotional and transformative contents as well. In other words, stories can reach the human heart and the human intellect in certain ways that are unavailable to other venues of discourse. This is why stories can be so effective in preaching. And so, yes, it could be more prudent to flee persecution; we know that we should never seek martyrdom outright. At the same time, the stories of courageous young women help remind modern disciples that the spiritual life requires a strong sense of asceticism, a dying to self, of sacrifice; and that, as Chrysostom described it earlier, "victory is in suffering evil for the sake of good." Or better, as Christ puts it, "anyone who loses his life for my sake will find it." In fact, anyone "who does not take up his [or her] cross and follow in my footsteps is not worthy of me."[71]

THE BODY AND THE SOUL

Thus, the stories of the virgin martyrs parallel Christ's instructions to his disciples in remarkable ways, reinforcing in the reader Christ's call to the way of discipleship. The outline of discipleship reported in the Gospels, especially Christ's instructions to the apostles found in chapter ten of Matthew, is reintroduced in the unique patterns of these narratives, providing a body to these stories that convey a strong meaning. That structure, which is the *literal sense* of these narratives, is also the foundation for the other senses; it is the body that also houses the spirit.

It is on this foundation of discipleship, then, that the other spiritual senses can be added, allowing multiple layers of meaning and insight in these stories to unfold. Indeed, in their commentaries on Matthew 10, it is very hard for the Fathers to stay with the strictly

---

71. Mt 10:38–39.

literal sense. Gregory the Great, for example, slips into the analogical sense while reflecting on the instruction to go and preach to the lost sheep of Israel: "Even if the gospel were to be silent, dearly beloved, the world now proclaims this message. Its ruins are its words. . . . It is as if the world itself reveals to us now that another kingdom is near, which will succeed it."[72] Jerome and Chrysostom both see clear moral requirements in the commands of Christ to take no staff, no money, and no supplies: "You are not then to move from house to house, looking constantly for better fare, which would vex those who would be receiving you and give you the reputation of gluttony and self-indulgence."[73] Hilary sees the apostles as being "other Christs" in the world, becoming a foretaste of redeemed humanity.[74] In biblical exegesis, the spiritual senses build upon the foundation of the literal sense. The same is also true in applying these senses to the stories of the virgin martyrs. From the foundation of discipleship the other senses can easily be determined. In both their virginity and suffering, the virgin martyrs allegorically portray the innocence and passion of Christ. As brides of Christ they are both an allegory for the Church and carriers of the Church's message of virtuous life; and as models of such a life, they lift up the whole body of Christ to the dwelling places of the angels. In order to see all this, however, we first have to understand the life to which Christ calls us. It is only when we are firmly planted in the details of discipleship that these other dimensions of holiness can be seen; it is only then that these stories can delight, teach, and sway the modern disciple into a deeper love of Christ and neighbor.

---

72. Gregory the Great, *Homily* 4.2, in Simonetti, *Matthew 1–13*, 195.

73. John Chyrsostom, *Homily* 32.5, *On Matthew*, in Simonetti, *Matthew 1–13*, 197.

74. Hilary of Poitiers, *On Matthew* 10.4, in Simonetti, *Matthew 1–13*, 195.

Chapter 4

The Lamb of God:
An Allegorical Reading

Still we honor the relics of the martyrs that we may adore Him whose martyrs they are. We honor the servants that their honor may be reflected upon their Lord who Himself says: "he that receiveth you receiveth me."

Saint Jerome[1]

Allegory teaches what you should believe.

Augustine of Dacia

One reason to apply the *four senses of Scripture* to the reading of the saints is that, as has been seen, similar questions arise in both biblical and hagiographic exegesis. Accounts that are contradictory, illogical, implausible, or simply dull, as in the case of the travelogue of the Israelites found in Numbers chapter 33, must be in the Scriptures for a reason, one that we are meant to discover.[2] Origen firmly believed that in such cases there must be a hidden, deeper intention beneath the obvious events being recounted. When preaching on Numbers 33, for example, he sees a spiritual significance to each and every place the Israelites stop in their journey through the desert.[3] The deeper intention of the sacred texts, therefore, brings the reader into the spiritual senses of allegory, anagogy, and tropology. In the reading of the virgin

---

1. Jerome, *Epistle* CIX.1, in W. H. Freemantle, trans., vol. 6, *Nicene and Post-Nicene Fathers, Second Series* (Buffalo: The Christian Literature Publishing Company, 1893), 212.

2. De Lubac, *History and Spirit*, 121.

3. See Origen, *Homily XXVII*, in Rowen A. Greer, trans., *Origen, Classics of Western Spirituality* (New York: Paulist Press, 1979), 245–69.

martyrs, the first of these, allegory, builds upon the literal sense, the bones of discipleship, and brings us to the very life of Christ, as can be seen in the story of Saint Agatha.

SAINT AGATHA

Jesus concludes his lengthy Sermon on the Mount by telling the crowds how he wants them to be disciples: "Everyone then who hears these words of mine and does them will be like a wise man who built his house upon the rock; and the rain fell, and the floods came, and the winds blew and beat upon that house, but it did not fall, because it had been founded on the rock."[4] It should come as no surprise that these are the very words the virgin-martyr Agatha is reported as saying when her enemies tried to persuade her with the temptations offered to those who give into worldly desires. The circumstances are quite familiar.

"The virgin Agatha," we are told, "was highborn and a great beauty, living in the city of Catania, where she worshiped God at all times and in all holiness."[5] Naturally both her beauty and her nobility attracted a particularly determined suitor, in this case the "baseborn, libidinous, greedy" worshipper of idols, the Roman consul, Quintianus. He was determined to have Agatha because she would satisfy all his needs. First, her beauty would satisfy his lust; second, her wealth would satisfy his need for economic stability and comfort; and finally, her noble title would satisfy his desire to be elevated to the elite levels of society, something even his own title seemed unable to do.

Seeing how determined she was in both refusing his offer of marriage and her Christian faith, Quintianus turned her over to a procuress, a "madam," who had nine daughters, all of whom were as "lascivious as their mother." These women were the ones who tried to entice Agatha into giving in to both the temptations of the flesh, and to the consul's proposal, by promising her pleasure, or alternatively,

---

4. Mt 7:24–25.

5. The story depicted here is based on Jacobus de Voragine, *Legenda aurea*, Maggioni critical edition, 39:256–61. Cf. Jacobus de Voragine, *The Golden Legend*, trans. William Granger Ryan, 1:154–57.

threatening her with pain. It is to them that Agatha echoes the teaching of Christ: "My determination is built on rock and founded on Christ! Your promises are raindrops; your threats are rivers; and however hard they beat upon the foundation of my house, it cannot fall."

The contest of wills between the prostitutes and the saint went on for some time. Eventually, the madam went to Quintianus and said, "It would be easier to split rocks or reduce iron to the softness of lead than to move or recall that girl's mind from its Christian intention." At hearing this, the story turns in a new direction, as Quintianus stops being her suitor and starts acting as her judge.

She is summoned before Quintianus who asks for the record, "What is your social standing?" She responds, "I am freeborn and of illustrious lineage, as my ancestry attests." The judge immediately retorts, "If you are so highborn, why does the way you live make you seem to be of servile status?" Her answer was just as quick: "I am the slave of Christ, therefore I show myself as a person in service." "If you are of noble birth," Quintianus asks again, "why do you call yourself a slave?" To which Agatha answers, "Because to be a slave of Christ is proof of the highest nobility."

Getting angrier by the minute, the judge orders Agatha to make a choice: either sacrifice to the gods or be tortured! Agatha replies by trying to bless her persecutor, if only to point out his own hypocrisy. "May your wife be like your goddess Venus," she says, "and may you be like your god Jupiter." The judge orders her to be slapped and yells at her, "Don't let your loose tongue insult your judge!" Agatha is amazed and says to the judge,

> I marvel that a sensible man like you can fall into such stupidity as to call gods those whose lives neither you nor your wife would want to imitate! Indeed, you consider it an insult if you are said to follow their example. If your gods are good, I've made a good wish for you; if you repudiate any association with them, then you agree with me!

Befuddled, Quintianus says, "What's the use of all this idle talk? Sacrifice to the gods or prepare to suffer!" To which the saint calmly replies:

> If you promise me the wild beasts, the sound of Christ's name will gentle them! If you try fire, angels will serve me with a healing dew from heaven! If you resort to wounds and torments, I have the Holy Spirit, through whom I make naught of all that!

At this point, she is thrown in jail so that she can stop talking and making a fool of the judge; she goes to prison rejoicing, as if she was "invited to a banquet."

The next morning, Agatha is offered another chance to sacrifice, and after refusing she is stretched out on the rack and tortured. Agatha yells out, "These pains are my delight." She sees in these tortures a parallel to the threshing out of wheat from chaff, a preparation for her entrance into heaven. This made Quintianus so angry that he ordered Agatha's breasts to be savagely twisted so she would writhe in pain; then he had them cut off. That night, while she sat in jail, an aged man entered her cell and told her he came to heal her wounds and restore her breasts. He said to her, "Though this mad consul has inflicted torments on you, the way you have answered him has tormented him even more." He then said that she should not be ashamed of him healing her, for he was an old Christian. Agatha, however, said that she had no need, for she had Christ who could, if he wished, restore her health at any time he wished. The elderly man responded, "I am his apostle, and he has sent me to you. Know that in his name, you are healed." And then Peter the apostle vanished, and Agatha was healed of all her wounds.

Peter must have disappeared in a blaze of light because the jailers all ran off terrified. Agatha found herself unguarded and free to leave, but she decided that she needed to stay lest she "lose the crown of patience," and also expose the guards to trouble. After four days, during which Agatha was not given any food or water, Quintianus returned, ordering her to offer sacrifice to the gods. She replied that he must be very stupid if he wanted her to sacrifice to stones and abandon the God of heaven who had healed her of all her wounds. He then asked who healed her, and she answered, "Christ, the Son of God." At the utterance of that name, Quintianus ordered Agatha to be stripped naked and rolled over broken pottery and burning coals. While such tortures were being inflicted, an earthquake shook the city, causing the palace to collapse, killing two of Quintianus's counselors.

The people reacted and started shouting at the consul that such horrors have been visited upon them because of his unfair treatment of Agatha. He threw her back into prison and tried to calm the riotous crowd. In jail, exhausted, Agatha knelt down in prayer and said, "Lord Jesus Christ, you created me, you have watched over me from infancy, kept my body from defilement, preserved me from love of the world, made me able to withstand torture, and granted me the virtue of patience in the midst of torments. Now receive my spirit and command me to come to your mercy." Upon finishing her prayer, she "called out in a loud voice and gave up her spirit." This was about the year 253, during the reign of the emperor Decius.

THE ALLEGORICAL SENSE

The report of Agatha's death can leave no question in the mind of the reader who the virgin martyr is imitating. These narratives are, after all, constructed on the pattern of discipleship, but are they simply imitating Christ, or is something more happening? Can the stories also be read on another level? As Augustine of Dacia helpfully points out, the allegorical sense teaches what you should believe. Read in such a light, the focus of the story is transformed; on the allegorical level, it becomes not so much a description of discipleship, but a depiction of the one the disciple follows. The allegorical sense does this by means of offering a pattern of its own called a "type." An element in the text, while maintaining its own meaning, can also symbolically, metaphorically, be understood as signifying something else; this is what Augustine calls a "sign."[6] Allegory and the use of "types" can be seen very clearly in Origen's homily on the *Sacrifice of Isaac*.

Origen begins by asking for the attention of those "who believe themselves faithful." "Observe each detail which has been written," he continues, "for, if one knows how to dig into the depth, he will find a treasure in the details, and perhaps also, the precious jewels of the mysteries lie hidden where they are not esteemed."[7] According to the *letter* of the text, the literal sense, questions arise as to why Abraham would not even hesitate to accept the command of the Lord to sacri-

---

6. Augustine, *De doctrina christiana*, I.2, in John E. Rotelle, ed., Edmund Hill, trans., *Teaching Christianity*, vol. I/11, *The Works of Saint Augustine : A Translation for the 21st Century* (Brooklyn, NY: New City Press, 1996), 106–7.

7. Origen, *Homily on Genesis*, 8, in Ronald E. Heine, trans., *Homilies on Genesis and Exodus*, vol. 71, *Fathers of the Church* (Washington, D.C.: The Catholic University of America Press, 1982), 136.

fice his son Isaac, the very son the Lord had promised would be the first of a whole nation of descendents as numerous as the stars. Abraham does not hesitate, and takes his son along with two servants on a three-day journey to the mountain where the sacrifice is to occur.

Origen tries to reconcile Abraham's acceptance of such a paradox. On the one hand, Abraham has absolute faith in God's promise of numberless offspring in and through his son Isaac; on the other hand, he accepts without question the command to sacrifice this very son, whom he loves so much. Origen states that Abraham was confident in God's ability to raise one up from the dead; and so by faith, he did not hesitate to follow God's command: "Abraham, therefore, hoped in the resurrection of Isaac and believed in a future which had not happened."[8]

Exactly on this point, though, Origen also sees a deeper truth in Abraham. Not only did he have faith and confidence in the possible resurrection of Isaac, but "Abraham knew himself to prefigure the image of future truth; he knew the Christ was to be born from his seed, who also was to be offered as a truer victim for the whole world and was to be raised from the dead."[9] Here then, an allegorical reading of the text brings this truer victim into focus. If Christ was to be born from Abraham's side, then Isaac stands in for him as the son of Abraham. Isaac as a "type" of Christ becomes even more pronounced as the events of the story unfold. After three days, they come to the mountain where Isaac carries the wood for the offering. "That Isaac carries on himself 'the wood for the holocaust' is a figure, because Christ also 'himself carried his own cross.'" Clement of Alexandria expands Isaac as a type of Christ:

> Isaac is another type too (he can easily be taken in this other sense), this time of the Lord. He was a son, just as is the Son (he is the son of Abraham; Christ, of God). He was a victim, as was the Lord, but his sacrifice was not consummated, while the Lord's was. All he did was to carry the wood of his sacrifice, just as the Lord bore the wood of the cross.[10]

8. Ibid., 137

9. Ibid, 137–38.

10. Clement of Alexandria, *Christ the Educator,* I.5.23, in Mark Sheridan, ed., *Genesis 12–50, Old Testament,* vol. 2, *Ancient Christian Commentary on Scripture* (Downers Grove, Ill.: InterVarsity Press, 2001), 105.

There is also the figure of Abraham in this story. For the three days they traveled, Origen imagines the torment Abraham must have gone through, the agony of being torn between the love he had for his son, and the love he had for God. In such a figure we also can see another "type," in this case, one that signifies God the Father. Caesarius of Arles states this specifically, "When Abraham offered his son Isaac, he was a type of God the Father."[11] Abraham wrestled between his love for his son and his love for God; is it too much to imagine the anguish of God the Father, who although he knew all, still must have wrestled between his love for his son, and his love for the world? Yet God the Father had faith in his Son, who, through the sacrifice of the cross, would save the world.

One last piece of allegory must be mentioned in this passage from Genesis, and that concerns the point of view of Isaac. Although in their commentaries, the Fathers often discuss the amazing faith of Abraham, our Father in faith, they rarely, if ever, discuss the faith of Isaac. Yet, Isaac had complete faith in his father. Although he raises a question about the lamb for the sacrifice they are to offer, he nonetheless trusts Abraham, even to the point of allowing him to bind him and lay him on the altar. Reading these events allegorically, it becomes clear that we are also to understand the faith of Christ, and his tremendous trust in the Father, even though he had some questions as well, as in the Garden of Gethsemane.

NEW TESTAMENT TYPES

In the Old Testament allegories, the types are said to foreshadow Christ, anticipating his eventual coming through the Incarnation. They are shadows in that they are pale comparisons to the fullness of truth which is Christ. As such, these Old Testament figures, like Isaac, set the scene for Christ, but are inferior to him. Nonetheless, they provide powerful insights into God's plan of salvation by helping the reader of Sacred Scripture see God's plan unfolding in the very history of his people.

The question now becomes, why are there no such counterparts to the Old Testament types after the Resurrection? One obvious

---

11. Caesarius of Arles, *Sermon* 84.2, in Sheridan, *Genesis 12–50, Old Testament*, 2:102.

answer is that there is no need for any, in that the fullness of the truth, the fullness of God's salvific plan is fulfilled and completed in Christ. This is perfectly true. At the same time, however, there is the observation Saint Paul made to the Corinthians, "For now we see in a mirror dimly."[12] Despite being in the post-Resurrection era, we still have not reached the time of Christ's second coming, when all shall be fulfilled in Him. It would seem reasonable that just as before the Incarnation there were figures that anticipated Christ's coming, there should also be figures or types that come after his Resurrection and reflect Christ's life, death, and Resurrection and anticipate his return.

In fact, these post-Resurrection or New Testament types are the saints. Whether they acted in this way in their historic, actual lives, or through stories that have been constructed around those lives, they still stimulate the Christian imagination leading others to see Christ. Each aspect of a saint's story aids the reader in seeing Christ, and teaches the reader not only what he is to believe, but in whom he is to have faith. The stories of the virgin martyrs accomplish such a task to an amazing degree, recalling Christ's innocence, suffering, strength, wit, nobility, faithfulness, service, and even his healing mission. In each of their stories we are taught who the savior is.

One simple way the stories of the saints recall the memory of Christ is through the use of special "biblical" numbers. In the case of the virgin martyrs, the favorite biblical number is the number three. Just as in the Genesis account of the Sacrifice of Isaac, where Abraham and his son travel for three days to the place of sacrifice, "the third day," as Origen recognizes, "is always applied to mysteries," especially to the mystery of Christ.[13] So, for example, Saint Cecilia's neck is hacked three times (the Trinitarian number), and she spends three days on her death bed in order to sanctify all those around her and to have her house dedicated as a church, allegorically post-figuring Christ's own three days in the tomb when he descended into hell and brought forth the salvation of all. Other numbers are significant as well; Saint Christina was shut up in a tower by her father with twelve women of waiting as her only company. Later, she is beaten up by twelve men, a hint that even the apostles abandoned the Lord at his

---

12. 1 Cor 13:12.

13. Origen, *Homily on Genesis* 8.4, in Origen, *Homilies on Genesis and Exodus*, 140.

darkest hour. Christina's story is also illuminating in that it is full of other biblical references from both the Old and New Testaments. In one of the many trials she has to undergo, she is tortured by being thrown into a blazing furnace, where for five days she walked about, singing with angels, unharmed just as Shadrach, Meshach, and Abednego did in the third chapter of *Daniel*.[14] These elements, however, are simple details that remind the reader of Christ. On the thematic level, the virgin-martyr narratives operate on a much stronger level of signification.

THE SUITOR

On the literal level, however, we have seen how through the narratives of the virgin martyrs, the disciple learns that following Christ means that he will face temptations from the world, temptations that will try to lure the disciple away from his dedication to Christ. Reading these stories through the spiritual sense of allegory, however, teaches the disciple why this has to be. It is not simply a case of remaining true to Christ, but that Christ himself underwent such temptations. The fundamental gift of Christ is the display of God's love for his creation, for humans. The very definition of this love, of charity, requires a turning away from self-interest and towards sacrifice for another. As Christ said to his disciples, "A man can have no greater love than to lay down his life for his friends."[15]

The stories of the virgin martyrs and their suitors are actually written with this stronger, spiritual sense in mind. They are not just simple stories of a disciple resisting the temptations of the world, but are even more "types" of Christ that show the epic battle between pure love, charity, and undiluted self-interest. These stories not only depict the temptations disciples face, but even more so, the temptations the teacher faces. In other words, the virgin martyrs and their struggles with suitors, which usually form the beginning of the story, signify the beginning of Christ's story as well—when Christ is led

---

14. Christina's story, as hagiographers have discovered, is actually the amalgamation of two separate stories about two female martyrs named Christina. See Herbert Thurston and Donald Attwater, *Butler's Lives of the Saints*, vol. 3 (Allen, Tex.: Christian Classics, 1995), 173–74.

15. Jn 15:13.

out by the spirit into the desert, and after forty days, faces the temptations offered by the devil himself.

According to the Gospel of Matthew, immediately after his baptism by John in the Jordan, Jesus is led by the Spirit "into the wilderness to be tempted by the devil."[16] In the trials they face, the virgin martyrs, as we have seen, are often sent out into a form of wilderness. The wilderness and the presence of the devil indicate a time of testing when the faith of the saint, and as such, the faith of Christ, will be tested by Satan. For the virgin martyrs, this place of testing can be the brothel that many, like Agnes, are thrown into. It could also be the time spent imprisoned and being tortured. For Agatha, the place of testing was in the house of the madam and her "lascivious daughters." There she was tormented with continual attacks, much like those we imagine Christ having to endure during his forty days in the desert. The madam and her girls continually tried to persuade Agatha of the foolishness of her ideas and dedication.

After the forty days, Christ found himself hungry; and so in his major offensive to tempt Jesus, the devil says to him, "If you are the Son of God, tell these stones to turn into loaves."[17] Jesus refuses the temptation. In the accounts of the virgin martyrs, several of them are thrown into prison and denied food and water. The emperor orders the virgin martyr, Eugenia, thrown into a cell without food and water for ten days. Katherine of Alexandria is treated in the same manner; Agatha too. However, in these stories, although the temptation of hunger must have been powerful, they are saved by heavenly powers. Agatha survives four days in prison without food or water, and is fine when she is dragged before Quintianus. This is after being healed by the Apostle Peter, and so we assume some form of miraculous strength was given to her in that visit. In the case of both Katherine and Eugenia, Christ himself comes to the virgin martyr and feeds her bread from heaven. Anastasia was held for two months without substance from her jailers, but we are told that Saint Theodora, who was martyred earlier, came and visited Anastasia and fed her this same bread from heaven. The fact that it is Theodora that brought the food is an interesting detail in that Theodora was a married woman who was

---

16. Mt 4:1–11.
17. Mt 4:3.

deceived by the devil into having an affair. After discovering the deception and her own weakness, she ran off to live a life of penance and was finally martyred in Alexandria.

The fact that the virgin martyrs seem to have been spared the temptation of hunger may seem somewhat at odds with the temptations Christ had to face in the desert. Here again, it must be remembered that these saints are post-Resurrection types of Christ and signify Christ after his victory over Satan. Indeed, many of the heavenly appearances depicted in the virgin martyr narratives seem to point directly to the end of Christ's temptations when the devil was foiled and "angels appeared and looked after him."[18] What allows Christ to resist Satan in the wilderness is his faith in his Father. In each temptation, Jesus responds by invoking the Father, the Lord God. By faith, the virgin martyrs respond in exactly the same way. Reading carefully, we notice that these accounts of being denied food are not really temptations at all; nowhere do the stories relate any aspect of temptation for food on the part of the virgin saint. Rather, the denial of food and water, combined with the fact that they receive heavenly food, acts as a direct signifier of Christ's victory over Satan even before the Cross, in that wilderness so long ago. Because we are on the far-side of the Resurrection, all the prophecies and promises have been fulfilled, and so any signification of Christ must incorporate this fact.

The exact same prophecies from Scripture that the devil uses to tempt Jesus actually are fulfilled in the virgin-martyr narratives. "If you are hungry, command these stones to turn into bread."[19] In other words, demand food to be brought to you out of nothing, out of thin air. Jesus responds to the devil, saying that "Man does not live on bread alone, but on every word that comes from the mouth of God."[20] That was not yet fulfilled until Christ, the Word of God, completed his work on earth. Now, however, the virgin martyrs show its fulfillment, and in so doing, they act as Christ acts. What more can be said than they were fed heavenly food? "My food," Christ tells his disciples, "is to do the will of him who sent me, and to accomplish his work."[21]

---

18. Mt 4:11.
19. Mt 4:3.
20. Mt 4:4.
21. Jn 4:34.

The same can also be seen in the second temptation of Christ. Satan tells Jesus to throw himself down off the parapet of the Temple, "for scripture says: 'He will put you in his angels' charge, and they will support you on their hands in case you hurt your foot against a stone.'"[22] As Saint Agatha told Quintianus, "If you try fire, angels will serve me with a healing dew from heaven! If you resort to wounds and torments, I have the Holy Spirit, through whom I make naught of all that!" This sentiment is echoed by each of the virgin martyrs and is reported actually to have occurred—an angel protects Agnes in the brothel; the Holy Spirit makes Lucy so heavy that no one can move her. In their cells, after experiencing horrific tortures, angels or saints come to minister to the martyrs' wounds. At one point in her story, a queen, intrigued by Katherine's convictions, goes to visit the saint, only to be greeted by "a cell filled with indescribable brilliance, and angels ministering to the virgin's wounds." A marvelous light also surrounded Margaret while she was in her cell; and in Euphemia's cell, there was a host of "shining virgins" surrounding the soon-to-be martyr. What was prophesized by Scripture, what was prefigured in the temptations of Christ in the desert are, in a post-Resurrection context, shown to have been fulfilled by Christ through the figure of the virgin martyr.

THE TRIALS

In the descriptions of the trials, where most of the dialogues take place, we also see how the virgin martyrs are a "type" of Christ. Many of the situations the saint finds herself in parallel situations Christ was in; the responses of the saints also parallel those of Jesus. One difference seems to be the fact that opposed to Christ's humble manner, all of these saints, once in front of the judge, seem to shout aloud, challenging the authorities in a very antagonistic way. But again, the sharp wit and cutting words of the virgin martyrs signify Christ from a post-victory perspective. As Christ himself said in the Gospel, "Do not suppose that I have come to bring peace on earth: it is not peace I have come to bring, but a sword."[23] In the virgin martyr these words are seen as fulfilled. Like Christ, in their contests with the state

---

22. Mt 4:6.
23. Mt 10:34.

officials, the virgin martyrs teach that the work of religion, the true work of God, is "that you believe in him whom he has sent."[24]

When Agnes yells at her suitor, "Be gone from me; go away you spark that lights the fire of sin, you fuel of wickedness, you food of death!," we recall the situation of Christ and Peter. In Agnes's rebuke of her suitor, we hear again Christ's strong words chastising Peter.[25] Both the saint and Christ chastise the person for thinking contrary to the ways of God. In essence both are saying, "Stop trying to steer me away from my dedication, from my path."

Agatha finds herself in a conversation with the Roman consul that is very similar to Christ's own conversations with the Pharisees. Agatha's use of clear thinking in her compliment to her persecutor when she says, "If your gods are good, I've made a good wish for you; if you repudiate any association with them, then you agree with me," points to Jesus' own attempts logically to persuade his opponents:

> "Show me the money for the tax." And they brought him a coin. And Jesus said to them, "Whose likeness and inscription is this?" They said, "Caesar's." Then he said to them, "Render therefore to Caesar the things that are Caesar's, and to God the things that are God's."[26]

There is also the time when the Sadducees tried to catch Jesus in a conundrum about the resurrection and divorce. Found in Matthew's Gospel immediately after the incident with the coins, the Sadducees asked Jesus if a woman has multiple husbands, whose wife would she be in heaven? Again, Jesus' quick and precise response throws his opponents, for "they were astonished at his teaching."[27]

Like Christ, when confronted with their opponents, the virgin martyrs use wit and wisdom to point out the logical flaws in their opponents' thinking and at the same time teach the truth. Katherine is forced into a debate with fifty of the wisest men in the world, gathered there by the emperor to rebuke her claims about Christ. In that contest of intelligence, she foils every attempt made by the wise men to expose the folly of her beliefs. Her wisdom is beyond reproach. She does so well, in fact, that all fifty of her opponents are reduced to

---

24. Jn 6:29.
25. Mt 16:23.
26. Mt 22:19–21.
27. Mt 22:33.

silence; in the end, they all become Christians. Lucy foils every attempt to entrap her with her own words. When commanded to offer sacrifice, Lucy responds by saying, "The sacrifice that is pleasing to God is to visit the poor and help them in their need." Here she signifies the teaching of Christ who answers the Pharisees' question about eating with tax collectors and sinners by saying, "Go and learn what this means, 'I desire mercy, and not sacrifice.'"[28] Since this very idea was prefigured in the words of the prophet Hosea— "For I desire steadfast love and not sacrifice, the knowledge of God, rather than burnt offerings"[29] —does it not seem sensible that it should appear again in the stories of the saints?

Along with their words, the virgin martyrs act as types of Christ in their behavior and compassionate response to certain situations. We hear of Saint Daria who scolds the lion protecting her, telling him he must not eat those who would attack her, rather he is to bring them to her and she will convert them. We hear of Agnes who brings back to life the very man who caused all her problems in the first place, combining Jesus' raising of Lazarus with his teaching and example of forgiving those who persecute you. The scene between the prefect whose son was restored to life, and Saint Agnes, can also be seen as a figuring of Christ's encounter with Pilate; both Pilate and the prefect realize the innocence of the one before them, but are either too afraid or too powerless to do anything about it.

SUFFERING

One of the most obvious ways the narratives of the virgin martyrs act as an allegory for Christ is found in their description of suffering and martyrdom. On the literal level, their suffering is an aspect of discipleship. However, the over-the-top accounts and descriptions of suffering and torture point to an allegorical understanding as well, suggesting not just the participation in (discipleship), but the actual passion of Christ. The amount of suffering portrayed, for example, in just the stories of martyrdom found in the *Golden Legend* is staggering, especially when we remember that the *Golden Legend*, by design,

---

28. Mt 9:13.
29. Hos 6:6.

was an abridgement of the longer accounts found in earlier versions of these stories. In all, Martha Easton has counted eighty-one different types of tortures described by Jacobus in the *Golden Legend*.[30] Many of these can be found in the virgin-martyr narratives. Cecilia is boiled in a bathtub, while Margaret was thrown into a tub of ice cold water after being burned all over her body by torches. Both Agatha and Christina had their breasts twisted with pinchers to the point of agonizing pain, only in the end to have them cut off. Apollonia, the only elderly virgin, was beaten so hard by a crowd that all her teeth came out (thus making her the patron of dentists!). Christina, as mentioned earlier, was stripped naked and beaten by twelve men—at her own father's command. Daria suffered many tortures and beatings; then she was thrown into a pit and crushed with stones.

Eugenia, who disguised herself as a male monk in order to lead a life of prayer, was accused of rape after she spurned the sexual requests of Melancia, the same woman she had healed earlier in the story. After proving her innocence by revealing herself to be a woman, Eugenia went to Rome where, after converting many to the faith, the emperor ordered her bound to a great stone and thrown into the Tiber. By God's grace she escaped unharmed, only to be seized again and thrown into a burning furnace. Again, she emerged and was thrown into a dark jail; on Christmas day, she was beheaded.

Other tortures inflicted upon these holy women included having molten lead poured onto them (Juliana and Justina); imprisonment and starvation (Anastasia, Katherine, Christina, Euphemia, Margaret, and Daria). Both Euphemia and Juliana were hung from their hair; Katherine, Agnes, Anastasia, Apollonia, Margaret, Lucy, and Christina all were burned—Christina on three separate occasions. Many were stripped naked, and several had their skin scraped off by rakes while they were hung up by the arms.

Six of the virgin martyrs (about a third of those described by Jacobus) were at one point placed upon a rack or wheel to stretch out their bodies to the point where "the marrow would spurt out."[31] The most famous of these devices was the one built to torture Katherine of

---

30. Martha Easton, "Pain, Torture and Death on the Huntington Library *Legenda Aurea*," in Sarah Salih, Samantha Riches, eds., *Gender and Holiness: Men, Women and Saints in Late Medieval Europe* (New York: Routledge, 2002), 50.

31. Jacobus de Voragine, *The Golden Legend*, 1:161.

Alexandria. The device consisted of four separate wheels all studded with "iron saws and sharp-pointed nails." Two of the wheels would go in one direction and two in the opposite direction, thus ripping apart the virgin's body while the saws and nails would cut into the flesh. Sometimes these wheels were designed either to be on fire, or have the flames of a fire beneath them lash up at the saintly bodies.

The tremendous suffering of Christ, who "takes away the sin of the world," [32] is echoed in the overwhelming accounts of suffering found in these narratives. These saints act as types of Christ, just as the earlier *Servant of the Lord* poems found in the book of Isaiah acted as a type of Christ. [33] The third *Servant* poem begins by reiterating the fact that God has given his servant a "well-trained tongue" so that he may speak to the weary about the glory of God (also seen in the virgin martyrs). It then goes on to illustrate the steadfastness of the *Servant of the Lord*:

> For my part, I made no resistance,
> neither did I turn away. I
> offered my back to those who struck me,
> my cheeks to those who tore at my beard;
> I did not cover my face
> against insult and spittle. [34]

It is obvious how the writers of the Gospels would read this and immediately see Christ. Although the virgin martyrs did not have beards that could be plucked, they certainly recall Christ when they, too, did not shield their faces and offered their backs to those who would beat them. In this third poem, the *Servant of the Lord* prefigures Christ, who is the one who will suffer greatly. This *servant* will endure a lot; but through it all, he adamantly adheres to God as his help and comfort. This same servant, who is Christ, is post-figured in the suffering of the martyrs, particularly the virgin martyrs.

This third *Servant* poem ends in a triumphant voice when the servant says to all those who oppose him: "This is your fate from my

---

32. Jn 1:29.

33. Traditionally, the four "Servant of the Lord" passages are Is 42:1–4, 49:1–7, 50:4–11, and 52:13–53:12.

34. Is 50:5–6.

hand: you shall lie down in a place of pain."[35] Although this fate may appear to be at odds with our normal picture of the loving Christ, it is nonetheless a valid part of the Suffering Servant and of Christ, who, at the final judgment will separate the sheep from the goats. To the goats, those on his left, he shall say, "Go away from me, with your curse upon you, to the eternal fire prepared for the devil and his angels."[36] In many of the narratives, the very miracle which saves the virgin martyr also kills her would-be prosecutors, those who are clearly marked as evil. When an angel of the Lord strikes the four-wheel contraption meant to tear Katherine apart, the splinters fly off in every direction and kill 4,000 pagan bystanders.

   In almost every story of the virgin martyrs, those most responsible for the torturing and execution of the saints come to a terrible end. Paschius, the prefect who sentenced Lucy, was dragged away in chains and executed by the new emperor. The prefect who tried to attack the three maiden servants of Anastasia is taken for a demon and is beaten up by the crowd. Quintianus, the prefect and suitor of Agatha, is kicked in the head by his horse and falls into a river; his body is never found. The headsman who killed Euphemia was devoured by a lion (not, however, the one which belonged to Daria). The prefect who tortured and killed Juliana went to sea with thirty-four men; they were cast into the sea by a storm and drowned. As if that were not enough, their bodies were tossed onto shore and were eaten by sea birds and wild beasts.

   All of these consequences prefigure the events of the second coming of Christ, who will restore justice, making right all the wrongs afflicted upon his witnesses as foretold in the seventeenth chapter of Revelation, where the great city of Babylon and the pagan nations are all destroyed. The stories told of the virgin martyrs, then, not only signify Christ in what he has done, but also in what he will yet accomplish. In this way these women martyrs *witness* to Christ and teach the reader about the one in whom he should place his faith.

---

35. Is 50:11(NAB).
36. Mt 25:41.

The Nobility of Christ

At work in these stories is a most amazing transformation. From very early on, the martyrs were identified with Christ. Ignatius of Antioch makes this connection explicit by yearning that his body might be like Christ's in the Eucharist. In his *Letter to the Romans* he writes: "I am God's wheat and I am being ground by the teeth of the wild beasts to make a pure loaf for Christ."[37] Indeed, it was believed by the early church that at the time of suffering, the martyr already coexisted with Christ, as we learn in the account of the martyrdom of Polycarp:

> [O]thers achieved such heroism that not one of them uttered a cry or a groan, thus showing all of us that at the very hour of their tortures the most noble of martyrs of Christ were no longer in the flesh, but rather that the Lord stood by them and conversed with them.[38]

The identification of the martyr with Christ was so strong that it appears that many sinners went to those in prison who were awaiting martyrdom in order to procure from them the forgiveness of their sins. This procedure was followed by so many that Tertullian lashed out at the practice and had to downplay the connection of Christ and the martyr by emphasizing that only God could forgive sins (and does so only through the church).[39]

In the case of the virgin martyrs, however, there is the added dimension of their virginity, which made their martyrdom even more captivating, and which partially explains the popularity of their cults and the production of these narratives. As can be seen in how these stories signify Christ, the combination of these two ways of holiness captured the imagination of many Christians. The gift of self that is inherent in the idea of virginity recreates the gift of Christ himself, who gave his entire life for us. As we know, however, Christ's gift is not limited to the laying down of his life on the cross; it goes far beyond that.

---

37. Ignatius of Antioch, *Epistle to the Romans*, 4; Ignatius of Antioch, "Epistles," in Cyril C. Richardson, ed. and trans., *Early Christian Fathers* (New York: Touchstone, 1996), 104.

38. *The Martyrdom of Polycarp*, 2, in Richardson, *Early Christian Fathers*, 149–50.

39. Tertullian, *De pudicitia* (On Modesty), XXII.

As Saint Paul relates in reproducing the great hymn found in the Letter to the Philippians, the gift of Christ begins with his *kenosis*, his self-emptying in the incarnation:

> So if there is any encouragement in Christ, any incentive of love, any participation in the Spirit, any affection and sympathy, complete my joy by being of the same mind, having the same love, being in full accord and of one mind. Do nothing from selfishness or conceit, but in humility count others better than yourselves. Let each of you look not only to his own interests, but also to the interests of others. Have this mind among yourselves, which is yours in Christ Jesus, who, though he was in the form of God, did not count equality with God a thing to be grasped, but emptied himself, taking the form of a servant, being born in the likeness of men.[40]

The nobility and beauty of the virgin martyrs reflect this understanding of total gift that is found in Christ. In Agatha's story, we find the heart of this grace when she is questioned by the consul Quintianus. When asked her social standing, Agatha replies that she is freeborn and of illustrious lineage; her ancestry attests to this fact. Quintianus rejoins by saying "If you are so highborn, why does the way you look make you seem to be of servile status?" And Agatha's response to that question echoes the gift Christ gave to the world. "I am the slave of Christ; therefore I show myself as a person in service. To be a slave of Christ is proof of the highest nobility." All of this must be seen as more than imitation; in the gift of themselves through their virginity, Agatha and the others are conforming to Christ in such a way as to be one with him. This is indicated within the stories by the saint claiming to be the bride of Christ; and, in the spiritual marriage of virginity, the virgin saint becomes one with her spouse.

The story of Saint Lucy also highlights Christ's gift to the world by making himself poor. After her mother consents to Lucy's desire to become a bride of Christ, the two of them sell all that would have been Lucy's dowry, and gave the proceeds to the poor—a literal reproducing of Christ's own poverty. Lucy made herself poor for his sake. And as the handmaid of the Lord, Lucy, through her dedication as a virgin, gave herself up to the service of others in Christ's name. As she said to the Roman official interrogating her, the true sacrifice

---

40. Phil 2:1–7 (RSV).

that God wants, is to be of service, to "visit the poor and help them in their need." In their gift of self and their service, the virgin martyrs naturally reflect Christ who said, "The Spirit of the Lord has been given to me, for he has anointed me. He has sent me to bring the good news to the poor."[41]

VIRGIN AND MARTYR

To read the legends of the virgin martyrs allegorically means to transform "the way in which these things are understood, even though the way they are named does not change."[42] The way Agnes, Lucy, Agatha, and the others are named is simply as *virgin martyrs*; but the joining of these two ways of holiness, virginity and martyrdom, combines to form a strong allegory of Christ. This is seen, first, in the total gift of self found in their declaration of virginity and the attitude of service this gift fosters; and second, in the witness given by their suffering and death. Like their prefiguring counterparts in the Old Testament, these stories are shadows in that they are inferior copies of the original story; nonetheless, they serve the purpose of teaching the disciple what he is to believe—the salvation that comes in the person Christ. In other words, the past—the once and for all salvific event of Christ—is kept alive in our memories by the stories we tell.[43] The stories of the virgin martyrs are told to each generation, not to eclipse the Gospel, but to help stimulate the Christian imagination, allowing us to see the Good News and inspiring the disciples of Christ continually to live out their faith, their belief, in Christ.

It is the unique combination of gift and sacrifice signified by virginity and martyrdom that allows these stories to *re*-present Christ. In these narratives, the virgin martyr is transformed into the exact likeness of Christ. What is truly amazing is that in a Christian context, which has been described as misogynistic and patriarchic, it is a *female* body which most typifies Christ. The popularity of the virgin martyrs among men and women alike in the first 1,500 years of the Church, demonstrates that people saw these women as something

---

41. Lk 4:18.

42. So Origen; see Henri de Lubac, *Medieval Exegesis*, 1:229.

43. Brevard S. Childs, *Memory and Tradition in Israel* (Naperville, Ill.: A. R. Allenson, 1962), 72. Childs writes, "The past is kept alive primarily by the story."

quite special, something worth remembering and holding on to. In the narratives, it is a female body which is broken, stabbed, burnt, and maimed. It is female breasts that are cut off, and the threat of rape is specifically used to terrorize a female body into submission. Yet, it is precisely these innocent female bodies which are transformed through suffering into the very image of Christ. When told the tale, one can see the body of Christ once more laid down for others; it is the cruci-fied one who is made *re*-presented in the body of a young girl. In a very powerful way, the weakest of all vessels, a young unmarried girl, becomes in the end, the King of Kings.

Chapter 5

A Body to Die For:
An Anagogical Reading

Although living in the flesh they were not weighted down by the allurements of the body, because of their affinity to the bodiless powers [they were] borne upwards in midair, they participated in the life of the celestial powers.

Saint Gregory of Nyssa[1]

Anagogy teaches where you will get relief.

Augustine of Dacia

The overwhelming amount of suffering, the long list of tortures, trials, imprisonment, and threats, all the things that the virgin martyr has to undergo, along with the sheer determination and energy required to go through them, can lead both the saint and the reader of her story to the point of exhaustion. All the epic struggles and events of the saint's story implicitly raise the question of Augustine of Dacia— where does one find relief? And indeed, many aspects of the stories of the virgin martyrs aid an anagogical reading by directing our attention specifically to the *telos*, to the end of Christian life—heaven. By hearing the virgin-martyr legends, like all stories of the saints, the reader should be *uplifted* by hope.

---

1. Gregory of Nyssa, *Vita S. Macrinae*, trans. Virginia Woods Callahan, in *Saint Gregory of Nyssa: Ascetical Works, vol. 58, Fathers of the Church* (Washington, D.C.: The Catholic University of America Press, 1967), 171.

ANAGOGY

The "lifting up" or the "building up" of the reader is the basic definition of the anagogical sense; it is the leading of a person (a mind, a
soul) from a lower level of understanding to a higher one. As described
by Hugh of St. Victor,

> Anagogy is an ascension, an elevation of the mind to contemplation of
> the divine. . . . [It is] finally, seeing the invisible through the visible
> signs. Sometimes, it is only through anagogy that the mind is drawn up
> to the pure, heavenly heights of contemplation.[2]

Given this definition, it should not be surprising to hear anagogical
language in the descriptions of Christ's Ascension, as in Saint Leo the
Great's homily for the feast:

> As therefore at the Easter commemoration, the Lord's Resurrection was
> the cause of our rejoicing; so the subject of our present gladness is His
> Ascension, as we commemorate and duly venerate that day on which
> the Nature of our humility in Christ was raised above all the host of
> heaven, over all the ranks of angels, beyond the height of powers, to sit
> with God the Father. On which Providential order of events we are
> founded and built up, that God's Grace might become more wondrous,
> when, notwithstanding the removal from men's sight of what was
> rightly felt to command their awe, faith did not fail, hope did not waver,
> love did not grow cold. For it is the strength of great minds and the
> light of firmly-faithful souls, unhesitatingly to believe what is not seen
> with the bodily sight, and there to fix one's affections whither you can-
> not direct your gaze.[3]

This upward movement contributes a major dimension to the
reading of the lives of the saints. The Venerable Bede, for example,
writes in his prologue to the *Life of Saint Cuthbert*, "[When] you
reverently hold the memory of this saintly father, your soul is lifted

---

2. Hugh of St. Victor, *Commentaria in Hierarchiam coelestem S. Dionysii Areopagitae*, in J.-P.
Migne, ed. (Paris) *PL* 175:941C. On Pseudo Dionysius see Paul Rorem, "The Uplifting
Spirituality of Pseudo-Dionysius," in Bernard McGinn, John Meyendorff, and Jean Leclercq,
eds., *Christian Spirituality: Origins to the Twelfth Century* (New York: Crossroads, 1985), 132–51.

3. Leo the Great, *Second Homily on the Lord's Ascension* (Sermon 74), trans. Charles Lett
Feltoe, vol. 12, *Nicene and Post-Nicene Fathers, Second Series* (Buffalo: The Christian Literature
Company, 1895), 188.

up to a higher place with longing for the heavenly kingdom."[4] This idea is constantly reinforced in the narratives of the virgin martyrs. For example, Agnes refuses to marry the prefect's son. Part of her response to her suitor points to the heavenly heights she seeks in and through her bridegroom: "He has placed a wedding ring on my finger, and a necklace of precious stones around my neck. . . . Already his chaste embraces hold me close, he has united his body to mine, and he has shown me incomparable treasures, and promised to give them to me if I remain true to him." Those treasures, of course, are found in heaven and not here on earth.

The purpose of an anagogical reading is to lift our eyes heavenwards, to delight the mind, and to enflame the soul to the point that it yearns to act according to this new goal. As Pope Leo says in this same homily, we are directed to gaze on "That which had never quitted the Father's side in descending to earth, and had not forsaken the disciples in ascending to heaven."[5] In other words, from the beginning, it was God's plan to lift Christ's disciples up to heaven after him.

The faith that comes with the Ascension of the Lord, and the hope it initiates in the hearts and minds of the disciples is very clear in the story of the saints, especially the martyrs. "For this Faith throughout the world," Leo reminds us, "not only men, but even women, not only beardless boys, but even tender maids, fought to the shedding of their blood."[6] In his homily Leo answers the question of where the virgin martyrs and the readers of their stories find relief; it is in knowing the reason behind all that occurs. Nothing, not "bonds, imprisonments, banishments, hunger, fire, attacks by wild beasts, refined torments of cruel persecutors," nothing can terrify the one who has faith in the promise of heaven.[7] Over and over again, the reader, the disciple, is reminded of this promise through the stories of the virgin martyrs, as can be seen in the case of one of the most famous virgin martyrs, Saint Cecilia.

---

4. "Pia sanctissimi patris memoria vestros animos ad desideria regni coelestis ardentius attollitis." So Bede, *Vita S. Cuthberti*; see Charles F. Altman, "Two Types of Opposition and the Structure of Latin Saints' Lives," *Medievalia et Humanistica* 6 (1975): 7.

5. Ibid.

6. Ibid.

7. Ibid.

SAINT CECILIA

Born into a noble Roman Christian family, Cecilia is said to have always been a woman of prayer who carried the Gospel of Christ in her heart. She desired to remain a virgin for Christ; but she was betrothed to a young man named Valerian, also of noble birth but from a pagan family. The day of her wedding, she prayed to the Lord that her desire to remain a virgin should be kept. All throughout this prayer, while her heart was singing to the Lord, the wedding musicians were playing for the guests. Then came the wedding night, when she and Valerian retired to the wedding chamber. Cecilia, still adamant in her desire to belong only to Christ, tells her new husband that she has a secret to confess to him. She tells him that she has "a lover, an angel of God, who watches over [her] body with exceeding zeal." She warns her husband, "if my angel senses that you are touching me with lust in your heart, he will strike you and you will lose the flower of your gracious youth. If, on the other hand, he knows that you love me with sincere love, he will love you as he loves me, and will show you his glory."[8]

Naturally, the young man wishes to see this angel, but he cannot. Cecilia tells him that if he wishes to see the angel, he must believe in the one true God and be baptized. Amazingly, he is convinced by her sincerity and goes out to meet the saintly pope, Urban, who is in hiding outside the city among the tombs of the martyrs. Urban greets him and hears how Cecilia has sent him. The Pope turns to the Lord in prayer saying, "Cecilia, your handmaid, has served you like a busy bee: the spouse whom she received as a fierce lion, she has sent to you as a gentle lamb."

At this point, Valerian experiences his first connection to this other world. After the Pope's prayer, an old man appears to the crowd; his garments are as white as snow, reflecting the purity of a martyr, and he carries a book written in gold letters. Although in the *Golden Legend* this man is not identified by name, he certainly is a figure from heaven, and we begin to sense that it must be Saint Paul because he begins to teach Valerian from words found in his book, the words from the Letter to the Ephesians: "There is one Lord, one faith, one

---

8. For the entire account of the legend of Cecilia, see Jacobus de Voragine, *Legenda aurea*, Maggioni critical edition, 165:1180–87. Cf. *The Golden Legend*, 2:318–23.

baptism, and one God who is Father of all."[9] When finished, this aged holy man asks Valerian if he believes in what he has just heard. Valerian replies enthusiastically, "There is nothing else under heaven that could be more truly believed!" With that the old man vanishes, and Valerian is baptized by Urban.

Valerian returns to find Cecilia talking to her angel, whom he can now see. The angel holds out two crowns made of roses and lilies for Valerian and Cecilia to take. The two are told that these crowns are from heaven and will never fade nor lose their fragrance as long as they shall remain pure; these crowns, they are told, cannot be seen by anyone "except those whom chastity pleases." The angel then asks Valerian, the new recruit of the heavenly kingdom, if there is anything he wishes. He asks that his brother could join them in the truth of Christ. The angel answers that his petition pleases the Lord; not only will his wish come true, but both he and his brother will be rewarded with the "palm of martyrdom," a testament to the perfection of charity within one who sides with the Lord.

It just so happens that Valerian's brother, Tiburtius, chooses to enter the room at this exact moment and notices a sweet fragrance (the fruit of charity entices others to charity). When he asks the source for this heavenly aroma, Valerian tells him that they have crowns made of flowers which he cannot see, and that if he wishes to see them, he would have to believe in the truth of Christ. At this point in the *Golden Legend*, Jacobus interrupts the story to reinforce the main point: Cecilia's story is not simply about a virgin and her betrothed, but has far more cosmic implications; it is about the conflict between heaven and earth. Jacobus highlights this theme by quoting Ambrose's preface for the liturgy on Cecilia's feast day:

> Saint Cecilia was so filled with the heavenly gift that she accepted the palm of martyrdom, cursing the world along with the pleasures of marriage. . . . A virgin led these men to glory and the world recognized how powerful commitment to chastity can be.[10]

The rejection of the world is at the heart of the discussion between Cecilia and Valerian, on the one hand, and his brother Tiburtius, on the other. But this discussion does not revolve around rejection of

---

9. Eph 4:5.

10. Jacobus de Voragine, *The Golden Legend*, 2:320.

worldly values concerning marriage or sexuality, as one might expect. Instead, it centers on the nature of authentic worship, the same debate that was occurring between Christianity and Roman society. Cecilia convinces her brother-in-law by plainly showing him that all idols were without feeling or speech. She then goes on to answer every one of his questions; in so doing, she unfolds for him the mystery of the Trinity, the necessity of Christ's passion, his Resurrection, and the promise of what is to come. Tiburtius declares, "Anyone who does not believe this is a brute beast." Cecilia responds joyfully, kissing Tiburtius on the breast and saying that not only has "the love of God made your brother my husband, [but] so has contempt for the idols made you my kinsman. Go therefore with your brother to be purified [baptized] and made able to see the faces of angels."

On their way to Pope Urban, Tiburtius recognizes that he has just switched sides. Speaking of Urban, he says to Cecilia and his brother: "If that man is found, he will be burned alive, and we will be caught in his flames; and while we are looking for God in heaven, we will bring burning fury upon us on earth!" Cecilia responds with the only weapon Christians were allowed to carry—faith. "If this life were the only life, you would be right in fearing to lose it; but there is another, better life, which is never lost, and which the Son of God has told us about."

After his baptism, Tiburtius and his brother devote themselves to works of mercy by burying the bodies of those whom the prefect Almachius had put to death because they refused to worship the Roman gods. It is not long before they themselves are caught and brought before the prefect. Here the clash between the two worlds comes to a head. Almachius summons the two brothers and asks them why they buried those who were condemned. Tiburtius's answer highlights the clash of worldviews:

> "Would that we might be slaves of those whom you call condemned! They despised what seems to be and is not, and found what is not seen to be, and is!"
> The prefect: "And what is that?"
> Tiburtius: "That which seems to be and is not is everything in the world that leads man to nonbeing. What is not seen to be and is, is the life of the righteous and the punishment of the wicked."[11]

---

11. Jacobus de Voragine, *The Golden Legend*, 2:320.

The prefect Almachius then turns to Valerian thinking that he would make sense since Tiburtius is obviously mad. Valerian only confirms what his brother said, using the example of men mocking those who work in the fields during the winter, only to be proved wrong when the summer harvest comes in. Almachius then asks, "So we, unconquered and unconquerable princes, will have eternal sorrow; and you, the rabble, will possess perpetual joy? Why do we go on arguing in circles? Offer libations to the gods and go scot-free!" The fact that Tiburtius and Valerian, along with all those the prefect had already condemned, refused to do such a simple and publicly beneficial act was incomprehensible to the prefect. The famous Roman historian Tacitus described this refusal on the part of the Christians as "hatred for mankind,"[12] which is what the prefect must have believed he was dealing with in these two brothers. And so, he ordered their execution.

The saga continues when the prefect Almachius saw a way to get hold of the brothers' possessions, thus adding to his personal treasury, an earthly concern that contrasts with Cecilia's and the two brothers' heavenly focus. The prefect called for Cecilia and demanded that she sacrifice to the idols or be sentenced to death. Her servants pleaded that she should yield to the prefect's wishes, but our saintly virgin refuses.

Almachius summons the virgin saint and demands to know what her status in life is. Cecilia responds saying, "I am freeborn and of noble decent." "No, I am asking about your religion," the prefect yells. Cecilia calmly answers, "Your interrogation began badly, because the one question called for two answers." Now very angry, the prefect says, "Where do your presumptuous answers come from?" "From a clear conscience and unfeigned faith," is her reply. This goes on for several minutes until the moment of truth arrives, and Almachius asks her, "Don't you realize that I hold the power of life and death over you?" At which point Cecilia laughs out loud saying, "Now I can prove that you have lied against what is known by everyone! You can indeed take life away from the living, but you cannot give life to the dead. Therefore you are a minister of death, not of life!" The power

---

12. Tacitus, *Annales*, 15.44: "*odium generi humani*," in Robert Louis Wilken, trans., *The Christians as the Romans Saw Them* (New Haven: Yale University Press, 1984), 49. Cf. Ysabel de Andia, "Martyrdom and Truth," *Communio* (Spring 2002): 70.

struggle is over before the prefect even realizes it. He indeed has some power, as a minister of the earthly city, but his power is not absolute, nor can his power compete against the heavenly power of Christ, who indeed was raised from the dead and had raised others back to life.

As if he sensed that he had lost, Almachius, the minister of death but not of life, angrily ordered Cecilia to be boiled alive in her own bath for a night and a day. Despite all the heat applied to the water, she was able to sit in perfect coolness, not even perspiring. Almachius then ordered her to be beheaded; but after three attempts, all the swordsman could do was leave a big gash in her throat. Cecilia lived on for three more days, asking that her possessions be given to the poor and her house be turned into a church. Cecilia then entered the heavenly kingdom which she had preached about so well.

Two Kingdoms

The image of Saint Cecilia preaching describes well the anagogical purpose of both her story and those of her sisters—the virgin martyrs. In these stories, several images and allusions are used to lift the reader's mind to the heavenly kingdom. In the story of Cecilia, all the elements are there: the unseen world of the angels, the struggle between the powers of this world and the next. These oppositions serve as vehicles to convey the anagogical sense; and, as Charles Altman suggested, the medieval Latin legends of the saints can be divided into two groups based on what type of opposition their plots employ.[13] The first group of narratives belongs to the martyrs and falls into what he classifies as a diametrical opposition between virtues (saint) and vices (persecutor). The second group of saints' lives belongs to the confessor saints, whose stories reveal a *"gradational* opposition." This type of opposition does not reject the secular world, as the martyr narratives do, but implies a gradual development from the secular to the spiritual.

Altman, however, exaggerates the distinction between the two types of hagiography. It is important to remember that the differences are of degree and subtlety. In the *passions* of the martyrs, the

13. Altman, "Two Types of Opposition and the Structure of Latin Saints' Lives," *Medievalia et Humanistica* 6 (1975): 1–11.

opposition between the two kingdoms is played out in the arena of religions—the state religion versus Christianity. In the *vitas* of the nonmartyrs, this battle is fought within the individual—opposing the temptations of the world to live a life of holiness. Of course, these are two sides of the same coin, for the battle of the individual against worldly desires is known as a bloodless or white martyrdom, while the battle of a martyr against the world of the state could not have come about without the individual overcoming her (or his) earthly temptations. Both sides of this coin illustrate a deep devotion to Christ and the fundamental struggle between the City of God and the Earthly City, fully described by Saint Augustine.

Remembering that the Christian understanding of history incorporates the broadest possible schema, that is the history of salvation, Augustine describes his philosophy of history as the slow but certain demise of the earthly city—the city of the unconverted pagans—and the patient yet certain rise of the City of God, the city of those converted to Christ.[14] This battle, this epic vision of history, is played out in each and every one of the legends of the virgin martyrs, where the reader is confronted by a single yet bold question, "Which side are you on?" In the very first part of her story, we learn that on the night that Saint Cecilia was to be married,

> While the musical instruments sounded, she sang in her heart to the Lord alone, saying: "Let my heart and my body be undefiled, O Lord, that I may not be confounded."[15]

In this passage (which is also the main reason she is the patron saint of musicians), Cecilia is praying to the Lord that she may remain a virgin in both heart and mind. Her fear is that in marriage, she will be torn between two worlds. She worries that her heart and her body would be split between her husband and her Lord, echoing the words of Saint Paul:

> In the same way an unmarried woman, like a young girl, can devote herself to the Lord's affairs; all she need worry about is being holy in

---

14. Augustine, *De civitate Dei*, I, Preface.

15. The English translation of the word *confounded* reflects perfectly the Latin verb used by Jacobus to describe Cecilia's prayer: "Fiat, domine, cor meum et corpus meum immaculatum, ut non confundar." Jacobus de Voragine, *Legenda aurea*, Maggioni critical edition, 165:1181.

body and spirit. The married woman, on the other hand, has to worry about the world's affairs and devote herself to pleasing her husband. [16]

In the life of virginity, therefore, Cecilia would be free to have a single-minded focus on the Lord. It is a theme repeated through all the tales of the virgin martyrs, and actually provides one way to define a saint—*single-hearted*. As Augustine commented, the fulfillment of Christ's commandment is having "single-hearted charity." [17] This is not to say that those who are married cannot be saints; rather, in her dedication to Christ, Cecilia desired to devote her whole self to the Lord through virginity. Virginity is only one of many possible means to holiness, but those who choose this route must guard it just as strongly as those who are married must protect their marriage vows through diligence and faithfulness. And so, Cecilia and the other virgin martyrs pray and work to maintain their virginity as an act of devotion and love, even when they are forced to enter into marriage against their wills. Anastasia, for example, feigned sickness at her marriage bed in order to dissuade her new husband, maintaining the deception so that she could go out and perform acts of charity. And when the emperor asks Katherine to tell him her ancestry, she replies "I am Katherine, only daughter of King Costus. Though born to the purple and quite well instructed in the liberal disciplines, I have turned my back on all that and taken refuge in the Lord Jesus Christ." [18]

Indeed, it is this turning their backs to the entire world that makes the virgin martyrs so intriguing; it is also the key reason they are put to death. As we know from the stories, although many times it is their beauty which initially attracts attention, it is their steadfast refusal to deny Christ by offering sacrifice to the pagan gods that leads to their deaths. These women are, and will always remain, focused solely on Christ and his kingdom, and on no other, come what may.

The anagogical opposition established in these narratives between the earthly and heavenly cities can be seen from the other

---

16. 1 Cor 7:34.

17. Augustine, *Exposition 2 of Psalm 31*, 5, in John E. Rotelle, ed., Maria Boulding, trans., *Expositions of the Psalms: 1–32*, vol. III/15, *The Works of Saint Augustine: A Translation for the 21st Century* (Brooklyn, N.Y.: New City Press, 2000), 367.

18. Jacobus de Voragine, *The Golden Legend*, 2:335.

side as well. Historically speaking, in the beginning, the Romans saw Christianity as simply another cult or religion that came from some backwater of the world. In fact, they had a hard time distinguishing it from Judaism, a much larger minority religion found within the empire.[19] When they did begin to notice, the Romans saw the Christians, as Robert Wilken describes it, as a burial society. These were social organizations which existed around the worship of a common deity and provided an outlet for friendships, gatherings, meals, conversations, and support. As a member in good standing, one was entitled to a decent burial at the club's expense. Given the association of the early Christians with the grave, this seemed a logical description.[20]

The Roman social structure was surprisingly tolerant of people's religious beliefs, incorporating many of the gods of those lands which it had conquered into its own religious system.[21] But there was a caveat: above all, the state cult must be maintained. People could experience religious freedom and worship whatever god they chose only to the extent that they also participated in the state religion.[22] During the upheaval of the civil war and the ensuing turmoil of the last century before Christ, the poet Horace wrote what many believed:

> You will continue to pay for your fathers' sins, O Roman, although you yourself are guiltless, until you have restored the temples and crumbling shrines of the gods and their statues, filthy with black smoke. You rule an empire because you acknowledge that you are subordinate to the gods. From them comes every beginning; attribute to them also every outcome. You neglected the gods, and they heaped on Italy many grievous calamities.[23]

The rebuilding of the temples and the restoration of shrines was both a religious and a civic duty. "It is religious in that the rebuilding of [a] temple was an act of piety towards the gods; but it was civic in that it

---

19. Suetonius, in his *The Lives of the Caesars*, makes a passing reference that "Because the Jews were continually causing disturbances at the instigation of Chrestus, Claudius expelled them from Rome." *Claudius* 25.4, in Jo-Ann Shelton, trans., *As the Romans Did: A Sourcebook in Roman Social History*, 2nd ed. (New York: Oxford University Press, 1998), 445.

20. Wilken, *The Christians as the Romans Saw Them*, 31–47.

21. For a few Latin sources on this, see Shelton, *As the Romans Did*, 367–68.

22. Wilken, *The Christians as the Romans Saw Them*, 58.

23. Horace, *Odes*, 3.6, in Shelton, *As the Romans Did*, 389.

was a public occasion involving the *populace as a whole* and was presided over by the representative of the people and the political head of the empire, the emperor."[24]

In a letter to the emperor written after Christianity was proclaimed the official state religion of the empire, the nobleman Symmachus pleaded that the altar to the goddess of Victory, which stood in the Senate for four centuries and "had symbolized the successful relationship between the Romans and the gods of the state cult," be restored.[25] His words give insight to the Roman mentality:

> It is reasonable to assume that whatever each of us worships can be considered one and the same. We look up at the same stars, the same sky is above us all, the same universe encompasses us. What difference does it make which system each of us uses to find the truth? It is not by just one route that man can arrive at so great a mystery.[26]

In this letter, Symmachus is obviously trying to nuance the monotheism of the newly founded state religion in a desperate attempt to restore the worship of the old gods who protected the city for so long. As a matter of fact, the clash between the heavenly and earthly cities can be symbolized in Symmachus's attempt to restore the pagan Altar of Victory because when he wrote his letter to the emperor Valentinian, he actually invoked the ire of Saint Ambrose, who unleashed two strongly worded letters of his own to the emperor arguing, naturally, against Symmachus' request.[27]

For the Roman, Christianity's insistence on a single god to the exclusion of all others seemed not only irrational, but dangerous. If the gods of the state cult were not worshiped, then the very social fabric of the community would begin to be ripped apart. In his letter, Symmachus argues that when, for example, the rites and honors due the Vestal Virgins were not maintained, the crops failed and a general famine struck the land.[28] Cicero wrote that "in all probability, disappearance of piety towards the gods will entail the disappearance of loyalty and social union among men as well, and of justice itself, the

---

24. Wilken, *The Christians as the Romans Saw Them*, 55.
25. Shelton, *As the Romans Did*, 390.
26. Symmachus, *Dispatches to the Emperor*, 3.10, in Shelton, *As the Romans Did*, 391.
27. Ambrose, *Letters XVII and XVIII*.
28. Symmachus, *Memorial*, 14, in Shelton, *As the Romans Did*, 416.

queen of all virtues."[29] He also wrote that if piety were gone, so too would religion and reverence disappear. "And when these are gone, life soon becomes a welter of disorder and confusion."[30] It should be no surprise that Augustine, a man who studied Cicero, would agree with the idea that without worship, confusion reigns. The only difference is that for Augustine, this worship was of the one true God, and the confusion came from the devil.

Inevitably, a clash arose between these two competing systems. Although Christianity was very much a minority religion, its clashes with the state-run religion would cause periodic retaliations on the part of the government. These intermittent persecutions formed the background of the narratives of the virgin martyrs. In the end, it was no longer a struggle between a virgin and her suitor; instead, it was a battle between two world views. In the debate with the prefect, Cecilia's brother-in-law Tiburtius highlights this clash of kingdoms when he says to the Roman official, "That which seems to be and is not is everything in the world that leads man to nonbeing. What is not seen to be and is, is the life of the righteous and the punishment of the wicked."

The virgin-martyr narratives are constantly teaching that very point, reminding the reader to keep his gaze on those things that cannot be seen, but are more real than anything that can be seen, as demonstrated in Cecilia's response to the crowd. When the people pleaded with her to remember her youth and beauty and not to give up such precious things, Cecilia points to the more heavenly gifts:

> Good folks, I am not losing youth but exchanging it, giving up clay and receiving gold, abandoning a hut for a palace, leaving a narrow corner of the street for a wide-open, light-filled plaza. If someone offered you a gold piece for a copper, would you not accept it readily?[31]

In these stories, then, the City of God and the City of Earth fight head to head, and their battlefield was the body of the virgin martyr.

---

29. Cicero, *De natura deorum*, 1.4, in Wilken, *The Christians as the Romans Saw Them*, 58–59.

30. Ibid.

31. Jacobus de Voragine, *The Golden Legend*, 2:322.

MYSTICAL UNION

It is not enough, however, for these stories simply to repeat the age-old battle between heaven and earth. A true anagogical reading of these narratives has to point even higher, to the ultimate end of this battle. They have to point to the victory already won in Christ, for not only does the anagogical sense show you where to find relief from this battle, it also teaches "what mark you should aim for."[32] The Second Vatican Council described how this mark is found in the Church herself, doing so in terms that could be directly applied to the virgin martyrs:

> On earth, still as pilgrims in a strange land, following in trial and in oppression the paths [Christ] trod, we are associated with his sufferings as the body with its head, suffering with him, that with him we may be glorified.[33]

Glorification, of course, is found in the fulfillment of the Christian life at the end of the pilgrimage. In a great majority of the stories of the virgin martyrs, the reader not only hears of the saint's passion and martyrdom, but he also hears a foreshadowing of the mystical end a Christian strives to attain—union with God.

The night before their deaths, for example, the two brothers Valerian and Tiburtius were placed in the custody of the guard Maximus, who, like the prefect, could not understand why they were willing to forfeit their lives. Maximus asks them, "How is it that you hasten to your deaths as to a banquet?" They answered him that if he would believe in Christ, then he would see their souls rise up to heaven when they were executed. Maximus responded that if their prediction came true, "May I be consumed by fiery lightening if I do not profess my faith in that one true God whom you adore." That same night, even before their deaths, Maximus and his whole household were instructed and baptized into the faith. At the hour of the two brothers' passion, Maximus did indeed see "shining angels and their souls going forth like virgins from the bridal chamber, the angels carrying them heavenwards," to the heavenly banquet.

---

32. Henri de Lubac, *Medieval Exegesis*,1:1. The original text reads: "quo tendas anagogia," which literally translated means "anagoagy—by which you may aim/ strive." However, Synan's version of "where you can get relief" conveys roughly the same idea, if in a more poetic fashion.

33. *Lumen gentium*, no. 7.

The mystical union that is the end of each Christian life is further demonstrated in these narratives by a description of how the virgin martyrs act as heavenly intercessors after their deaths. The miracles associated with them demonstrate their closeness to the Lord. And so, we hear, for example, of Saint Margaret who, before her death, prays that women in difficult childbirth may call upon her and that through such a prayer, the Lord would remember Margaret's faithfulness and grant the birth of a healthy child. Apollonia is the patron saint of dentists after having all her teeth kicked out of her head. Agatha and Lucy both become patrons of the cities where they had suffered martyrdom. In the story of Katherine of Alexandria, we hear that after she died, milk, not blood, flowed from her wounds, and angels came and carried her body to Mount Sinai, where they gave her an honorable burial. A monastery exists there now, built by the emperor Justinian, and a healing oil is said to still issue from her body.

The miracles, the heavenly visits of angels, saints, and even of Christ himself, and the miraculous events that occur after the saint's death, all answer the question of where one finds relief. The end of this earthly pilgrimage, the *telos* of Christian life, is found in the Lord. All the mystical aspects of these stories are meant to invoke in the reader the hope of that life to come, all the while reminding him that it begins now, in this life. In the Church, in the body of Christ, the disciple finds himself participating in this union with God, the same union the virgin martyrs illustrate in the various details of their stories. As such, the legends of the virgin martyrs not only delight the reader, but also teach him the mark he should be aiming for — the goal is heaven, and the means to this end is faith, the faith found in and through the Church.

THE CHURCH

One of the ways in which the virgin martyrs have captured the imagination of the Church can be seen in the countless works of art and in hundreds of writings that tell the virgin-martyr's story, the suffering of an innocent young woman at the hands of a greedy, lustful, and power-hungry pagans, the epitome of everything foreign and evil, is a hard story to resist. It is a story that has been told and retold in books and movies of our own time, where the villain constantly desires the heroine; and when she refuses, he makes her suffer. (In the old villain movies, he would tie her to the railroad tracks.) In the case of the virgin martyrs, however, these romantic motifs are different; they point to a higher goal, to a greater degree of love.

Part of the reason why the virgin martyrs captured the imagination of the Church is due to the unique quality of the virgin body itself. Maud Burnett McInerney notes that twenty of the twenty-four female martyrs in the *Golden Legend* are virgins (not counting the 11,000 that accompanied Ursula). This has special significance, in that the virgin body has always been a sign of purity and integrity, and when associated with the divine, it holds a singular power.[34] It is this unique aspect that sets the virgin martyr stories apart from the other legends of the saints. In the virgin martyr there is a unique relationship, not only to Christ, but also to the rest of us. In her suffering and torment, we see the body of Christ undergoing torture and death. In her pledge of virginity we see her as the bride of Christ; and both of these descriptions—the *body of Christ* and *the bride of Christ*—were terms first applied to the Church.[35] And so, in the story of the virgin martyr, we see a microcosm of the Church: "You are," Amborse writes of the virgin, "all the more fit to be compared with the Church."[36]

Like the virgin martyrs themselves, the Church must be pure, faithful, and willing to be a sacrifice for the sake of others. This, of course, can only be accomplished through grace, but part of that grace involves seeing what has been taught anagogically—that this world is merely a transitional one, there is another kingdom that the Christian, and the Church, must strive for. In other words, part of the grace offered to the Church, through the revelation of Christ, is an eschatological understanding. To be sure, this same eschatological understanding is at the heart of the Church herself, as the Fathers of the Second Vatican described:

> It is of the essence of the Church that she be both human and divine,
> visible and yet invisibly equipped, eager to act and yet intent on contem-

---

34. Maud Burnett McInerney, "Rhetoric, Power, and Integrity in the Passion of the Virgin Martyr," in Kathleen Coyne Kelly and Marina Leslie, eds., *Menacing Virgins: Representing Virginity in the Middle Ages and Renaissance* (Newark: University of Delaware Press, 1999), 50–70.

35. See 2 Cor 11:2; Eph 5:22–33; Eph 4:12; Rom 12:5; 1 Cor 12:27.

36. Ambrose, *De virginitate*, XII.68, In James Shiel, trans., *Given to Love*, 101.

plation, present in this world and yet not at home in it; and she is all these things in such wise that in her the human is directed and subordinated to the divine, the visible likewise to the invisible, action to contemplation, and this present world to that city yet to come, which we seek.[37]

It is no coincidence that Saint Cecilia asks for her home to be converted into a church, the earthly component of the heavenly city. Nor is it a coincidence that Saint Agnes was especially honored in the liturgical calendar by having two feast days. The first, the 21st of January, commemorates her actual martyrdom. The second is a week later, on the 28th, and emphasizes the anagogical nature of the virgin martyr stories; this second feast commemorates how, eight days after her death, Agnes's parents saw their daughter on her way to her heavenly home. At her grave,

> [They] saw a chorus of angels clothed in shining gold garments, and in their midst Agnes, similarly clad and with a lamb whiter than snow standing at her right hand. Agnes consoled them: "Do not mourn my death, but rejoice and be glad with me, because I now have a throne of light amidst all these holy ones."[38]

The lamb, of course, is Christ, and the two are in their wedding procession.[39] Agnes is to have a "throne of light" as the bride of Christ; she is to be queen to the king of heaven himself.

Saint Augustine lays out one example of how the Church herself is understood to be such a queen. There are some texts, he says, that obviously concern Christ and his Church. One such text is Psalm 45, which describes a king, *the fairest of the sons of men*, and his queen, who stands *at* [his] *right hand, arrayed in the gold of Ophir.* Augustine identifies this queen with the Church, who is "joined to so great a Husband in spiritual marriage and divine love."[40]

"I do not suppose," Augustine continues, "that anyone is so foolish as to believe that it is some mere woman who is here praised and described." Obviously this psalm is describing a wife fit for such a man who is *anointed by God with the oil of gladness above [his] fellows.* These "fellows," Augustine tells us, are those Christians "out of whose

37. *Sancrosanctum concilium,* 2.
38. Jacobus de Voragine, *The Golden Legend,* 1:103.
39. Cf. Rev 19:7.
40. Augustine, *De civitate Dei,* XVII.16, 805.

unity and concord that 'queen' is formed who in another psalm is called 'The city of the great King' (Psalm 48:2)," and in others Mount Zion, the holy city, Jerusalem—all eschatological names for the Church of God.[41] The enemy of this heavenly city, Augustine goes on to tell us, is the Devil's city, Babylon:

> which means "confusion." Yet this queen among all nations is redeemed from that Babylon by regeneration, and passes from the worst king to the best; that is, from the devil to Christ.[42]

And as we have seen, this description is echoed in the discussion on authentic worship between Cecilia and her brother-in-law.

As the microcosm of the Church, we hear in the stories of the virgin martyrs how this Queen, the Church, was created; how she conquered the confusion called Babylon; and how she passed over from the kingdom of the devil to the kingdom of God. Everything that happens to the virgin martyr happens to the Church, and everything that describes these saints describes the Church. Through the lens of the virgin martyrs, we come to see how beautiful, noble, faithful, pure, and sacrificing the Church is (and is called to be). And, just as we receive a foretaste of what is to come through the stories of the virgin martyrs, we also know that it is in and through the Church that the Kingdom of God begins in the City of Earth which is transformed into the Queen of heaven.

THE VIRGIN MARTYR

The uniqueness of the virgin martyrs lies in the way she uplifts those who follow her life. In the story of Saint Justina, for example, we see the purity of faith exhibited in the purity of the virgin body; we realize that what the saintly virgin undergoes is the same struggle the Church herself experiences. Converted by listening to the deacon Proclus, the holy virgin-martyr Justina dedicated herself to Christ. Her father was a pagan priest, and so it was with some trepidation that Justina's mother told him of Justina's newfound faith as they were preparing for bed. That night, both father and mother had a dream in

---

41. Augustine, *De civitate Dei*, XVII.16, 805–6. Cf. Ps 48; Heb 12:22; Rev 21:2.
42. Augustine, *De civitate Dei*, XVII.16, 806.

which Christ, accompanied by his angels, told them to come to him, and he would give them the kingdom of heaven. The next day, her parents were baptized alongside their daughter.

Of course, the story does not end there. A certain young man named Cyprian, whose parents consecrated him at a young age to the devil, became enamored with our virgin saint. Note already, the two kingdoms are set up in opposition. Unable to cast a spell of love on her by himself, this man enlisted the help of a demon. Each time, the demon was thwarted by the faith of Justina, who simply made the sign of the cross and the demon had to flee. Exasperated, Cyprian recruited an even stronger demon, who was equally unsuccessful. Finally, he called upon the prince of demons. At first, this prince of demons seemed to have some success; he tempted Justina by quoting Scripture. Disguised as a fellow virgin committed to Christ, the devil asked, "Is it not true that God has told us to be fruitful and multiply? I am afraid that if we remain virgins, we will be going against God's command." Justina hesitated for a moment, but then she quickly came to herself and recognized who it was that was actually posing the question. "So she shielded herself with the sign of the cross, and then blew on the devil, causing him to melt like a candle."

The struggle with Cyprian and his league of demons is the struggle of the Church. The Church is constantly being assailed by the devil and all sorts of evil; but she is to remain true to her bridegroom, refusing to fall into the temptations of the world. The Church is also called to be a light to the world, bringing the good news of Christ. Like Christ, the Church is to be the incarnational witness of God's love, working towards bringing the world into the kingdom of God. In other words, the Church is to help bring about the conversion of the city of earth, leading it into the city of God. In the end, Cyprian confronted the devil and his inability to win Justina. He forced the devil to confess that the reason he failed was because the one who was crucified is greater. Realizing that he was on the losing side of the battle, Cyprian left the devil and followed Justina, becoming a disciple of Christ.

Together, Cyprian and Justina, like the Church, faced the ultimate threat. The Roman prefect heard of these two holy people and had them brought before him. He asked if they were willing to offer sacrifice to the gods; they steadfastly refused. After withstanding all the temptations of the devil, Justina was not about to dilute her faith in Christ by offering honor to the pagan gods; she remained true to the end, pure in her faithfulness to her bridegroom. Justina was thrown into a cauldron of boiling pitch, wax, and fat along with her one time persecutor, Cyprian. The boiling liquid, however, had no affect on the two saints; and so, the pagan priest came over to the caldron and cried out to his gods, Hercules and Jupiter. Immediately, fire poured out of the caldron and consumed the priest completely. As for Cyprian and Justina, they were taken out and beheaded.

The life of Justina displays how the virgin martyr is unique precisely in her capacity as *both* virgin and martyr. In their stories, these holy women offer the ultimate sacrifice, not because they are fearful of losing their virginity; on the contrary, they offer their lives because they realize that there are far more vital issues involved. As a virgin, the virgin martyr's "purity" represents the purity of faith which the Church possesses. To choose not to die, to offer incense to a pagan god, would mean a denial of Christ. Her faith would no longer be pure; her faith would no longer be single-hearted. The purity of her body was of paramount importance, not because of some narrow-minded understanding of sexuality, nor any other sociological reading of the texts, such as the defense of male property rights over women, but because the purity of that body reflected the purity of her faith.

This is why, in the stories, God always protected the saint's virginity. God was constantly on watch, jealously guarding her virginity at every step because, on one level of the story, her virginity represented the purity of the Church, who is always faithful to God. It is true that Cyprian and all martyrs die for their faith; but in the virgin martyrs, this element of purity is added, which corresponds not to the virgin herself, but to the entire people of God. This ecclesial dimension is present in the narratives of the virgin martyrs in a way that is not found in any of the other martyr legends. In the end, the body which the virgin martyr dies for is not her own body, but rather the Body of Christ.

Chapter 6

Brides of Christ:
A Tropological Reading

That which makes people blessed is not being close to upright and holy people by blood relationship, but being united with them by obeying and imitating their doctrine and way of life.

Saint Augustine[1]

Morality teaches what you ought to do.

Augustine of Dacia

One of the more fantastic and entertaining scenes found in the legends of the virgin martyrs is Saint Margaret confronting a demon disguised as a man. This demon was the agent of evil sent to entice Margaret away from Christ and into the arms of her persecutor, the prefect Olybrius. Recognizing him for what he was, Margaret grabs the demon by the head, throws him to the ground, and plants her right foot on his neck. In a strong and controlled manner, she tells the demon, "Lie still at last, proud demon, under the foot of a woman."[2] The demon, having utterly failed in his mission, reports back to the prefect, who is now even more frustrated and enraged.

This was not, however, Margaret's first experience in fighting the devil. Earlier, while sitting in prison after being hung on a rack and beaten by rods, a hideous dragon entered her cell and swallowed

---

1. Augustine, *De virginitate*, 3, in John E. Rotelle, ed., Ray Kearney, trans., vol. I/9, *Marriage and Virginity: The Excellence of Marriage, Holy Virginity, the Excellence of Widowhood, Adulterous Marriages, Continence, The Works of Saint Augustine: A Translation for the 21st Century* (Hyde Park, N.Y.: New City Press, 1999), 69.

2. Jacobus de Voragine, *The Golden Legend*, 1:369.

her up whole. Unfazed and with absolute trust, Margaret simply made the sign of the cross and the dragon burst into countless pieces; she stepped out from the middle of the carnage unscathed. In telling of this, however, the author of the *Golden Legend* warns the reader that the swallowing of the maiden and the bursting open of the dragon should be "considered apocryphal and not to be taken seriously."[3] Nonetheless, he includes it in the text because the point being made is quite straightforward: in this world, the Christian who desires holiness has to contend with the temptations and interference of the devil.

THE MORAL OF THE STORY

The story of Margaret fighting with the devil sets the stage for the last of the *four senses*, the moral or tropological reading of these stories. For most readers the tropological sense is the easiest one to comprehend; after all, it asks the basic question, what is the moral of the story? One major reason the stories of the saints should be read and preached is to teach us moral lessons and behaviors that we are to imitate. Unfortunately, sometimes it can be difficult to discern exactly what aspects of these saintly stories we are to imitate. In reading the virgin martyrs, are we to imitate their virginity, their radical stance against all authority, their willingness to die?

In her *Study of the Bible in the Middle Ages*, the Church historian, Beryl Smalley, observes that in the twelfth century the tropological sense took an interesting turn. Up until that time, tropology had a narrow focus: it dealt with how the biblical passage applied to the individual; but in the twelfth century, the tropological sense was expanded. "Instead of dealing mainly with the virtues and vices at war in the individual soul, [tropology moved to describe] external things, such as the behavior of groups, or types, and religious and social abuses." By expanding the use of the moral sense beyond the application to the individual, the preacher was understood to be holding up a mirror to society as a whole, showing the people "who they are, and what they ought to be"; he would do so by providing stories mixed with humor and satire, and the congregation would "delight in a spectacle which

---

3. Ibid., 1:369.

[was] both funny and edifying."[4] A tropological reading, therefore, can be applied either to the individual soul or to the greater society.

On the level of the individual, traditional tropological interpretation of the narratives of the virgin martyrs concentrated on the virtue of purity. As would be expected, the virgin martyrs were presented, in particular, as role models to young women. For religious women confined to the cloister, the virgin-martyr stories provided a strong moral to remaining steadfast in the vocation of a virgin. However, these stories were also applied to young women preparing for or early in their marriage. In these cases, the steadfastness and faithfulness of the "bride of Christ" was to be imitated by the young bride. In the early years of the fifteenth century, for example, Christine de Pisan wrote a guide book for raising young women, called *The Treasure of the City of Ladies*, in which she suggests that young women should read the lives of the virgin martyrs because they are outstanding stories of "women . . . whose fair lives serve as excellent examples for every woman above all other [sources] of wisdom."[5] Similarly, in William Caxton's translation of *The Book of the Knight of the Towers*, a work addressed to three daughters of the knight, the father tells his daughters to always keep in mind the lives of Saint Katherine, Saint Margaret, and other virgin martyrs, "For they surmounted many grete temptacions (sic)."[6]

Underneath such advice is the unstated supposition that the temptations the young women constantly faced were sexual temptations, an interpretation that appears to be supported by the narratives themselves. Through the copious miracles reported, it seems that the hagiographer (and therefore the Church) is saying that even God preferred these women to remain "pure" and "intact." The variety of miracles and events which sustain such a reading are numerous and, in some cases, quite amazing. We have Lucy, who is saved from gang rape by the Holy Spirit making her absolutely unmovable; Agnes is

4. Beryl Smalley, *The Study of the Bible in the Middle Ages* (Notre Dame, Ind.: University of Notre Dame Press, 1978), 245.

5. Quoted in Katherine J. Lewis, Noel M. James, and Kim M. Phillips, *Young Medieval Women* (Phoenix Mill: Sutton Publishing, 1999), 38.

6. Quoted in Katherine J. Lewis, "The Life of St Margaret of Antioch in Late Medieval England: A Gendered Reading," in R. N. Swanson, ed., *Gender and Christian Religion: Papers Read at the 1996 Summer Meeting and the 1997 Winter Meeting of the Ecclesiastical History Society*, *Studies in Church History* (Rochester, NY: Boydell Press, 1998), 141.

rescued by an angel blinding her would-be attacker; and the three virgin servants of Anastasia, who were saved by God who deprived the prefect of his senses, so that he satisfied his lust with the pots and pans of the kitchen, believing them to be the maidens.

To modern ears, of course, these miracles sound far-fetched. However, these miracles have occurred again, and in modern times. Consider an example from Korea: In 1839, two sisters, both Christians, were arrested along with others, in an attempt by the Korean authorities to crush the Christian faith, just as the Romans tried centuries before. These two young girls, Kim Huo-im Columba and Kim Hyo-ju Agnes, both named after saints, were stripped naked by government officials and thrown into a cell with hardened criminals for two days. The idea was to torture them through gang rape. Yet, even though they left the criminals unsupervised, and even may have encouraged them, not one of them approached the two women; both Agnes and Columba went unmolested. Eventually, though, the two were tortured severely and finally beheaded. They are now remembered as two of the 103 martyrs of Korea.[7] Also, recall one part of Saint Lucy's story, when, sentenced to the brothel, no one, not even a team of one thousand oxen, could budge her, a part of the story that cannot, of course, be historically verified. As incredible as this sounds, there was a similar case reported in 1961. In Garabandal, Spain, during the summer of 1961, four visionaries claiming to be seeing the Virgin Mary were immovable. Each one became so heavy that the strongest men in the village could not lift them an inch off the ground.[8]

In the legends of the virgin martyrs, God also works indirectly, through people and animals, to save his maidens from losing their virginity. We see that Daria is protected by a fierce, man-eating lion; and the Virgin of Antioch is saved by a knight who enters the brothel, as if to have his way only to exchange clothes with the saint, allowing her to leave unharmed. Later, as the knight is in jail awaiting execution for being a Christian, she finds him; together they both win the crown of martyrdom. Citing all the miracles that protect the virgin martyr from rape, a traditional tropological reading of these stories is one that promotes the virtue of individual purity above all others

---

7. Kim Chang–seok Thaddeus, *Lives of 103 Martyr Saints of Korea* (Seoul, Korea: Catholic Publishing House, 1984), 64 and 86–87.

8. Randall Sullivan, *The Miracle Detective* (New York: Atlantic Monthly Press, 2004), 181.

On the other hand, a contemporary tropological reading of the virgin martyrs avoids discussing the individual virtues; instead, it advances an understanding of the societal issues these stories depict. Such an interpretation believes that these stories can actually articulate a strong counterpoint to a male-dominated religious system. The fact is that these stories describe female saints standing up to male judges, just as much as they depict torture and death. The narratives of the virgin martyrs convey intelligent, clever, and unintimidated young women who get the better of their male antagonists. This leads many contemporary readers to see the virgin martyrs as the "pioneers of women's freedom." One such reader puts it this way:

> In the virgin martyrs, feminine weakness becomes strength, feminine loquacity becomes eloquence, and this strength and eloquence have a single object: to put the virgin herself beyond the roles and limitations of a society that casts women as silent, passive child bearers.[9]

Such an interpretation, however, seems to ring false for two reasons. First, if society (and presumably the male-dominated Church is a significant participant of this society) desired women to be "silent, passive child bearers," why would the Church promote such stories of the virgin martyrs who were anything but silent and passive? Certainly, there is no evidence that bishops and priests preached on the virgin martyrs, calling on women to follow their example and stand up to male authority, which would have meant resisting the very preachers who were spreading such a message! Second, defining the virgin martyrs as such pioneers of women's freedom fails to explain how these female saints were role models for all of society. The sheer amount of artwork dedicated to the virgin martyrs that can be seen throughout medieval Europe demonstrates how Saint Margaret and the other virgin martyrs were seen as role models for people across the population, not simply for women. For example, devotion to Saint Katherine of Alexandria in England alone "can be detected across the period and among all classes within medieval society." Various aspects of her story made her the patron saint of different guilds, societies, and institutions, in addition to appealing to the general public;

---

9. Maud Burnett McInerney, "Rhetoric, Power, and Integrity in the Passion of the Virgin Martyr," in Kathleen Coyne Kelly and Marina Leslie, eds., *Menacing Virgins: Representing Virginity in the Middle Ages and Renaissance* (Newark: University of Delaware Press, 1999), 63.

devotion to Saint Katherine was so prominent that, in some way fathomable only to medieval genealogists of the time, she was said to be related to the royal family themselves.[10]

Like all the virgin martyrs, Margaret and Katherine had to face a variety of temptations, all of which serve the tropological sense of the story by teaching the reader what "he ought to do." One of the strongest moral lessons of these narratives, of course, is that none of these frail, young girls ever gave in to the temptation to run. Each one of them resisted the temptation to flee, even when threatened with torture, rape, and death. At the same time, and in a hundred different ways, these saints resisted the temptations of despair, anxiety, fear, loneliness, doubt, and the need for acceptance, along with resisting the temptations voiced by those around them, such as lust, luxury, wealth, comfort, and the temptation to "think of your beauty, your youth," and not let them "go to waste."

The "moral" of the stories, therefore, calls for the listener to imitate the virgin martyrs in how they succeeded in resisting all temptations, rebuking the devil and all his works, either on the level of the individual or in the social realm. To apply the words of Richard of St. Victor, these stories resonate with the "honorable elements of morals" which are "inscribed on the human heart."[11] It is a concept that is clearly stated by Jacobus de Voragine in his telling of the story of the virgin martyr Katherine of Alexandria.

SAINT KATHERINE OF ALEXANDRIA

The daughter of a king, Katherine was very well educated in the liberal arts, knowing all the philosophies of the time.[12] There is no mention in the *Golden Legend* how she became a Christian, but implied in her intelligence and wisdom is the idea that she must have seen the truth of the faith from an early age. One day, she was alone in the palace, surrounded by all its riches and servants which, we are told, held no sway over her, when she heard commotion coming from the town.

---

10. Katherine J. Lewis, *The Cult of St Katherine of Alexandria in Late Medieval England* (Woodbridge, Suffolk: Boydell Press, 2000), 63–79.

11. Henri de Lubac, *Medieval Exegesis*, 2:131.

12. The legend of Saint Katherine is from Jacobus de Voragine, *Legenda aurea*, 168:1205–15. Cf. *The Golden Legend*, 2:334–41.

She quickly learned that the emperor was in Alexandria and had summoned the entire town to offer sacrifice to the gods and to root out and persecute the Christians. Indignant, Katherine quickly went out of the house, arming herself with the sign of the cross to confront the emperor directly.

She went up to him and said: "Both the dignity of your rank and the dictates of reason counseled me, Emperor, to present my greeting to you if you were to acknowledge the Creator of the heavens and renounce the worship of false gods." Such determination and resolve quickly impressed the emperor; and Katherine held him there, in front of the entrance to the temple. She prevented him from entering the temple and offering sacrifice by letting out a stream of reasoned arguments as to why he should worship the one true God. "You wonder at this temple built by the hands of artisans. You admire the precious ornaments that in time will be like dust blown before the face of the wind. Marvel rather at the heavens and the earth, the land and the sea and all that is in them." The list goes on, and finally Katherine says to the emperor, "Take note of all these things, and then ask, and learn, who it is who has brought all these into being."

With these and many more arguments, the emperor became intrigued and wanted to engage her in stimulating debate, but he knew that the duties of his office and his religion required him to offer sacrifice at that time. He finally managed to pull himself away, but only after he ordered the guards to arrest her and place her in prison. That way, he thought, at least he would be able to have a future conversation with her.

Later, the emperor summoned Katherine and began to debate her, a prospect he found both mentally engaging and personally invigorating. Once again he was deeply impressed with Katherine's wisdom, but now he also noticed her beauty. He asked her who she was, and about her family and background. Katherine responded by saying that she was the only daughter of King Costus; she told the emperor that although she was "born to the purple and quite well instructed in the liberal disciplines, I have turned my back on all that and have taken refuge in the Lord Jesus Christ." She then said to the emperor that his gods were quite useless, "When called upon in times of need, they offer no aid; in times of tribulation they give no comfort, and when in danger they offer no defense."

The emperor quickly realized that he could not answer all of Katherine's claims, and so he summoned the fifty wisest philosophers in the empire. When all had arrived from the four corners of the world, they assembled and asked the emperor what he wanted. He explained that there was a young girl "who has no equal in understanding and prudence. She refutes all our wise men and declares that all our gods are demons. If you can refute her, then you shall be able to go home rich and famous." All fifty of the world's greatest thinkers started to laugh, saying that any one of their students could perform such a task. Their smugness, however, was short-lived. After hours and hours of debate, the philosophers finally threw up their hands in surrender; all their arguments were exhausted. They returned to the emperor and said that they could not succeed; in fact, they found her arguments so convincing that they said to the emperor, "We are all converted to Christ!" The emperor erupted into a fury and ordered the execution of all fifty, but with words of encouragement from Katherine, their resolve for Christ was firm, and they went off, jumping into the flames set for them.

The emperor then turned his attention back to Katherine. He begged her to think carefully and remember her youth; he offered her the highest place in the empire, second only to the empress herself. Naturally, she refused. "I am the bride of Christ," she said, "and nothing, not even bribes, enticements or torture, and the threat of death will tear me away from his love." The emperor once again burst into a rage and had Katherine locked away for twelve days, while he went away on official business. While locked up, none other than the empress herself came to see Katherine, inspired by the saint's steadfastness and ability to stand up against her husband and the wisest men of the realm. Katherine instructed her in the faith, and she was converted to Christ. While this was going on, the two hundred soldiers assigned to guard both Katherine and the empress, listened outside the door. From what they overheard, they too came to believe in Christ; they knelt before Katherine and acknowledged their faith.

Because the emperor ordered Katherine to be held in the cell without food or water, Christ sent angels to her with food from heaven. On the night before the emperor returned, Christ himself came to visit her. "Be constant, Katherine," Christ told her, "for I am with you." The next day, after failing in his attempts to persuade

Katherine to change her mind, the emperor resorted to torture. Katherine told him that this was fine with her, because she wanted to offer her body and blood to Christ just as Christ had offered his body and blood for her. The emperor's men built a unique machine consisting of four counter-rotating wheels, each studded with iron saws and sharp nails meant to tear Katherine's flesh to shreds. Before they could get her on the device, however, Katherine prayed to the Lord, asking him to destroy it for the sake of his glory and the conversion of souls. Immediately an angel of the Lord struck the contraption so hard that it was completely shattered, the shrapnel flying in all directions, killing four thousand pagans where they stood.

Eventually Katherine was killed by being beheaded, but not before the queen went to her husband and berated him for his cruelty. Remaining doggedly stubborn in his own conviction, the emperor ordered the queen, his own wife, tortured and executed for her Christian beliefs. After the queen's death, the chief guard secretly buried her body. The emperor caught wind of the guard's secret actions and summoned him for an explanation. The guard confessed his Christian motives; and right then, all the other guards who were converted by Katherine came up and stood beside their chief, declaring that they too were Christians. The emperor ordered that all two hundred should be executed. In the end, however, the emperor himself did not escape punishment. In the story relating the events around the finding of the True Cross, we learn how eventually the emperor was punished for these and other sins when he met Constantine in battle at the Albine Bridge, which we know of as the Milvian Bridge. Trying his hand at deception, the emperor, Maxentius, the one who had Katherine killed, designed a false bridge; but when the battle began, he forgot his own plan, and ran onto the false bridge. It collapsed, of course, and he fell into the river; his body lost in the waters forever.[13]

After reporting the story of the virgin-martyr Katherine of Alexandria, the author of the *Golden Legend* offers his own moral interpretation as to what the reader should learn and imitate in this great saint. There are five things that he finds admirable in Katherine: first her wisdom, second her eloquence, third her constancy, fourth her chastity, and fifth her privileged dignity. Katherine's wisdom is

---

13. Jacobus de Voragine, *The Golden Legend* (*Legenda aurea*), 1:279–80.

evident throughout the narrative, but especially in how she turned away from all things material and human and desired only God. Her eloquence flows naturally from her wisdom, but it too is always used to preach one thing, Christ, and her preaching was, as we have heard, quite convincing. In all this Katherine remained constant in her faith, even in the most trying and desperate of times. She remained steadfast in her devotion to the Lord.

In the purity of her chastity, we see how Katherine remained true despite all the areas of temptation that normally test a virtuous heart to the breaking point, areas such as having abundant wealth, the opportunity for intimate relations, the temptations of youth, and having both freedom and beauty. Note that these temptations all occurred before she was put on trial or even known by the emperor; there were no miraculous interventions preventing her from succumbing to temptations earlier in her life, when she lived in the palace of her father. There were, however, many areas in which Katherine was protected by the miraculous intervention of God, all occurring after she was arrested; and these help describe the fifth area in which we are to admire and imitate this saint.

All of the miracles experienced by Katherine, the feeding in jail, the breaking up of the wheels of torture, the visitation of Christ himself, all these protections point to a privileged dignity, a special affiliation between the saint and Christ. Not only was she His bride, but they shared the close bond of friendship. Ultimately, each Christian is to experience the same dignity, the same relationship with Christ; and this special status as friends of God calls each disciple to live a more dignified, a more virtuous life. In the story, this dignity is described in terms of Katherine's devotion to God; but even more so, the miracles she experiences—which are meant to remind the reader of the miracles he himself has experienced—demonstrate God's radical devotion to his friends.

TROPOLOGY

Nevertheless, it must be conceded that in the end it is difficult to imitate the virgin martyrs. The virtues promoted by the story of Saint Katherine, wisdom, eloquence, virginity, all seem quite specific to a certain vocation and not all that applicable to the general Christian public. Although it is true that the last virtue, remembering our privileged dignity as children of God, is something that every Christian is to do, ascertaining such a concept from all the miracles and extraordinary events of the legends of the virgin martyrs requires a lot of thought and reflection (and even then, it might still be a stretch). One would hope that the tropological sense, the sense that teaches the reader what he ought to do, would be simpler, more straightforward, universal, and obvious. Despite all that has been said already, the question remains, what, exactly, are we to imitate in these eccentric virgin martyrs?

Originally, *tropologia* meant "speech turned around," referring to something like a metaphor or a twist of phrase. It had no connotations of moral conversion. Eventually, in the hands of biblical scholars like Origen, *tropologia* would come to mean "speech turned around toward us, i.e., toward our ways of behaving."[14] A tropological reading is one that sways the reader into change, into a deeper conversion of heart. Even then, however, we should avoid thinking that the tropological sense simply depicts a moral code or a set of behaviors that we should duplicate. Rather, to understand the unique and distinct moral teachings of the Christian faith, we first have to encounter the mystery of Christ. It is from this encounter that Christian moral behavior results; as the ninth century Benedictine Abbott and Archbishop Rabanus has said, "one is not made to come to faith by the virtues, but rather one is brought to pursue the virtues by means of faith."[15] A tropological reading of the virgin-martyr stories, therefore, has to begin from the same starting point as the other senses—that is, it begins with having faith in Christ.

Fundamental to all the stories of the virgin martyrs is desire. There is the desire of the people around, including some of the parents, who tell their daughter to stop her behavior and marry well; there are also the lustful desire of the suitor and the desire of the official that the virgin martyr relent and sacrifice to the pagan gods. Chief among all these desires, though, is the desire of the young saint to remain true to her bridegroom, Christ, to maintain her faith in him. This intention forms the heart of any tropological reading.

---

14. De Lubac, *Medieval Exegesis*, 2:129.
15. Ibid., 2:128.

Leo the Great, for example, ends his homily on the Ascension by moving his listeners from the *uplifting* events gleaned from the anagogical sense to the more immediate moral implications, telling them how they should remain true to Christ: "And so, dearly beloved, let us rejoice with spiritual joy, and let us with gladness pay God worthy thanks and raise our hearts' eyes unimpeded to those heights where Christ is." Of course, once our hearts have been uplifted, the pope continues, they should never again "be pressed down by earthly affections." For Leo, the root of earthly affections is the evil weed of avarice, from which comes all sorts of evils:

> Let us then, dearly beloved, resist this pestilential evil and '"follow after charity," without which no virtue can flourish, that by this path of love whereby Christ came down to us, we too may mount up to Him, to Whom with God the Father and the Holy Spirit is honour and glory for ever and ever. Amen. [16]

To follow charity is to follow Christ; it means to stay true to that love. In a tropological reading of the virgin martyrs, this idea is reinforced over and over again. The saints are consistently being pulled by tempters who try to make them abandon their desire to remain true to Christ, who remained true to them.

There is one more desire that should be considered in these stories, and that is the desire for the listener of the story. Built into the telling of these tales is the desire to lead the listener away from the temptations of the self, the "earthly affections," and towards the desire to remain true to Christ. As discussed in the previous chapter, this is one reason for the popularity of these saints; devotion to the virgin martyrs was very popular because their stories led a variety of groups and peoples to seek them out as intercessors. In the case of Saint Margaret, this role was even woven into the narrative. As noted earlier, right before she was to be killed, Margaret specifically mentions those who would listen to her story. She prayed "devoutly for herself and for her persecutors and for all who would honor her memory and invoke her, adding a prayer that any woman who invoked her aid when faced

---

16. Leo the Great, *Second Homily on the Lord's Ascension (Sermon 74)*, trans. Charles Lett Feltoe, vol. 12, *Nicene and Post–Nicene Fathers Second Series* (Buffalo: The Christian Literature Company, 1895), 189.

with a difficult labor would give birth to a healthy child."[17] Implicit in her prayer is the assumption that the listener actually *heard* the story of Margaret and was *moved* to a deeper faith in Christ. The desire for the listener is that he or she may be moved to a deeper love of God by imitating the intense faith of the virgin martyr. The effect of this desire for the listener can be seen directly in the life of Saint Thérèse of Lisieux.

THE VIRGIN MARTYRS AND THE *LITTLE FLOWER*

In her autobiography, *The Story of a Soul*, the Carmelite nun, Thérèse, described her trip to Rome in 1887, a trip that changed her life in several ways. One aspect of her visit to the Eternal City might not seem very significant at first glance, but as it relates to the virgin martyrs, it should not go unnoticed. At one point in her narrative, Thérèse tells us how she had a desire to have a souvenir from the catacombs; and so, she and her sister fell back, letting the tour group go ahead of them. Together, they slipped into the ancient tomb of Saint Cecilia. As Thérèse tells us:

> Before my trip to Rome I'd had no particular devotion for that Saint, but on visiting her home that had been changed into a church, the place of her martyrdom, and on learning that she had been proclaimed the queen of harmony, not because of her beautiful voice or her talent for music, but in memory of the *virgin's song* that she sang to her Heavenly Bridegroom who was hidden in the depths of her heart, I felt for her more than devotion: It was the true *tenderness of a friend*. . . . She became my favorite Saint, my intimate confidante. . . . Everything about her delighted me, especially her *abandon*, her boundless *trust* that rendered her capable of making virgins of souls who never desired any other joys than those of the present life.[18]

Here is an example of how the stories of the virgin martyrs promote and deepen the faith of Christian disciples. When she visited the sites and heard the stories associated with Cecilia, Thérèse was

---

17. Jacobus de Voragine, *The Golden Legend*, 1:370.

18. Thérèse of Lisieux, *The Story of a Soul*, trans. Robert J. Edmonson (Brewster, Mass.: Paraclete Press, 2006), 147 (italics added). One of Thérèse's first poems was on Saint Cecilia. See Thérèse of Lisieux, *The Poetry of Thérèse of Lisieux*, trans. Donald Kinney (Washington, D.C.: Institute of Carmelite Studies, 1996), 43–45.

moved into a deeper faith, one that would continue to unfold in her own spiritual and moral development. Inspired by the example of Saint Cecilia and many others, Thérèse would eventually accept her own suffering with dignity and come to understand how, as she put it, her vocation was to love.

Thérèse reflected on this vocation over and over again in her writings, especially in her letters and poetry. Thérèse enjoyed a special correspondence with a seminarian and future missionary named Maurice Bellière, who wrote to the monastery of Lisieux asking for the prayers of one of the nuns, as he began his studies for the priesthood. The Mother Superior assigned Thérèse to be his spiritual sister. In one letter to him dated June 21, 1897, Thérèse wrote a simple description of her "little way,"[19] repeating the same idea she found so attractive in Saint Cecilia: "I try to be no longer occupied with myself in anything, and I *abandon* myself to what Jesus sees fit to do in my soul (emphasis added)."[20] She says something quite similar to another spiritual brother, the Reverend Adolphe Roulland, a missionary to China. Sometimes, she told him, the great spiritual treatises she knows she should read actually cause her head to hurt and her soul to dry up. At those times, she drops them and turns to the Sacred Scriptures. "Then all seems luminous to me; a single word uncovers for my soul infinite horizons, perfection seems simple to me; I see it is sufficient to recognize one's nothingness and to *abandon* oneself as a child into God's arms."[21]

What Thérèse had learned was that abandonment is an essential virtue necessary for faith. Christ told his disciples this very truth when he said to them that if they wanted to follow him, they would

---

19. Thérèse's "little way" is found throughout her autobiography and describes her simple approach to spirituality. It is based simply on love and trust where she teaches that our focus should be doing ordinary things extraordinarily and with the single intention of love.

20. Thérèse of Lisieux, *General Correspondence*, Centenary ed., vol. 2, trans. John Clarke (Washington, D.C.: Institute of Carmelite Studies, 1982), 1134.

21. Ibid., 2:1094, (emphasis added). Cf. Thérèse's letter to her sister Celine: "I cannot think without delight of the dear little *St. Cecilia*; what a model for the little lyre of Jesus. . . . In the midst of the world, plunged into the center of all dangers, at the moment of being united with a young pagan who longs only for profane love, it seems to me that Cecilia would have to tremble and to weep . . . but no, while hearing the sounds of the instruments that were celebrating her nuptials, *Cecilia was singing in her heart.* . . . What abandonment!" Thérèse of Lisieux, *General Correspondence*, 2:850–51 (emphasis added).

have to deny themselves daily and take up their crosses. [22] In other words, in order to follow the will of Christ, as Thérèse teaches in her "little way," the disciple has to abandon his own will. This requires a great courage and trust on the part of the disciple, which is something else Thérèse admired in Saint Cecilia. On her deathbed Thérèse is reported as saying, "I prefer the saints who feared nothing, like Saint Cecilia, who allowed herself to be married and feared nothing." [23]

In the end what Thérèse learned to imitate from the story of the virgin martyr Cecilia was the virtue of *fortitude*, the courage of discipleship. Fortitude, however, was just half of the picture, for abandonment to the will of God not only requires a strong dose of the gift of fortitude, it also requires a genuine love, the gift of *charity*. For Thérèse, this sense of abandonment is the "delectable fruit" of the tree of love, and is seen most clearly in the Eucharist when Christ himself abandoned his life for the sake of those he loved. This sense of giving oneself totally for others, Thérèse continues, has to take root in one's soul. [24]

These two virtues, then — fortitude and charity, or in Saint Thérèse's words, trust and love — are the two major virtues that the reader "ought to" imitate after encountering the virgin martyrs. Thérèse herself heard these stories in the Divine Office; she learned the story of Saint Cecilia for the first time when she visited the saint's tomb and church in Rome. From these stories, she learned to imitate the abandonment of any self-centered desires and to embrace the will of Christ, who is love. From the experience of that love, she received great courage and strength. For Thérèse, these virtues were a deeply valued gift. In a poem addressed to Saint Cecilia, Thérèse notices how humans have an advantage over the angels in heaven: they can imitate the self-sacrifice of Christ that defines true charity. [25] Only human beings, made in the image of God, have the capacity for this gift of self, the total abandonment of the self to Christ that Thérèse admires so much in Cecilia, and by extension, to the other virgin martyrs. It is also what she most desperately desired to imitate. At the end of her poem she addresses Cecilia directly:

---

22. Matt 16:24.
23. Thérèse of Lisieux, *General Correspondence*, 2:829 n. 10.
24. Thérèse of Lisieux, *The Poetry of Thérèse of Lisieux*, 206–8.
25. Ibid., "Saint Cecilia," 45.

Cecilia, lend me your sweet melody.
I would like to convert so many hearts to Jesus!
Like you, I would like to sacrifice my life.
I would like to give him both my blood and my tears . . .
Obtain for me to taste perfect abandonment,
That sweet fruit of love, on this foreign shore.
O my dear saint! soon, far from earth,
Obtain for me to fly beside you forever. [26]

The fortitude and the charity needed to undergo such suffering as Thérèse desires may seem contrary to any healthy sense of life, but it is just the opposite. By seeking the suffering she is speaking of, Thérèse desires to imitate not only the virgin martyrs, but the one they, in turn, are imitating—Christ and his perfect love.

Another virgin martyr that was close to Thérèse's heart was Joan of Arc, the fifteenth-century French warrior saint. It cannot be a coincidence that two of the three heavenly visitors Joan received in her mystical visions were the virgin martyrs, Katherine of Alexandria and Margaret of Antioch, who help teach her the meaning of sacrifice and love. [27] In Thérèse's understanding, Joan's fighting may have saved France and brought about the coronation of a king, but all this was "only fleeting glory." Joan's true glory, the glory that won her a crown in heaven was "her virtues, her love." [28] And those became evident in her subsequent suffering. [29]

Still, it is not enough simply to seek suffering; in fact, there is no virtue in suffering for the sake of suffering, which both Thérèse and the virgin martyrs understood. Suffering is for the sake of sacrifice; it is for the sake of love as Christ demonstrated in the gift of the cross. As Thérèse said in her prayer at the end of her poem to Saint Cecilia, the goal of suffering is to "convert so many hearts to Jesus!" Or, as she writes in her "Canticle for the Canonization for Joan of Arc:"

Sweet Martyr, our monasteries are yours.
You know well that virgins are your sisters,

---

26. Ibid.

27. See Donald Spoto, *Joan: The Mysterious Life of the Heretic Who Became a Saint* (New York: HarperSanFrancisco, 2007), 14–18. Cf. Paul Burns, *Butler's Lives of the Saints*, 5:173.

28. Donald Spoto, *Joan: The Mysterious Life*, "Canticle to Obtain the Canonization of the Venerable Joan of Arc," 48.

29. Ibid., "To Joan of Arc," 200.

And like you the object of their prayers
Is to see God reign in every heart.[30]

Through all this, we can see that what Thérèse saw in the narratives of
the virgin martyrs was the same vocation to love that she herself felt
and imitated. For Thérèse, the moral of Saint Cecilia and Joan of Arc
was the lesson of self-abandonment, fortitude, and charity. Thérèse
perceived these gifts, these virtues, explicitly in the stories of the virgin martyrs. How Thérèse thought of the virgin martyrs may be
summed up in a line for a play she wrote depicting the life of Joan of
Arc; Joan says, "If I am honored in Heaven, it is not for having been
an illustrious warrior, but because I united virginity with
martyrdom!"[31]

VIRGIN AND MARTYR

Again, as was the case with the other three senses of reading, the
combination of virginity and martyrdom results in a very powerful
expression of Christian discipleship. In the moral reading of these
saints, this combination shows the reader that what is required is an
abandonment of self that leads to fortitude and charity, to great trust
and love in Christ. This abandonment can be seen in each and every
one of the virgin martyr narratives, from Katherine who went out
from a palace full of riches, comforts, security, and even authority, to
Lucy's abandonment of her dowry for the sake of the poor, and
Agnes's forfeiting of the earthly treasures offered her for the promise
of heavenly treasures.

The gift of fortitude that accompanies such abandonment is
also very clear in these narratives. How else can one explain the abun-
dance of courage and strength demonstrated by these young girls?
They faced every kind of cruelty, torture, and pain; they experienced
the mocking of the crowds, and, sometimes, even of their own families. Nevertheless, they remained resolute and courageously faced
every challenge with the conviction of Christ's love. This holds true
even in the troubling few cases where it appears the virgin martyr
actually commits suicide, as we see in the story of Saint Pelagia.

---

30. Ibid., "Canticle to Obtain the Canonization of the Venerable Joan of Arc," 49.
31. Ibid., 46.

Ambrose himself used Pelagia's story in his treatise *On Virginity*, as he tried to answer a question from his sister about Pelagia's apparent suicide. [32] Pelagia was alone in her family house in Antioch when the persecutions of Christians began. Knowing her to be a Christian, the crowds came and surrounded her house, demanding her surrender. Pelagia strongly suspected, because of past occurrences, that the men surrounding her house desired to have their way with her, so before this would happen, she asked permission from them to prepare herself for death. They agreed, and so Pelagia climbed the stairs of her house and dressed herself in a bride's dress, and then calmly, threw herself out the window. After she died, the men, denied their lustful intentions, went after Pelagia's mother and sisters, who, while being chased, walked into a river hand in hand and drowned. [33]

The question posed to Ambrose from his sister Marcellina was if such an act, which appears to be suicide, could be a cause for merit or condemnation. Earlier, in the second book of *On Virginity*, Ambrose explicitly laid out the case that a virgin who was raped or forced against her will in any manner was not guilty of any sin; indeed, she was still considered a virgin. [34] From their stories, the virgin martyrs certainly knew that there would be no sin, no disgrace, on their part if they were raped. The answer as to the merits or sinfulness of a virgin causing her own death cannot be discerned on the level of virginity or purity; this

---

32. Ambrose, *De virginibus*, III.32–38, 114–15.

33. Ramsey notes that Ambrose's version of the Pelagia legend is a combination of the legend of Saint Pelagia and a different story of a mother and her three daughters (*De virginibus*, nn. 49, 224). Eusebius reports a similar story of a mother and her three daughters from Antioch who threw themselves into the river to preserve their chastity. See Eusebius, *Ecclesiastical History*, VIII.12, in G. A. Williamson, trans., *The History of the Church from Christ to Constantine* (New York: Penguin Books, 1989), 269–70.

In fact, there are several different Pelagias; the Pelagia of Antioch whom Ambrose discusses is not the same Pelagia reported in the *Golden Legend*. The Pelagia found in the *Golden Legend* (2:230–32) is obviously based on a translation of an original Syriac text which tells the story of a woman of Antioch named Pelagia who was extravagantly dressed wearing the finest silks and jewels. She was a prostitute and her beauty was beyond compare. The way in which she places so much care in her appearance shames the holy bishop Veronus (Nonnos in the Syriac version) who says that he does not spend so much energy pleasing the Lord as this woman does pleasing her costumers. After hearing a homily by the same bishop, however, Pelagia is converted from her sinful ways. She sells all that she has and gives the money to the poor and then goes off into the desert. There she puts on the robe of a hermit and spends her years in prayer and fasting. She eventually dies not as a martyr, but in her cave while she slept. For the original Syriac version see Sebastian P. Brock and Susan Ashbrook Harvey, *Holy Women of the Syrian Orient*, vol. 13, *Transformation of the Classical Heritage* (Berkeley: University of California Press, 1987), 40–62.

34. Ambrose, *De virginibus*, II.24, 97.

is also the opinion of Saint Augustine. Augustine understood suicide always to be a definite sin.[35] However, if for some reason, a woman was under the mistaken impression that there was some disgrace in being such a victim, and she does end up committing suicide in order to avoid such a disgrace, Augustine asks, "What person of human feeling, then, would refuse to forgive those women who for this reason slew themselves rather than suffer in such a way?"[36]

The answer to Marcellina's question, then, has to be found elsewhere. Ambrose suggests that the answer is found in looking, not at Pelagia's suicide, but at her desire to remain true to the oath she had made to Christ when she became his bride. In his reading of the story, it was Pelagia's constancy, her steadfastness that required such a drastic response. This is an answer that Augustine supports as well. In the *City of God*, Augustine introduces the pagan story of Regulus, who was a Roman general captured by the Carthaginians.[37] He swore an oath while captive to return to his enemy after he served as an ambassador for a prisoner exchange. Regulus does return, after arguing against the prisoner exchange, even though his people begged him not to, realizing it meant his certain death. He does so out of a sense of devotion. He had made an oath, and even though he was a captive, he had made it freely. He returned to fulfill that oath, even though it meant certain death; to do otherwise meant dishonoring both himself and the gods.

Although never directly stated by Augustine, implicitly, Regulus's desire to remain true to what he promised to his gods, is the same devotion displayed by those virgin martyrs who actually commit suicide instead of being raped. They made an oath, a promise, to be true to their bridegroom. To them, even though they knew no sin was involved, they desired to maintain that vow to the end, whatever may come. Despite the fact that the story of the virgin martyrs, even those few who committed suicide, may have some connection to similar romantic stories and perceptions of antiquity,[38] the strength and

35. Augustine, *De civitate Dei*, I.20, 32–33.

36. Ibid., I.17, 26–27.

37. Ibid., I.15, 23–26.

38. See Kate Cooper, *The Virgin and the Bride: Idealized Womanhood in Late Antiquity* (Cambridge, Mass.: Harvard University Press, 1996). Cooper argues that the romantic stories of antiquity were designed to support and foster loyalty to the *polis* and the common good (20–44) and that these stories and the culture that produced them directly influenced the Christian

courage reported in the narratives of the virgin martyrs is distinctly Christian. This resolve is why the Church claimed them as martyrs. Luckily only a few of the virgin martyr narratives involve a saint committing suicide, for both Ambrose's and Augustine's attempts to justify these actions appear problematic and not necessarily convincing.

Nevertheless, the virtue of fortitude must always be accompanied by the greater virtue of charity. Through the abandonment of will, all the virgin martyrs remain constant in their love and dedication to Christ, and that love also overflows towards others. Saint Thérèse of Lisieux saw this most clearly in her life, as well as in the stories of the saints, chiefly, as the hunger for souls, the desire "to see God reign in every soul." This is natural enough; the bride of Christ is not selfish, but desperately yearns for others to find the true peace and happiness that come from being united to the source of all love. In the story of Saint Katherine, we see this desire in amazing detail. Katherine sets out, "armed with the sign of the cross," to stop the persecutions of Christians and to win the emperor over to Christ. Although she fails in this task, along the way, she does manage to win over the fifty wisest men in the world, the emperor's wife, along with two hundred guards and soldiers.

The courage and love demonstrated in the narratives of the virgin martyrs still inspires people today, especially in more recent years, as the vocation to consecrated virginity has grown, albeit on a small scale. In the prescribed homily for the Rite of Consecration of a Virgin, the Bishop speaks of the consecrated virgin as having "the dignity of being a bride of Christ." The Bishop reminds all those in attendance, especially the virgin, that the Church is also called the Bride of Christ; this dignified name was extended to virgins by the Fathers of the Church because they were "a sign of the great mystery of salvation, proclaimed at the beginning of human history, and fulfilled in the marriage covenant between Christ and his Church." The bishop, echoing the words of the early fourth-century bishop Methodius of Olympus, says that the motherhood of the virgin will be like

---

notion of virginity. On virgins and suicides in antiquity see Anton J. L. van Hooff, *From Autothanasia to Suicide: Self-Killing in Classical Antiquity* (New York: Routledge, 1990), 22–26. On Pelagia specifically, see Brock and Harvey, *Holy Women of the Syrian Orient*, 40.

the motherhood of the Church, bearing much fruit "so that a great family of children may be born, or reborn, to the life of grace."[39]

Through their stories being told over the centuries, the virgin martyrs have proved their own motherhood and fruitfulness. These brides of Christ model for everyone who reads their stories the Christian vocation of love; it is a vocation that impels the disciple to remain true, trusting with great courage that all Christ has promised shall come to pass. The moral of these stories, then, the virtues the reader is to imitate are the abandonment of will to God, the practice of fortitude, and charity above all. In the end, these stories teach us that what we ought to do is work towards love—the same lesson Thérèse of Lisieux learned from these stories. In one poem, she wrote down the responses of Saint Agnes which she learned from hearing the story several times through the Divine Office:

> So I fear nothing, neither sword nor flame.
> No, nothing can trouble my ineffable peace,
> And the fire of love which consumes my soul
>   Shall never go out![40]

---

39. *The Revised Order of Blessing an Abbot or Abess, of Consecration to a Life of Virginity, and of the Blessing of Oils* (Washington, D.C: International Committee on English in the Liturgy (ICEL), 1971), 24–24a. Cf. Methodius, *The Symposium*, IV.1–8, *trans.* Herbert Musurillo (Westminster, Md.: Newman Press, 1958), 58–67.

40. Thérèse of Lisieux, *The Poetry of Thérèse of Lisieux*, "The Responses of Saint Agnes," 138.

Chapter 7

Conclusion

By celebrating the passage of these saints from earth to heaven, the Church proclaims the Paschal Mystery achieved in the saints who have suffered and been glorified with Christ; she proposes them to the faithful as examples drawing all to the Father through Christ, and through their merits she pleads for God's favors.

Sacrosanctum concilium, 104

The stories of the virgin martyrs, when read as part of a specific genre of literature with its own rules and purposes, allow us to capture the way in which they teach Christ and the Good News. Applying the ancient practice of the *four senses of Scripture* to the narratives found in the *Golden Legend*, the *passions, poems, and lives of the virgin martyrs* enables these stories to be reintroduced into the teaching and preaching of the Church. At the same time, such an adaptation maintains the correct respect for historical criticism; it also permits these stories to work in the way they were meant to work. The stories that surround the names of the virgin martyrs were meant to edify the people of God; they were meant to capture the imagination of the Christian people and by so doing, teach them the truths of the faith, sway them to believe those truths, and to delight them into putting those truths into practice. All this was meant to draw the reader into a deeper relationship with Christ and his Church. The proof of the effectiveness of these stories to do just that can be seen in a return to the story of Maria Goretti; she knew these stories and lived out the charity of the virgin martyrs in her own life.

Saint Maria Goretti

Maria Goretti's death has been read by the Church as a brave act which defended her chastity against the threat posed by her would-be rapist. She is a martyr in defense of a virtue, which begs the question of any other interpretation of her holiness.[1] How can her death be seen in any other light than that which the Church herself proposes? As journalist Kenneth Woodward observes, "Maria Goretti continues to be held up as the heroic embodiment of the church's sexual ethic."[2] The very man who initiated this interpretation of Maria Goretti's life is also the one who points to an alternative reading. In his homily at the canonization mass of Saint Maria Goretti in 1950, Pope Pius XII, who three years earlier called upon those who wished to protect public morality to look towards the model of Maria Goretti, asked the people of God this insightful question:

> Why is it that when you read or listen to the story of her brief life, which reminds you of the limpid narrative of the Gospels in the simplicity of its details, in the color of its circumstances, in the sudden violence of death with which it closes—why does this story move you even to tears? Why has Maria Goretti so quickly conquered your hearts, and taken the first place in your affections?[3]

The Pope, of course, knew the answer. The story of Maria Goretti directs us to the Lord, a fact supported by the very details of her story.[4]

---

1. As Saint Thomas Aquinas explains, "the sufficient motive for martyrdom is not only confession of faith, but any other virtue, not civic but infused, that has Christ for its end." S.T. suppl. 96.6, ad 9, vol. V, trans. Fathers of the English Dominican Province (Chicago: Benzinger Brothers, 1992), 2979.

2. Kenneth L. Woodward, *Making Saints: How the Catholic Church Determines Who Becomes a Saint, Who Doesn't, and Why* (New York: Simon and Schuster, 1996), 123.

3. Pius XII, *Allocution on Maria Goretti*, April 28, 1947, in *Acta Apostolicae Sedis*, 39:352–58, in Godfrey Poage, C.P., trans., *In Garments All Red* (Chicago: Paluch Publications, 1950), 15.

4. See Paul Burns, *Butler's Lives of the Saints*, 7:41–42. For a good summary of the historical evidence and the details of Maria Goretti's canonization, see Nadia Tarantini, *Processo Goretti, I Libri Dell'unità* (Rome: L'Unità, 1994). See also, Congregatio pro Causis Sanctorum, *A Proposito Di Maria Goretti: Santità E Canonizzazioni* (Vatican City: Libreria Editrice Vaticana, 1986). In this document the Congregation for the Causes of Saints refutes the many errors and misrepresentations of a certain Giordano Bruno Guerri's 1985 book about Maria Goretti entitled *Povera santa, povero assassino*.

Even on the literal level, the story of Maria Goretti is the story of love and forgiveness, the great lessons she learned from the liturgy and from the stories of the saints. As she was being attacked, Maria's concern was not the defense of her purity, or even the state of her soul. She knew *she* committed no sin in being raped. Instead, her concern was for Alessandro, her attacker. When the process for her beatification began, all those who were involved were interviewed, including Alessandro. He testified that during the attack, Maria was distressed for his soul; she pleaded with him not to commit such a terrible sin. Her anxiety was for him, for the other and not for herself. When Alessandro yelled at Maria "Why will you not give in?" Maria answered, "Because it is a sin, God forbids it. You will go to hell, Alessandro; you will go to hell if you do it."[5] In his extreme rage, Alessandro stabbed her fourteen times.

As those who promote Maria as the martyr for purity have pointed out, her story does indeed have a tropological bent. Maria Goretti does die for the sake of a virtue, but it is important to understand which virtue that is. The charity that one must possess in order to be so profoundly focused on the one who is attacking takes on a supernatural dimension, one that remained as Maria lay on her deathbed. She was constantly forgiving Alessandro and praying on his behalf. Her response also required true fortitude. Like all rapists, Allessandro was relying on Maria's fear, hoping to use it to subdue her into submission. Maria, however, does not show fear. The virtue of fortitude, always closely linked to charity, expanded Maria's heart, giving her the love and the strength not only to remain true to Christ, to follow his will always, but even more so, it gave her the courage to be true to Christ's love. "No one," we are reminded by Christ, "has greater love than this, to lay down one's life for one's friends."[6] Maria took Christ at his word: "But I say this to you, love your enemies and pray for those who persecute you."[7]

---

5. In 1929, Alessandro testified in the process of Maria Goretti's beatification where he stressed that "Maria's appeals had been for the safety of his soul and that she had urged him not to commit such a grave sin." Burns, *Butler's Lives of the Saints*, 7:42. Cf. Pietro DiDonato, *The Penitent* (New York: Hawthorn, 1962).

6. Jn 15:13.

7. Mt 5:44.

Maria's supernatural gifts of charity and fortitude were fruits of her relationship with Christ. She knew Christ from the reading of the Gospel during the liturgies she attended, from her training to receive the sacraments, and from the many stories of the saints she had heard over her few short years. She knew him well enough to follow his commandment of love. Even when she faced the ultimate price for that obedience, she never forgot the one who was going to kill her. In the end, Maria imitated the martyrs in the sacrifice of their lives for the sake of Christ; and in so doing, she joined their ranks, and her story became another beautiful allegory of Christ's sacrifice of love.

The anagogical aspects of Maria's story are just as prevalent as the other senses. Reminiscent of the first Agnes, this new Agnes appeared to Alessandro while he was in prison. She came to him in a dream and offered him lilies, a sign not only of her purity; in offering them to her attacker, she was telling him of her forgiveness and her desire for his conversion, his own purity. In the dream, Maria was dressed all in white, the bride of Christ, and was standing in a garden, an Eden-like space that invokes heaven. Finally, when she gave the lilies to Alessandro, each one burst into a gentle, pure white flame — the intense flame of pure *caritas*, of love. This vision, which came to him in a dream unlike any other, was also an invitation to him to enter into the peace of Christ, and a call for him to imitate her in pure love of Christ and others. When he was arrested, Alessandro vehemently denied the charges against him. It was only after being confronted with the overwhelming testimony compiled against him that he even admitted to the crime. Once in jail, he grew more and more restless and was filled with rage — even to the point of attacking a priest. He was violent, angry, and inconsolable. Maria's invitation not only offered him the comfort of her forgiveness, but the presence of the Lord himself. From that point forward, Alessandro became a model prisoner. After serving twenty-seven years of his thirty-year sentence, Alessandro was set free for good behavior. He spent the rest of his life in a Capuchin monastery in penance and service to God.[8]

---

8. For the story of Alessandro, see DiDonato, *The Penitent*. Although it has been persistently said that Alessandro was present at Maria's beatification and/or canonization, it is not true. Maria's mother and several other family members were at both, but Alessandro, although reconciled with the family, remained in his monastery for the ceremonies.

Maria's heavenly visit accomplished the exact mission of
Christ, reconciliation. It reminds the reader of the ultimate goal of
that reconciliation—union with God, entrance into the heavenly
Jerusalem. The story of Maria Goretti cannot simply end with her
death; if it does, the result is that she died only for the sake of protecting her virginity. Instead, her story must be remembered as ending in
the hope that springs from forgiveness and charity; it must end with
the hope of heaven, just as Christ's story ends with his hope of being
one with his people.[9]

CRISIS OF IDENTITY

It is precisely the loss of this anagogical sense that has led to a certain
crisis of identity on the part of most people, a crisis that is particularly
acute in what some are calling the postmodern age. Sarah Coakley of
Harvard Divinity School has suggested that "the obsessive interest in
the 'body' which has been such a marked feature of late twentieth-
century Western culture hides a profound eschatological longing; only
a *theological* vision of a particular sort, [she suggests,] can satisfy it."[10]
"From this perspective," Coakley continues, "the quest for longevity,
beauty, health, sexual performance—bespeak a prevailing denial of
death."[11] In truth, this denial is an inadequate attempt, albeit an
unconscious one, to fill the void left by the rejection of the Christian
narrative of the resurrection. Once, in western culture, the Resurrection provided the hope of escaping that one thing we fear most—
death. With the secularization of culture, and the denial of any
religious mega-narratives, this hope has been lost. The eschatological
teachings of Christianity once provided an answer to the question of
identity. It is not a coincidence that when this eschatological teaching
has been diminished or even lost by some, so too have the stories of
the virgin martyrs been either dismissed, lost, or reduced to a single
focus, that of the female body.

One of the means the Church has employed in disseminating
the eschatological teaching of the Resurrection, which gives definition

9. See Jn 17.

10. Sarah Coakley, "The Eschatological Body: Gender, Transformation, and God," *Modern Theology* 16, no. 1 (2000): 61.

11. Ibid., 63.

to human identity, is through the use of hagiography. The reading of the legends of the virgin martyrs through the medieval technique of the *four senses* demonstrates how this can happen, and can aid in restoring that function as well. Each and every saintly narrative directly points to Christ and his message of salvation, the reconciliation of the individual and God, of heaven and earth. And, as we have learned from the anagogical sense, in doing so, the stories of the saints constantly remind us that our true identity is that of pilgrims; we are pilgrims on this journey of reconciliation and love.

As Kenneth Cragg, the former assistant Anglican bishop of Jerusalem, has observed, a pilgrimage is a unity of three terms, "place, folk, and story."[12] A pilgrimage is defined first and primarily in terms of geography, of place; it is a journey from one place to another. A pilgrimage, however, is more than a journey; it is also a journey that is defined by people, those left behind, those encountered along the way, and those met at the end. In the Christian life, all three types of people help to shape, for better or worse, a person's journey either towards or away from God. Some of the people a Christian meets along the way, and one hopes, at the end of the pilgrimage, are saints. Finally, added to place and people, a pilgrimage is defined by story; it is a journey engaged in response to a story.[13] In the Christian context, it is a journey taken in response to the story of Christ or one of his saints.

These three things, place, people, and story, when joined together, also give shape and definition, Cragg observes, to human life.[14] In other words, all three are components necessary for coming to a true sense of identity. The lives of the saints help to fill in that identity by continually repeating, in imaginative and inspiring ways, the story that answers the questions of purpose and destiny. The evangelical invitation offered by these stories is the invitation to enter into the mystery of Christ's life. To be sure, reading these stories, one can say, is entering into a pilgrimage in itself, a journey that helps teach the reader his true identity, the true purpose of his life: to be one with God.

---

12. Kenneth Cragg, "Jesus, Jerusalem, and Pilgrimage Today," in Craig G. Bartholomew and Fred Hughes, eds., *Explorations in a Christian Theology of Pilgrimage* (Burlington, Vt.: Ashgate, 2004), 3.

13. Paul Elie, *The Life You Save May Be Your Own: An American Pilgrimage* (New York: Farrar, Straus and Giroux, 2003), x.

14. Cragg, "Jesus, Jerusalem, and Pilgrimage Today," 3.

SOME APPLICATIONS

This evangelical invitation, the pilgrimage into union, is not only offered through the strange and fascinating tales of the virgin martyrs, but is found in each and every hagiographic narrative. Each and every saint, whether their stories are mostly historically accurate or mostly inventive exercises, invites the Christian pilgrim into this mystery. They do so precisely because these stories of the saints are strange and do not fit into our conventional cultural understanding. Towards the end of his book, *Theology and Social Theory*, John Milbank argues that theology, and how we think of theology, needs to be reworked. He writes:

> the claim is that *all* theology has to reconceive itself as a kind of "Christian sociology": that is to say, as the explication of a socio-linguistic practice, or as the constant re-narration of this practice as it has historically developed. The task of such a theology is not apologetic, nor even argument. Rather it is to tell again the Christian *mythos*, pronounce again the Christian *logos*, and call again for Christian *praxis* in a manner that restores their freshness and originality. It must articulate Christian difference in such a fashion as to make it strange.[15]

How Milbank wants theology to be reworked can also be applied to the way the reading of the lives of the saints needs to be rethought, for both theology and hagiography share the same purpose— they are to make Christ strange. The saints present to the world the Christian alternative. Through their holy lives, through their very bodies, through the stories that surround their names, the saints demonstrate to others an alternate way, not only to comprehend the world, but to live in it. The saints do this by making themselves strange—in all senses of the word: odd, different, baffling, unknown, unfamiliar, unexpected, extraordinary, and intriguing. The saints present such a strange presence in such a way that they literally cause a disruption of perception. It is in that disruption that the saint reveals the uniqueness of Christ and his Gospel, and invites our response. By representing the uniqueness of Christianity, by making it different from all other "truths," the saint is really making Christianity strange to the

---

15. John Milbank, *Theology and Social Theory: Beyond Secular Reason*, Signposts in Theology (Cambridge, Mass.: Blackwell, 1993), 381.

world. Yet, at the same time, this strangeness, this difference of the saint's faith, almost paradoxically, makes following Christ very appealing, a truth demonstrated over and over again, by the number of people who came to Christ after being touched in some way by the story of a saint.

In order for these stories to be so effective, however, they have to be read; but the credulity that seems to be required, the apparent lack of historical truth, and the "over-the-top" events in these stories, all combine to present a major barrier to people reading them. By applying the method of the *four senses of scripture* to the stories of the virgin martyrs, these barriers can be removed, and can teach a way of reading that helps to unlock the wonderful strangeness and beauty of the invitation these stories offer. As we have learned, the reduction of the virgin martyrs, such as Maria Goretti, to a moral example of chastity, although partially valid, is simply inadequate. The Christ-like features of Maria's story—of sin, death, new life and resurrection, of conversion and redemption—all point to the mystery of Christ. Although she was the stimulus for Alessandro's desire, eventually, through her visit to him in a dream, she became the vehicle that redirected that desire into a longing for God. This is the transformation that the Church offers, through God's grace, to all. The story of Maria Goretti is actually an invitation to move beyond the self and enter into the divine.

The method of the *four senses* is not limited, of course, to the narratives of the virgin martyrs. It can be applied to the stories of all the saints. For example, the famous *Life of St. Antony* by Athanasius, can be read through the lenses of the *four senses*. Very briefly, on the literal level, Antony was a man who wanted to follow the dictates of the Gospel explicitly, and so he goes off to the desert to confront the devil and conquer the inordinate desires that led him away from God. The literal sense is the "obvious" sense of the text, and so beyond that basic description of Antony's life, there is the understanding from this masterpiece that each person must, to some degree, come to an ascetical life if they desire to follow the Lord.

Moving into a deeper encounter with the text, the allegorical sense can easily be applied. Antony, of course, is the "father of monasticism," and as such, he is the archetype of a monk; he is the model to which all monks aspire and who inspires all monastic reforms. Antony is also an obvious "type" of Christ, and his temptations match those of Jesus. Since Antony is not divine, his fight with the devil takes a lifetime, whereas Christ's encounter with temptations only took forty days; nonetheless, Antony serves as a guide for the spiritual life. The three stages of Antony's life are a direct corollary to the three stages of the spiritual perfection first described by Evagrius Ponticus and then (Pseudo) Dionysius.[16] Antony first lived in a tomb, then moved to a fortress, and finally to the mountain, allegorical of the purgative, illuminative, and unitive stages. The purgative stage is when one *dies* to one's sinful ways represented by the tomb; the illuminative is when one is enlightened and *strengthened* by Christ, the fortress; and the unitive stage is when one is in mystical union with God, long symbolized by being on the "mountain of God." These three stages can also be considered the anagogical thrust of the work, being as they are the ascent to the dwelling place of God. This is further validated by the advice Antony delivers to his disciples: "Therefore do not fear them [the demons], but rather draw inspiration from Christ always, and trust in him. And live as though dying daily."[17]

Tropologically, the story of Saint Antony is straightforward; the reader is called to imitate Antony in desiring God alone. Through a life of self-denial and ascetic training, Antony was able to excel in virtue and even be free from the fear of death. Wishing to inspire terror in the Christians, the authorities in Alexandria selected a few prominent Christians to be tried and executed, and Antony went to the city to lend spiritual support to those selected. Because of his virtue and the inner strength that comes from such a life, Antony was incapable of being intimidated by the prefect.

> When the judge saw the fearlessness of Antony and of those with him, he issued the order that none of the monks were to appear in the law court, nor were they to stay in the city at all. All others thought it wise to go into hiding that day, but Antony took this so seriously as to wash his upper garment and to stand in the next day in a prominent place in front, and to be clearly visible to the prefect. When, while all marveled at this, the prefect, passing by with his escort, saw him, he stood there

---

16. Louis Bouyer, *Introduction to Spirituality*, trans. Mary Perkins Ryan (Collegeville, Minn.: Liturgical Press, 1961), 244.

17. Athanasius, *The Life of Antony and the Letter to Marcellinus*, trans. Robert C. Gregg (New York: Paulist Press, 1980), 97.

calmly, demonstrating the purposefulness that belongs to us Christians.[18]

Finally, the life of Saint Antony describes well the ideal all Christians are called to, holiness. The descriptions of Antony's humility, wisdom, and miraculous powers are all reported in order to show what holiness can mean and how beautiful a life a saint can have. Antony's final home is on the mountain of Colzim, which is still called Saint Antony's mountain, and the mountain has always been the spiritual symbol of meeting between a person and God.[19] For Antony to live on a sacred mountain meant more than just an encounter with the Lord; it meant a state of union with him. Because of this union, Antony was able to perform all the miracles reported by Athanasius; because Antony was one with God, he acted in concert with him. This, then, is a beautiful description uncovered by an anagogical reading of the text of his life.

In addition, Antony always kept the goal of the pilgrimage of life always in mind. First, he taught his disciples to perform a daily examination of conscience, so that they could grow closer to perfection in charity, and to be ready at a moment's notice if the Lord called them that night.[20] And second, he always practiced and taught others to "live as though dying daily." He would teach his students not to get caught up in the trappings and temptations of this world; rather they should work on being prepared for the next.[21]

On the surface, such interpretations as these, drawing on the *four senses*, might seem obvious, even somewhat basic. However, just as the *four senses*, when applied to Scripture, can produce layer after layer of interpretation, insight, and amazement, so, too, can they produce such results in the reading of hagiography. In addition, what is useful is that such a methodology respects the integrity of the text itself. These stories are read not in the same way as fairy tales and mythology, as quaint stories with a moral, but in a way similar to reading Scripture; the reader is expecting insight and ultimately conversion

---

18. Ibid., 66.

19. James Cowan, *Desert Father* (Boston: Shambhala, 2004), 7–8. On the mountain as a holy place see, Joseph Ratzinger (Pope Benedict XVI), *Jesus of Nazareth*, trans. Adrian J. Walker (New York: Doubleday, 2007), 309.

20. Cowan, *Desert Father*, 72–73.

21. Cowan, *Desert Father*, 95.

of life. Questions of credulity, such as how to understand Antony's constant combat with demons, are not so much laid aside, as seen within the context of the narrative and the deeper, underlying truth it conveys.

In truth, if the purpose of hagiography is to be upheld, these stories cannot help but be read at least allegorically. It is obvious that the dragon Saint George fights is the devil and that all the trials of the martyrs are proof, not only of their commitment to God, but the fact that they survived is proof of God's commitment to them. However, through a more conscious application of these senses, not just a cursory allegorical reading, even more can be gleaned. There is the matchmaker motif in George, when the saint, after subduing the dragon, unites the princess and her entire village to Christ. In Ardo's famous *Life of Saint Benedict, Abbot of Aniane and of Inde*, one can see how the Rule of the first Saint Benedict had become an allegorical key to Christ: "[Benedict of Aniane] was inflamed with love of the Rule of Benedict, and like a new athlete just back from single combat, he entered the field to fight publicly."[22] A close tropological reading of the same text produces an awareness of how, although never stated, the corporal and spiritual works of mercy form the foundation of Benedict's holiness.

MAKING CHRIST STRANGE

The application of the *four senses* to the stories of the saints does not remove their strangeness, but it does allow the reader to enter more deeply into that strangeness. It is this strangeness that stimulates the imagination, and moves a reader into a more profound relationship with the text, which ultimately, can lead to a more profound relationship with Christ. It is in the strange stories of the saints that our hearts are set on fire. Re-reading the lives of the virgin martyrs and the other saints of the Church through the *four senses* rescues them from the obscurity of social constructs or mythical tales and recaptures their edifying purpose. For it is through their stories of dedication, suffering, defiance, sacrifice, love, courage, forgiveness, and even

22. Ardo, "The Life of Saint Benedict, Abbot of Aniane and of Inde," in Thomas F. X. Noble and Thomas Head, eds., *Soldiers of Christ* (University Park, Pa.: Pennsylvania State University Press, 1995), 220.

death that the hope of the victory of Christ is told once more. Somewhere, at some previous time, these saints lived and breathed; and although we know that their stories do not portray their lives accurately, we nonetheless know that they somehow were so extraordinary that people remembered their names, and saw them as being very close to Christ. Today, they act in the same way; today, it is their strange and compelling stories, handed down to us through the centuries, that allow the virgin martyrs and all the saints to be once again ambassadors of Christ to men and women alike, and can lead us to our true identity as children of heaven. It seems there is still, after all, a large place for these holy women, and all the saints, in our modern world.

Bibliography

Magisterium

Ancyra, Council of. *The Canons of the Council of Ancyra*. Translated by
Henry R. Percival. Vol. XIV, *Nicene and Post–Nicene Fathers,
Second Series*. Buffalo: The Christian Literature Company, 1900.

Catechism of the Catholic Church. 2nd ed. Washington, D.C.: United States
Catholic Conference Inc.—Libreria Editrice Vaticana, 1994.

Congregatio pro Causis Sanctorum. *A Proposito di Maria Goretti: Santità
e Canonizzazioni*. Città del Vaticano: Libreria Editrice Vaticana,
1986.

Pius XII. *On Holy Virginity: Encyclical Letter Issued March 25, 1954*.
Washington, D.C.: National Catholic Welfare Conference,
1954.

Pontificia Commissione Biblica. *L'interprétation de la Bible dans l'Eglise*.
Vatican City: Libreria Editice Vaticana, 1993. Translation: *Origins* 23:29 (January 6, 1994).

Sacra Congregatio pro Cultu Divino. *Ordo Consecrationis Virginum; Editio Typica*. Vatican City: Libreria Editrice Vaticana, 1978.

Second Vatican Council. *Lumen gentium. The Dogmatic Constitution on the
Church* (November 21, 1964). Translation by Douglas G. Bush-
man, The Sixteen Documents of Vatican II, 123–195. Boston:
Pauline Books, 1999.

―――. *Sacrosanctum concilium. The Constitution on the Sacred Liturgy*
(December 4, 1963). Translation by Douglas G. Bushman, The
Sixteen Documents of Vatican II, 47–84. Boston: Pauline
Books, 1999.

Liturgical Texts

The Gelasian Sacramentary. Liber Sacramentorum Romanae Ecclesiae. Edited by H. A. Wilson. Oxford: Clarendon Press, 1894.

International Committee on English in the Liturgy (ICEL). *The Revised Order of Blessing for an Abbot or Abess, of Consecration to a Life of Virginity, and the Blessing of Oils.* Washington, D.C.: International Committee on English in the Liturgy (ICEL), 1971.

The Liturgy of the Hours: According to the Roman Rite. IV vols. New York: Catholic Book Pub. Co., 1976.

Missale Romanum: Editio Princeps (1570). Edited by Manlio Sodi and Achille M. Triacca. Ed. anastatica/ed, *Monumenta Liturgica Concilii Tridentini; 2.* Cittáa del Vaticano: Libreria Editrice Vaticana, 1998.

Missale Romanum: Ex Decreto Sacrosancti Oecumenici Concilii Vaticani II Instauratum Auctoritate Pauli Pp. VI Promulgatum. Editio typica. ed. Vatican City: Liberia Editrice Vaticana, 1975.

Missale Romanum: Ex Decreto Ss. Concilii Tridentini Restitutum S. Pii V Pontificis Maximi Jussu Editum, Clementis VIII, Urbani VIII. Et Leonis XIII. Auctoritate Recognitum. Rome: Sumptibus et typis Societatis S. Joannis Evang. Desclée, Lefebure et soc., 1907.

Sacramentarium Leonianum. Edited by Charles Lett Feltoe. Cambridge, UK: Cambridge University Press, 1896.

Le Sacrementaire Grégorien, Ses Principales Formes d'après les plus Anciens Manuscrits. Ed. Comparative. Edited by Jean Deshusses. Fribourg: Editions Universitaires, 1971.

Church Fathers and Patristic Texts

Ambrose. *De officiis.* Translated by Ivor J. Davidson. 2 vols, *The Oxford Early Christian Studies.* New York: Oxford University Press, 2001.

———. *De virginibus.* Translated by Boniface Ramsey, *Ambrose, Early Church Fathers.* London; New York: Routledge, 1997.

————. *De virginitate.* Translated by James Shiel, *Given to Love.* Chicago: Scepter, 1963.

————. *Saint Ambrose: Letters.* Vol. 26. Fathers of the Church. Translated by Sister Mary Melchoir Beyenka. Edited by Roy Joseph Deferrari. New York: Fathers of the Church, Inc., 1954.

Athanasius. *The Life of Antony and the Letter to Marcellinus.* Translated by Robert C. Gregg. New York: Paulist Press, 1980.

Augustine. *Confessiones.* Translated by R. S. Pine–Coffin, *Confessions.* Baltimore: Penguin Books, 1961.

————. *De civitate Dei.* Translated by R. W. Dyson, *The City of God against the Pagans: Cambridge Texts in the History of Political Thought.* New York: Cambridge University Press, 1998.

————. *De continentia.* Translated by Ray Kearney. Edited by John E. Rotelle. Vol. I/9, *Marriage and Virginity: The Eexcellence of Marriage, Holy Virginity, the Excellence of Widowhood, Adulterous Marriages, Continence. The Works of Saint Augustine: A Translation for the 21st Century.* New York: New City Press, 1999.

————. *De doctrina Christiana.* Translated by Edmund Hill. Edited by John E. Rotelle. Vol. I/11, *Teaching Christianity. The Works of Saint Augustine: A Translation for the 21st Century.* New York: New City Press, 1996.

————. *De virginitate.* Translated by Ray Kearney. Edited by John E. Rotelle. Vol. I/9, *Marriage and Virginity: The Excellence of Marriage, Holy Virginity, the Excellence of Widowhood, Adulterous Marriages, Continence. The Works of Saint Augustine: A Translation for the 21st Century.* New York: New City Press, 1999.

————. *Expositions of the Psalms: 1–32.* Translated by Maria Boulding. Edited by John E. Rotelle. Vol. III/15, *The Works of Saint Augustine: A Translation for the 21st Century.* New York: New City Press, 2000.

————. *Sermons 273–305a (on the Saints).* Translated by Edmund Hill. Edited by John E. Rotelle. Vol. III/8, *The Works of Saint*

Augustine: A Translation for the 21st Century. New York: New City Press, 1994.

————. *Sermons on the Old Testament (1–19).* Translated by Edmund Hill. Edited by John E. Rotelle. Vol. III/I, *The Works of Saint Augustine: A Translation for the 21st Century.* New York: New City Press, 1990.

Cassian, John. *Collationes.* Translated by Boniface Ramsey, *Confrences.* Vol. 57, Ancient Christian Writers. New York: Paulist Press, 1997.

Cyprian. *De Habitu Virginum.* Translated by Sister Angela Elizabeth Keenan, S.N.D. Edited by Roy J. Deferrari, *Treatises.* Vol. 51, Fathers of the Church. Washington, D.C.: Catholic University of America, 1958.

Damasus. *Damasi Epigrammata.* Edited by Max Ihm. Lipsiae: in aedibvs B. G. Tevbneri, 1895.

Deferrari. *Saint Ambrose: Letters.* Vol. 26, Fathers of the Church. New York: Fathers of the Church, Inc., 1954.

Egeria. *Itinerarium Egeria.* Translated by George E. Gingras, *Diary of a Pilgrim. Vol. 38,* Ancient Christian Writers. New York: Newman Press, 1970.

Ephrem the Syrian. *Ephrem the Syrian: Hymns,* Classics of Western Spirituality. Edited by Kathleen E. McVey. New York: Paulist Press, 1989.

Eusebius. *Ecclesiastical History.* Translated by G. A. Williamson, *The History of the Church from Christ to Constantine.* New York: Penguin Books, 1989.

Gregory of Nyssa. *De virginibus.* Translated by Virginia Woods Callahan, *Saint Gregory of Nyssa: Ascetical Works.* Vol. 58, Fathers of the Church. Washington, D.C.: Catholic University of America Press, 1967.

————. *Vita S. Macrinae.* Translated by Virginia Woods Callahan, *Saint Gregory of Nyssa: Ascetical Works.* Vol. 58, Fathers of the Church. Washington, D.C.: Catholic University of America Press, 1967.

Gregory the Great. *Forty Gospel Homilies.* Translated by Dom David Hurst. Kalamazoo, Mich.: Cistercian Publications, 1990.

Ignatius of Antioch. "Epistles." In *Early Christian Fathers*, 87–120. New York: Touchstone, 1996.

Jerome. *Epistles.* Translated by W. H. Freemantle. Vol. VI, *Nicene and Post–Nicene Fathers, 2nd Series.* Buffalo: The Christian Literature Publishing Company, 1893.

Justin Martyr. *The Second Apology.* Translated by Leslie William Barnard, *St. Justin Martyr: The First and Second Apologies.* Vol. 56, Ancient Christian Writers. New York: Paulist Press, 1997.

Leo the Great. *Second Homily on the Lord's Ascension (Sermon 74).* Translated by Charles Lett Feltoe. Vol. XII, Nicene and Post–Nicene Fathers Second Series. Buffalo: The Christian Literature Company, 1895.

"The Martyrdom of Polycarp." In *Early Chirstian Fathers*, edited by Cyril C. Richardson, 149–58. New York: Touchstone, 1996.

Maximus of Turin. *Sermon 56.* Edited by J. P. Migne, *Patrologiae cursus completus. Series Latina*, Vol. 57:537–542. Paris, 1847.

Methodius. *The Symposium: A Treatise on Chastity.* Translated by Herbert Musurillo, S.J. Westminster, Md.: Newman Press, 1958.

Minucius Felix. "Octavius." In *Tertullian and Minucius Felix.* The Loeb Classical Library, edited by T. E. Page. New York: G. P. Putnam's Sons, 1931.

Origen. *De principiis.* Translated by Rowan A. Geer, *Origin.* Classics in Western Spirituality. New York: Paulist Press, 1979.

———. *Homilies on Genesis and Exodus.* Translated by Ronald E. Heine. Vol. 71, Fathers of the Church. Washington, D.C.: Catholic University of America Press, 1982.

Prudentius. *The Poems of Prudentius.* Translated by Sister M. Clement Eagan. Vol. 43, Fathers of the Church. Washington, D.C.: Catholic University of America Press, 1962.

Pseudo–Clement. *Ad Virgines*. Translated by B.P. Pratten. Vol. VIII, Ante–Nicene Fathers. Buffalo: The Christian Literature Publishing Company, 1886.

Tertullian. *Apologeticum*. Translated by Sister Emily Joseph Daly. Edited by Rudolph Arbesmann et al., *Tertullian: Apologetical Works and Minucius Fellix: Octavius*. Vol. 10, Fathers of the Church. New York: Fathers of the Church, Inc., 1950.

———. *De pudicitia (La Pudicité)*. Edited by Claudio Micaelli and Charles Munier, *Sources Chrétiennes No 394–395*. Paris: Cerf, 1993.

———. *De resurrectione Carnis*. Translated by Dr. Holmes. Vol. III, Ante–Nicene Fathers. Buffalo: The Christian Literature Publishing Company, 1885.

———. *De virginibus velandis*. Translated by S. Thelwell. Vol. IV, Ante–Nicene Fathers. Buffalo: The Christian Literature Publishing Company, 1885.

Ancient Roman Authors

Aulus Gellius. "Attic Nights." In *As the Romans Did: A Sourcebook in Roman Social History*, edited by Jo–Ann Shelton, 427–28. New York: Oxford University Press, 1998.

Cicero, Marcus Tullius. *De natura deorum*. Translated and edited by H. Rackham. The Loeb Classical Library, edited by T. E. Page. New York: G. P. Putnam's Sons, 1933.

Dionysius of Halicarnassus. "Roman Antiquities." In *As the Romans Did: A Sourcebook in Roman Social History*, edited by Jo–Ann Shelton, 427–28. New York: Oxford University Press, 1998.

Horace. "Odes." In *As the Romans Did: A Sourcebook in Roman Social History*, edited by Jo–Ann Shelton, 389. New York: Oxford University Press, 1998.

Symmachus. "Dispatches to the Emperor." In *As the Romans Did: A Sourcebook in Roman Social History*, edited by Jo–Ann Shelton, 390–91. New York: Oxford University Press, 1998.

Tacitus. "Annals." In *As the Romans Did: A Sourcebook in Roman Social History*, edited by Jo–Ann Shelton, 408–09. New York: Oxford University Press, 1998.

Medieval Authors

Ardo. "The Life of Saint Benedict, Abbot of Aniane and of Inde." In *Soldiers of Christ*, edited by Thomas F. X. Noble and Thomas Head, 215–54. University Park, Pa.: Pennsylvania State University Press, 1995.

Chaucer, Geoffrey. *The Canterbury Tales: A Verse Translation*. Translated by David Wright. Oxford [Oxfordshire]: Oxford University Press, 1985.

———. *The Works of Geoffrey Chaucer: A Facsimile of the William Morris Kelmscott Chaucer*. Edited by John T. Winterich. New York: The World Publishing Company, 1958.

Dante Alighieri. *Epistola a Cangrande*. Edited by Enzo Cecchini, *Biblioteca Del Medioevo Latino*. Firenze: Giunti, 1995.

Hugh of St. Victor. *Commentaria in Hierarchiam coelestem S. Dionysii Areopagitae*. Edited by J. P. Migne, *Patrologiae cursus completus. Series Latina*, Vol. 175:923–1154. Paris, 1854.

———. *Didascalicon*. Translated by Jerome Taylor, *Hugh of St. Victor: Didascalicon, a Medieval Guide to the Arts*. New York: Columbia University Press, 1961.

Thomas Aquinas. *Summa Theologiae*. Translated by Fathers of the English Dominican Province. Chicago: Benzinger Brothers, 1992.

Jacobus de Voragine and the *Golden Legend*

Bertini Guidetti, Stefania. *Il Paradiso e la Terra: Iacopo Da Varazze e il suo Tempo: Atti del Convegno Internazionale, Varazze, 24–26 Settembre 1998*. Tavarnuzze (Firenze): SISMEL: Edizioni del Galluzzo, 2001.

Caxton, William. "Introduction." In *The Golden Legend*, edited by George V. O'Neill. Cambridge: Cambridge University Press, 1914.

Del Corno, Carlo. "La 'Legenda Aurea' e la Narrativa dei Predicatori." In *Jacopo da Varagine: Atti del I Convegno di Studi, Varazze, 13–14 Aprile 1985*, edited by Giovanni Farris, Benedetto Tino Delfino, 27–49. Cogoleto [Ge.]: Edizioni SMA, 1987.

Dunn–Lardeau, Brenda. *Legenda Aurea–– La Légende Dorée (Xiiie–Xve S.): Actes du Congrès International de Perpignan (Séances "Nouvelles Recherches sur la Legenda Aurea")*. Montréal: Ceres, 1993.

————. *Legenda Aurea, Sept Siècles de Diffusion: Actes du Colloque International sur la Legenda Aurea, Texte Latin et Branches Vernaculaires à l'université du Québec à Montréal, 11–12 Mai 1983*. Montréal: Bellarmin, 1986.

Farris, Giovanni, Benedetto Tino Delfino, and Centro studi Jacopo da Varagine. *Jacopo da Varagine: Atti del I Convegno di Studi, Varazze, 13–14 Aprile 1985, Atti e Studi (Centro Studi Jacopo da Varagine); 1*. Cogoleto (Ge.): Edizioni SMA, 1987.

Fleith, Barbara. "The Patristic Sources of the *Legenda Aurea*: A Research Report." In *The Reception of the Church Fathers in the West*, edited by Irena Backus, 231–87. Leiden: E. J. Brill, 1997.

————. *Studien Zur* Überlieferungsgeschichte *Der Lateinischen Legenda Aurea*. Bruxelles: Société des Bollandistes, 1991.

Fleith, Barbara, and Franco Morenzoni. *De la Sainteté a L'hagiographie: Genèse et usage de la Légende Dorée, Publications Romanes et Françaises, 229*. Genève: Droz, 2001.

Jacobus de Voragine. *The Golden Legend: Readings on the Saints*. Translated by William Granger Ryan. 2 vols. Princeton, NJ: Princeton University Press, 1993.

————. *Legenda aurea*. Edited by Giovanni Paolo Maggioni. 2a ed. 2 vols, *Millennio Medievale 6*. Tavarnuzze: SISMEL: Edizioni del Galluzzo, 1998.

————. *Legenda aurea.* Edited by Thomas Graesse. Osnabruck: Otto Zeller Verlag, 1969.

O'Neill, George V. "Preface." In *The Golden Legend by William Caxton.* Cambridge: Cambridge University Press, 1914.

Pasotti, Innocenzo. *Il Beato Giacomo da Varazze (Jacopo da Varagine).* Cogoleto: Tip. SMA, 1974.

Reames, Sherry L. *The Legenda Aurea: A Reexamination of its Paradoxical History.* Madison: University of Wisconsin Press, 1985.

Richardson, Ernest Cushing. *Materials for a Life of Jacopo da Varagine.* New York: H. W. Wilson, 1935.

Ryan, William Granger. "Introduction." In *The Golden Legend: Readings on the Saints,* xiii–xviii. Princeton, NJ: Princeton University Press, 1993.

Books and Articles

Adam, Adolf. *The Liturgical Year: Its History and Its Meaning after the Reform of the Liturgy.* New York: Pueblo Pub. Co., 1981.

Altman, Charles F. "Two Types of Opposition and the Structure of Latin Saints' Lives." *Medievalia et Humanistica* 6 (1975): 1–11.

Andia, Ysabel de. "Martyrdom and Truth." *Communio* Spring (2002).

Anson, John. "Female Transvestites in Early Monasticism." *Viator* 5 (1974): 1–32.

Bachrach, Bernard S. *The Medieval Church: Success or Failure?* New York: Holt Rinehart and Winston, 1972.

Badcock, F. J. "*Sanctorum Communio* as an Article in the Creed." In *Acts of Piety in the Early Church,* edited by Everett Ferguson, 96–117. New York: Garland Pub., 1993.

Barmann, Lawrence F., and C. J. T. Talar. *Sanctity and Secularity During the Modernist Period: Six Perspectives on Hagiography around 1900,*

Subsidia Hagiographica; No 79. Bruxelles: Société des Bollandistes, 1999.

Bartlett, Anne Clark. *Male Authors, Female Readers: Representation and Subjectivity in Middle English Devotional Literature*. Ithaca: Cornell University Press, 1995.

Beckwith, Sarah. *Christ's Body: Identity, Culture, and Society in Late Medieval Writings*. London: Routledge, 1993.

Bennett, Ralph Francis. *The Early Dominicans; Studies in Thirteenth-Century Dominican History*. Cambridge: Cambridge University Press, 1937.

Bergman, Susan. *Martyrs: Contemporary Writers on Modern Lives of Faith*. Maryknoll, NY: Orbis Books, 1998.

Bloch, H. R. "Chaucer's Maiden Head: 'The Physician's Tale and the Poetics of Virginity." *Representations* 28 (1989): 113–34.

Bloch, Marc. *The Historian's Craft*. New York: Alfred A. Knopf, 1963.

Blumenfeld–Kosinski, Renate. "Review of De la Sainteté à L'hagiographie." *Speculum* 78, no. 3 (2003): 879–81.

Bouyer, Louis. *Introduction to Spirituality*. Translated by Mary Perkins Ryan. Collegeville, MN: Liturgical Press, 1961.

Breton, Valentin Marie. *The Communion of Saints; History, Dogma, Devotion*. Translated by Robert Elliott Scantlebury. St. Louis, Mo.: B. Herder, 1934.

Brock, Sebastian P., and Susan Ashbrook Harvey. *Holy Women of the Syrian Orient*, Vol. 13. Transformation of the Classical Heritage. Berkeley: University of California Press, 1987.

Bronfen, Elisabeth. *Over Her Dead Body: Death, Femininity, and the Aesthetic*. Manchester, UK: Manchester University Press, 1982.

Brown, Peter. *The Body and Society: Men, Women, and Sexual Renunciation in Early Christianity*. New York: Columbia University Press, 1988.

——. *The Cult of the Saints: Its Rise and Function in Latin Christianity*, *Haskell Lectures on History of Religions No. 2.* Chicago: University of Chicago Press, 1981.

——. "The Saint as Exemplar in Late Antiquity." In *Saints and Virtues*, edited by John Stratton Hawley. Berkeley: University of California Press, 1987.

Brown, Raymond E., and Sandra M. Schneiders. "Hermeneutics." In *The New Jerome Biblical Commentary*, edited by Raymond E. Brown, S.S., Joseph A. Fitzmyer, S.J. and Roland E. Murphy, O.Carm., 1146–65. Englewood Cliffs, NJ: Prentice Hall, 1990.

Bugge, John M. *Virginitas: An Essay in the History of a Medieval Ideal*, *Archives Internationales D'histoire Des Idées: Series Minor, 17.* The Hague: Martinus Nijhoff, 1975.

Burke, Ronald. "Sanctity and Secularity During the Modernist Period." *Catholic Historical Review* 86, no. 4 (2000): 698–99.

Burns, Paul. *Butler's Lives of the Saints.* New full ed. 12 vols. Collegeville, MN: Liturgical Press, 1998.

Burrus, Virginia. *Chastity as Autonomy: Women in the Stories of the Apocryphal Acts*, Vol. 23. Studies in Women and Religion. Lewiston, NY: Edwin Mellen Press, 1987.

Butler, Alban. *Lives of the Fathers, Martyrs and Other Principal Saints Compiled from Original Monuments and Other Authentic Records.* London: Joseph Booker, 1833.

Bynum, Caroline Walker. *The Resurrection of the Body in Western Christianity, 200–1336*, *Lectures on the History of Religions, New Ser., No. 15.* New York: Columbia University Press, 1995.

Cantalamessa, Raniero. *Virginity: A Positive Approach to Celibacy for the Sake of the Kingdom of Heaven.* New York: Alba House, 1995.

Caplan, Harry. *Of Eloquence: Studies in Ancient and Mediaeval Rhetoric.* Edited by Anne King and Helen North. Ithaca: Cornell University Press, 1970.

Cardman, Francine. "Acts of the Women Martyrs." In *Women in Early Christianity*, edited by David M. Scholer. New York: Garland Publishers, 1993.

Carr, John. *Saint Maria Goretti: Martyr for Purity*. Dublin: Clonmore and Reynolds, 1950.

Cavalieri, Pio Franchi de. *S. Agnese nella Tradizione e nella Leggenda*. In commission der Herder'schen verlagshandlung zu Freiburg im Breisgau und der buchhandlung Spithöver zu Roma, 1899.

Cazelles, Brigitte. *The Lady as Saint: A Collection of French Hagiographic Romances of the Thirteenth Century*, Middle Ages Series. Philadelphia: University of Pennsylvania Press, 1991.

Childs, Brevard S. *Memory and Tradition in Israel*. Naperville, IL: A. R. Allenson, 1962.

Clark, Elizabeth A. *Ascetic Piety and Women's Faith: Essays on Late Ancient Christianity*, Studies in Women and Religion. Vol. 20. Lewiston, NY: Edwin Mellen Press, 1986.

———. "Foucault, the Fathers, and Sex." *Journal of the American Academy of Religion* 56 (1998): 619–41.

———. *Jerome, Chrysostom, and Friends: Essays and Translations*, Studies in Women and Religion ; Vol. 2. Lewiston, NY: Edwin Mellen Press, 1979.

———. *Women in the Early Church*. Collegeville, MN: Liturgical Press, 1990.

Coakley, Sarah. "The Eschatological Body: Gender, Transformation, and God." *Modern Theology* 16, no. 1 (2000): 61–73.

Cooper, Kate. *The Virgin and the Bride: Idealized Womanhood in Late Antiquity*. Cambridge, MA: Harvard University Press, 1996.

Cormack, Margaret. *Sacrificing the Self: Perspectives on Martyrdom and Religion*, The Religions American Academy of Religion. Oxford: Oxford University Press, 2002.

Cowan, James. *Desert Father: A Journey in the Wilderness with Saint Anthony.* Boston: Shambhala, 2004.

Cragg, Kenneth. "Jesus, Jerusalem, and Pilgrimage Today." In *Explorations in a Christian Theology of Pilgrimage*, edited by Craig G. Bartholomew and Fred Hughes, 1–16. Burlington, Vt.: Ashgate, 2004.

Dahl, Nils Alstrup. *Jesus in the Memory of the Early Church: Essays.* Minneapolis: Augsburg Pub. House, 1976.

Dahmus, John W. "A Medieval Preacher and His Sources: Johannes Nider's Use of Jacobus De Voragine." *Archivum Fratrum Praedicatorum* LVIII (1988): 123–76.

Daniélou, Jean, ed., and Herbert Musurillo, ed. *From Glory to Glory; Texts from Gregory of Nyssa's Mystical Writings.* Translated and edited by Herbert Musurillo. New York, Scribner 1961.

Delcourt, Marie. *Hermaphrodite: Myths and Rites of Bisexual Figure in Classical Antiquity.* Translated by Jennifer Nicholson. London: Studio Books, 1961.

Delehaye, Hippolyte. *The Legends of the Saints.* Portland, Ore.: Four Courts Press, 1998.

———. *The Legends of the Saints. With a Memoir of the Author.* New York: Fordham University Press, 1962.

———. *Les Légendes Hagiographiques.* Bruxelles: Société des Bollandistes, 1927.

———. *Les Origines du Culte des Martyrs.* 2. éd., rev. ed, *Subsidia Hagiographica*, 20. Bruxelles: Société des Bollandistes, 1933.

———. *The Work of the Bollandists through the Centuries.* Princeton, NJ: Princeton University Press, 1922.

De Lubac, Henri. *Medieval Exegesis.* Translated by Mark Sebanc. Grand Rapids, Mich.: W. B. Eerdmans, 1998.

———. *History and Spirit: The Understanding of Scripture According to Origen.* Translated by Anne Englund Nash. San Francisco: Ignatius Press, 2007.

DiDonato, Pietro. *The Penitent*. New York: Hawthorn, 1962.

Donovan, Kevin. "The Sanctoral Calendar." In *The Study of the Liturgy*, edited by Cheslyn Jones, Geoffrey Wainwright, Edward Yarnold, and Paul Bradshaw, 472–84. New York: Oxford University Press, 1993.

Dubay, Thomas. *And You Are Christ's: The Charism of Virginity and the Celibate Life*. San Francisco: Ignatius Press, 1987.

Duprâe, Louis K., Don E. Saliers, and John Meyendorff. *Christian Spirituality: Post–Reformation and Modern*. World Spirituality; Vol. 18. London: SCM Press, 1990.

Earl, James W. "Typology and Iconographic Style in Early Medieval Hagiography." In *Typology and English Medieval Literature*, edited by Hugh T. Keenan. New York: AMS Press, 1992.

Easton, Martha. "Pain, Torture and Death on the Huntington Library *Legenda Aurea*." In *Gender and Holiness: Men, Women and Saints in Late Medieval Europe*, edited by Sarah Salih Samantha Riches. New York: Routledge, 2002.

Elie, Paul. *The Life You Save May Be Your Own: An American Pilgrimage*. New York: Farrar, Straus and Giroux, 2003.

Elizabeth of the, Trinity. *I Have Found God: Complete Works*. Translated by Anne Englund Nash. Edited by Conrad De Meester. Centenary ed. Washington, D.C.: ICS Publications, 1984.

Elliott, Alison Goddard. *Roads to Paradise: Reading the Lives of the Early Saints*. Hanover, NH: University Press of New England, 1987.

Elm, Susanna. *Virgins of God: The Making of Asceticism in Late Antiquity*. New York: Oxford University Press, 1994.

Eschenburg, Johann Joachim. *Manual of Classical Literature*. Translated by N. W. Fiske. 2d ed. Philadelphia: Edward C. Biddle, 1847.

Ferzoco, George. "The Context of Medieval Sermon Collections on Saints." In *Preacher, Sermon and Audience in the Middle Ages*, edited by Carolyn Muessig, 279–92. Boston: Brill, 2002.

Fuller, Michael J. K. "Martyrs: Icons of Christ the Suffering Servant, Icons of Suffering Christians." *Chicago Studies* 43, no. 1 (2004): 37–47.

———. "To Edify the People of God: A New (Old) Method of Reading Medieval Hagiography." *Chicago Studies* 44, no. 3 (2005): 284–94.

Gaunt, Simon. *Gender and Genre in Medieval French Literature*. Cambridge: Cambridge University Press, 1995.

Gaylord, Alan T. "Reflections on D. W. Robertson, Jr., and 'Exegetical Criticism'." *The Chaucer Review* 40, no. 3 (2006): 311–33.

Gerould, Gordon Hall. *Saints' Legends*. Boston: Houghton Mifflin, 1916.

Gibbon, Edward. *The History of the Decline and Fall of the Roman Empire*. Edited by David Womersley. 3 vols. New York: Penguin, 1994.

Ginther, James R. *"Laudat sensum et significationem*: Robert Grosseteste on the Four Senses of Scripture." In *With Reverence for the Word: Medieval Scriptural Exegesis in Judaism, Christianity, and Islam*, edited by Jane Dammen McAuliffe, Barry D. Walfish, and Joseph W. Goering, 237–55. Oxford: Oxford University Press, 2003.

Goering, Joseph W. "An Introduction to Medieval Christian Biblical Interpretation." In *With Reverence for the Word: Medieval Scriptural Exegesis in Judaism, Christianity, and Islam*, edited by Jane Dammen McAuliffe, Barry D. Walfish, and Joseph W. Goering, 197–203. Oxford: Oxford University Press, 2003.

Goldberg, P. F. P. "Pigs and Prostitutes: Streetwalking in Comparative Perspective." In *Young Medieval Women*, edited by Katherine J. Lewis, Noel M. James, and Kim M. Phillips. Stroud/Gloucestershire, UK: Sutton Publishing Ltd., 1999.

Gravdal, Kathryn. *Ravishing Maidens: Writing Rape in Medieval French Literature and Law*, New Cultural Studies Series. Philadelphia: University of Pennsylvania Press, 1991.

Griffiths, Paul. "The Limits of Narrative Theology." In *Faith and Narrative*, edited by Keith E. Yandell, 217–36. Oxford: Oxford University Press, 2001.

———. *Religious Reading: The Place of Reading in the Practice of Religion.* New York: Oxford University Press, 1999.

Hall, Stuart G. "Women among the Early Martyrs." In *Martyrs and Martyrologies: Papers Read at the 1992 Summer Meeting and the 1993 Winter Meeting of the Ecclesiastical History Society*, edited by Diana Wood. Oxford: Published for the Ecclesiastical History Society by Blackwell Publishers, 1993.

Harvey, Susan Ashbrook. "Women in Early Byzantic Hagiography: Revising the Story." In *That Gentle Strength: Historical Perspectives on Women in Christianity*, edited by Lynda L. Coon et al. Charlottesville: University Press of Virginia, 1990.

Heffernan, Thomas J. *Sacred Biography: Saints and Their Biographers in the Middle Ages.* New York: Oxford University Press, 1988.

Hellmann, J. A. Wayne, O.F.M. Conv. "Spiritual Writing, Genres Of." In *The New Dictionary of Catholic Spirituality*, edited by Michael Downey. Collegeville, MN: The Liturgical Press, 1993.

Hennecke, Edgar, Wilhelm Schneemelcher, and R. McL. Wilson. *New Testament Apocrypha.* Translated by R. Mc. L. Wilson. 2 vols. Philadelphia: Westminster Press, 1965.

Hill, Harvey. "Review of Hippolyte Delehaye: Hagiographie Critique et Modernisme." *Theological Studies* 62, no. 4 (2001): 836–38.

Hinnebusch, William A. *The History of the Dominican Order.* 2 vols. Staten Island, NY: Alba House, 1973.

Howe, E. Margaret. "Interpretations of Paul in *the Acts of Paul and T hecla*." In *Pauline Studies: Essays Presented to Professor F. F. Bruce on His 70th Birthday*, edited by F. F. Bruce, Donald Alfred Hagner, and Murray J. Harris. Devon, UK: Paternoster Press, 1980.

Huppâe, Bernard Felix, and D. W. Robertson. *Fruyt and Chaf; Studies in Chaucer's Allegories.* Princeton, NJ: Princeton University Press, 1963.

Ignatius of Loyola. *Autobiography.* Translated by George E. Ganss, *Ignatius of Loyola: The Spiritual Exercises and Selected Works.* Classics of Western Spirituality. New York: Paulist Press, 1991.

Innes–Parker, Catherine. "Sexual Violence and the Female Reader: Symbolic 'Rape' in the Saints' Lives of the Katherine Group." *Women's Studies* 24 (1995): 205–17.

Irigaray, Luce. "Equal to Whom." In *The Postmodern God: A Theological Reader,* edited by Graham Ward, 198–213. Oxford: Blackwell, 1997.

Jameson, Fredric. *The Political Unconscious: Narrative as a Socially Symbolic Act.* Ithaca: Cornell University Press, 1981.

Jensen, Anne. *God's Self–Confident Daughters: Early Christianity and the Liberation of Women.* Translated by Jr. O. C. Dean. 1st ed. Louisville, KY: Westminster John Knox Press, 1996.

Joassart, B. *Hippolyte Delehaye: Hagiographie Critique et Modernisme.* Bruxelles: Société des Bollandistes, 2000.

John Paul II. *The Theology of the Body: Human Love in the Divine Plan.* Boston: Pauline Books & Media, 1997.

Johnson, Luke Timothy. "Imagining the World Scripture Imagines." *Modern Theology* 14, no. 2 (1998): 165–80.

Kasper, Walter. "The Unity and Multiplicity of Aspects in the Eucharist." *Communio* 12 (Summer 1985): 115–38.

Keating, James, and David M. McCarthy. "Moral Theology with the Saints." *Modern Theology* 19, no. 2 (2003): 203–18.

Kellner, Karl Adam Heinrich. *Heortology; a History of the Christian Festivals from Their Origin to the Present Day.* London: K. Paul, Trench, Trèubner & Co., Limited, 1908.

Kelly, Jamesetta, O.P. *Life and Times as Revealed in the Writings of St. Jerome Exclusive of His Letters.* Washington, D.C.: The Catholic University of America Press, 1944.

Kelly, J. N. D. *Early Christian Creeds.* New York: David McKay Company, 1972.

Kelly, Kathleen Coyne, and Marina Leslie. *Menacing Virgins: Representing Virginity in the Middle Ages and Renaissance.* Newark: University of Delaware Press, 1999.

Kim Chang–seok, Thaddeus. *Lives of 103 Martyr Saints of Korea.* Seoul, Korea: Catholic Publishing House, 1984.

Kitchen, John. *Saints' Lives and the Rhetoric of Gender: Male and Female in Merovingian Hagiography.* New York: Oxford University Press, 1998.

Kuhn, Thomas S. *The Structure of Scientific Revolutions.* 3rd ed. Chicago: University of Chicago Press, 1996.

Larson, Wendy R. "The Role of Patronage and Audience in the Cults of Sts. Margaret and Marina of Antioch." In *Gender and Holiness: Men, Women, and Saints in Late Medieval Europe*, edited by Samantha and Sarah Salih Riches. New York: Routledge, 2002.

Leclercq, Jean. *The Love of Learning and the Desire for God: A Study of Monastic Culture.* 3rd ed. New York: Fordham University Press, 1982.

Lee, Alvin A. "Old English Poetry, Mediaevel Exegesis, and Modern Criticism." In *Typology and English Medieval Literature*, edited by Hugh T. Keenen, 43–70. New York: AMS Press, 1992.

Lewis, Katherine J. *The Cult of St Katherine of Alexandria in Late Medieval England.* Woodbridge, Suffolk: Boydell Press, 2000.

———. "The Life of St Margaret of Antioch in Late Medieval England: A Gendered Reading." In *Gender and Christian Religion: Papers Read at the 1996 Summer Meeting and the 1997 Winter Meeting of* the Ecclesiastical History Society, edited by R. N. Swanson, 129–42. Rochester, NY: Boydell Press, 1998.

——. "Model Girls? Virgin–Martyrs and the Training of Young Women in Late Medieval England." In *Young Medieval Women*, edited by Katherine J. Lewis, Noel M. James, and Kim M. Phillips. Stroud/Gloucestershire, UK: Sutton Publishing Ltd., 1999.

Lewis, Katherine J., Noel M. James, and Kim M. Phillips. *Young Medieval Women*. Stroud/Gloucestershire, UK: Sutton Publishing Ltd., 1999.

Liere, Frans van. "The Literal Sense of the Books of Samuel and Kings; from Andrew of St. Victor to Nicholas of Lyra." In *Nicholas of Lyra: The Senses of Scripture*, edited by Philip D. W. Krey and Lesley Smith, 59–81. Boston: Brill, 2000.

Lifshitz, Felice. "Beyond Positivism and Genre: 'Hagiographical' Texts as Historical Narrative." *Viator* 25 (1994): 95–113.

Likoudis, James. "Patroness of Purity—St. Maria Goretti, Virgin and Martyr." *Lay Witness* 4, no. 4 (2002): 22–23, 51.

Lupton, Julia Reinhard. *Afterlives of the Saints: Hagiography, Typology, and Renaissance Literature*. Stanford, CA: Stanford University Press, 1996.

Lysaught, M. Therese. "Witnessing Christ in Their Bodies: Martyrs and Ascetics as Doxological Disciples." *Annual of the Society of Christian Ethics* 20 (2000): 239–62.

MacConastair, Alfred. *Lily of the Marshes: The Story of Maria Goretti*. New York: MacMilian, 1951.

Maier, Gerhard. *Biblica Hermeneutics*. Translated by Robert W. Yarbrough. Wheaton, IL: Crossway Books, 1994.

Martimort, Aimè Georges. *The Church at Prayer: An Introduction to the Liturgy*. New ed., 4 vols. Collegeville, MN: Liturgical Press, 1985.

Mayeski, Marie Anne. "New Voices in the Tradition: Medieval Hagiography Revisited." *Theological Studies* 63 (2002): 690–710.

McGinn, Bernard, John Meyendorff, and Jean Leclercq. *Christian Spirituality: Origins to the Twelfth Century*. New York: Crossroad, 1985.

McGinn, Bernard, John Meyendorff, and Jill Raitt. *Christian Spirituality: High Middle Ages and Reformation*. New York: Crossroad, 1987.

McGuckin, John Anthony. "Martyr Devotion in the Alexandrain School: Origen to Athanasius." In *Martyrs and Martyrologies: Papers Read at the 1993 Summer Meeting and the 1993 Winter Meeting of the Ecclesiastical History Society*, edited by Diana Wood. Oxford: Published for the Ecclesiastical History Society by Blackwell Publishers, 2002.

McInerney, Maud Burnett. *Eloquent Virgins from Thecla to Joan of Arc*. New York: Palgrave Macmillan, 2003.

———. *I Am No Woman but a Maid: The Rhetoric of Virginity from Thecla to Joan of Arc*. New York: Palgrave, 2002.

———. "Rhetoric, Power, and Integrity in the Passion of the Virgin Martyr." In *Menacing Virgins: Representing Virginity in the Middle Ages and Renaissance*, edited by Kathleen Coyne Kelly and Marina Leslie, 50–70. Newark: University of Delaware Press, 1999.

McNamara, Jo Ann. "Sexual Equality and the Cult of Virginity in Early Christian Thought." *Feminist Studies* 3, no. 3/4 (1976).

———. *Sisters in Arms: Catholic Nuns through Two Millennia*. Cambridge, MA: Harvard University Press, 1996.

Meltzer, Francoise. "Re–Embodying: Virginity Secularized." In *God, the Gift and Postmodernism*, edited by John D. Caputo and Michael J. Scanlon, 260–81. Bloomington: Indiana University Press, 1999.

Meredith, Anthony. *Gregory of Nyssa, The Early Church Fathers*. London: New York: Routledge, 1999.

Metz, Johannes Baptist, Edward Schillebeeckx, and Marcus Lefébure. *Martyrdom Today*. New York: Seabury Press, 1983.

Milbank, John. *Theology and Social Theory: Beyond Secular Reason, Sign-posts in Theology*. Oxford, UK; Cambridge, MA: Blackwell, 1993.

———. *The Word Made Strange: Theology, Language, Culture*. Cambridge, MA: Blackwell, 1997.

Moody, Margaret Anne. *A Natural Passion: A Study of the Novels of Samuel Richardson* Oxford: Clarendon Press, 1974.

———. "Introduction," in Samuel Richardson, *Pamela*. Edited by Peter Sabor. New York: Penguin, 1981.

Morrill, Bruce T. *Anamnesis as Dangerous Memory: Political and Liturgical Theology in Dialogue*. Collegeville, MN: Liturgical Press, 2000.

Murphy, William F., Jr. "Mystery before Morality in Delubac's *Medieval Exegesis.*" *Josephinum Journal of Theology* 10, no. 1 (2003): 132–39.

Musurillo, Herbert. *The Acts of the Christian Martyrs*. Oxford: Clarendon Press, 1972.

Noble, Paul R. "The *Sensus Literalis*: Jowett, Childs, and Barr." *The Journal of Theological Studies* 44, no. Part I (1993): 1–23.

Norris, Kathleen. *Amazing Grace: A Vocabulary of Faith*. New York: Riverhead Books, 1998.

———. *The Cloister Walk*. New York: Riverhead Books, 1996.

———. *Dakota: A Spiritual Geography*. New York: Ticknor & Fields, 1993.

Nugent, Sister M. Rosamond. *Portrait of the Consecrated Woman in Greek Christian Literature of the First Four Centuries*. Washington, D.C.: The Catholic University of America Press, 1941.

O'Loughlin, Thomas. "Introduction." In *Hippolyte Delehaye, the Legends of the Saints*, v–xix. Portland, OR: Four Courts Press, 1998.

Ommeslaeghe, Flor van. "The *Acta Sanctorum* and *Bollandist Methodology.*" In *The Byzantine Saint: University of Birmingham Fourteen-*

the Spring Symposium of Byzantine Studies, edited by Sergei Hackel. London: Fellowship of St. Alban and St. Sergius, 1981.

Owst, G. R. *Literature and the Pulpit in Medieval England*. New York: Barnes and Noble, 1961.

Percy, Walker. "Another Message in the Bottle." In *Signposts in a Strange Land*, edited by Patrick H. Samway. New York: Farrar, Straus, and Giroux, 1991.

Perham, Michael. *The Communion of Saints: An Examination of the Place of the Christian Dead in the Belief, Worship, and Calendars of the Church, Alcuin Club Collections*. London: Published for the Alcuin Club by S.P.C.K., 1980.

Perrin, Joseph–Marie, O.P. *La Virginité Chrétienne*. Translated by Katherine Gordon. Westminster, MD: Newman Press, 1956.

Poage, Godfrey, C.P. *In Garments All Red*. Chicago: Paluch Publications, 1950.

Potter, Giselle. *Lucy's Eyes and Margaret's Dragon: The Lives of the Virgin Saints*. San Francisco: Chronicle Books, 1997.

Ratzinger, Joseph. *Jesus of Nazareth*. New York: Doubleday, 2007.

Reno, R. R. "The Bible Inside and Out." *First Things* 182 (April, 2008), 13–15.

Riches, Samantha J. E. "St. George as a Male Virgin Martyr." In *Gender and Holiness: Men, Women and Saints in Late Medieval Europe*, edited by Samantha Riches and Sarah Salih, 65–85. New York: Routledge, 2002.

Riches, Samantha, and Sarah Salih. *Gender and Holiness: Men, Women, and Saints in Late Medieval Europe*. New York: Routledge, 2002.

Robertson, D. W. *Essays in Medieval Culture*. Princeton, NJ: Princeton University Press, 1980.

————. *A Preface to Chaucer; Studies in Medieval Perspectives.* Princeton, NJ: Princeton University Press, 1962.

————. "Translator's Introduction." In Augustine, *On Christian Doctrine.* Upper Saddle River, NJ: Prentice Hall, 1958.

Robertson, D. W., and Bernard Felix Huppâe. *Piers Plowman and Scriptural Tradition.* Princeton, NJ: Princeton University Press, 1951.

Rorem, Paul. "The Uplifting Spirituality of Pseudo–Dionysius." In *Christian Spirituality: Origins to the Twelfth Century,* edited by Bernard McGinn, John Meyendorff and Jean Leclercq, 132–51. New York: Crossroads, 1985.

Ruether, Rosemary Radford. "Misogynism and Virginal Feminism in the Fathers of the Church." In *Women in Early Christianity,* edited by David M. Scholer, 262–95. New York: Garland, 1993.

Salih, Sarah. *Versions of Virginity in Late Medieval England.* Woodbridge, Suffolk, UK; Rochester, NY: D. S. Brewer, 2001.

Salisbury, Joyce E. *Church Fathers, Independent Virgins.* London: New York: Verso, 1991.

Schèussler Fiorenza, Elisabeth, and M. Shawn Copeland. *Violence against Women.* Maryknoll, NY: Orbis Books, 1994.

Schulenburg, Jane Tibbetts. *Forgetful of Their Sex: Female Sanctity and Society, ca. 500–1100.* Chicago: University of Chicago Press, 1998.

Seybolt, Robert Francis. "The *Legenda Aurea,* Bible, and *Historia Scholastica.*" *Speculum* 21 (1946): 339–42.

Shaw, Teresa Marie. *The "Burden of the Flesh:" Fasting and the Female Body in Early Christian Ascetic Theory.* Ann Arbor, Mich.: University Microfilms International, 1992.

Shearman, Rev. Thomas, C.S.S.R. *The Veneration of Saint Agnes, V.M.: Mary's Waiting Maid.* New York: Benzinger Brothers, 1908.

Sheridan, Mark, ed. *Genesis 12–50, Old Testament*, Vol. 2, Ancient Christian Commentary on Scripture. Downers Grove, Ill.: InterVarsity Press, 2001.

Shore, Sally Rieger, and Elizabeth A. Clark. *John Chrysostom: On Virginity; against Remarriage, Studies in Women and Religion. V. 9.* Lewiston, NY: Edwin Mellen Press, 1983.

Simonetti, Manlio, ed. *Matthew 1–13, New Testament* Vol.1a. Ancient Christian Commentary on Scripture. Downers Grove, Ill.: InterVarsity Press, 2001.

Simpson, Jane. "Women and Aceticism Inthe Fourth Century: A Question of Interpretation." In *Women in Early Christianity*, edited by David M. Scholer. New York: Garland Publishing, 1993.

Smalley, Beryl. *The Study of the Bible in the Middle Ages.* Notre Dame, IN: University of Notre Dame Press, 1978.

Smith, Right Rev. Abbot. *Life of Saint Agnes, Virgin and Martyr.* London: Burns Oates and Washbourne, 1906.

Stenzel, Eileen J. "Maria Goretti: Rape and the Politics of Sainthood." In *Violence against Women*, edited by Elisabeth Schussler Fiorenza and M. Shawn Copeland. Maryknoll, NY: Orbis Press, 1994.

Straw, Carole. "A Very Special Death:' Christian Martyrdom in Its Classical Context." In *Sacrificing the Self: Perspectives on Martyrdom and Religion*, edited by Margaret Cormal. Oxford: Oxford University Press, 2002.

Suelzer, Alexa, S.P., and John S. Kselman, S.S. "Modern Old Testament Criticism." In *The New Jerome Biblical Commentary*, 1113–29. Englewood Cliffs, NJ: Prentice Hall, 1990.

Sullivan, Patricia A. "A Reinterpretation of Invocation and Intercession of the Saints." *Theological Studies* 66 (2005): 381–400.

Sullivan, Randall. *The Miracle Detective.* New York: Atlantic Monthly Press, 2004.

Swanson, R. N., ed. *Gender and Christian Religion: Papers Read at the 1996 Summer Meeting and the 1997 Winter Meeting of the Ecclesiastical History Society, Studies in Church History*, 34. Woodbridge, Suffolk, UK; Rochester, NY: Published for the Ecclesiastical History Society by the Boydell Press, 1998.

Sweetman, Robert. "Beryl Smalley, Thomas of Cantimpré, and the Performative Reading of Scripture." In *With Reverence for the Word: Medieval Scriptural Exegesis in Judaism, Christianity, and Islam*, edited by Jane Dammen McAuliffe, Barry D. Walfish, and Joseph W. Goering. Oxford: Oxford University Press, 2003.

Swidler, Leonard. *Aufklärung Catholicism 1780–1850: Liturgical and Other Reforms in the Catholic Aufklärung*. Edited by Stephen D. Crites. Vol. 17, American Academy of Religion: Studies in Religion. Missoula, Mont.: Scholars Press, 1978.

Synan, Edward. "The Four 'Senses' and Four Exegetes." In *With Reverence for the Word: Medieval Scriptural Exegesis in Judaism, Christianity, and Islam*, edited by Jane Dammen McAuliffe, Barry D. Walfish, and Joseph W. Goering. Oxford: Oxford University Press, 2003.

Talar, C.J.T. "Hippolyte Delehaye: Hagiographie Critique et Modernisme." *Catholic Historical Review* 87, no. 3 (2001): 520–22.

Tarantini, Nadia. *Processo Goretti, I Libri Dell'unità*. Rome: L'Unità, 1994.

Thaden, Robert H. von, Jr. "Glorify God in Your Body: The Redemptive Role of the Body in Early Christian Ascetic Literature." *Cistercian Studies Quarterly* 38, no. 2 (2003): 191–209.

Thérèse of Lisieux. *General Correspondence*. Translated by John Clarke. 2 vols. Washington, D.C.: Institute of Carmelite Studies, 1982.

———. *The Poetry of Thérèse of Lisieux*. Translated by Donald Kinney. Washington, D.C.: ICS Publications, 1996.

———. *The Story of a Soul: A New Translation*. Translated by Robert J. Edmonson. Complete and unabridged ed., *Living Library*. Brewster, MA: Paraclete Press, 2006.

Thurston, Herbert J., and Donald Attwater. *Butler's Lives of the Saints*. Complete ed., 4 vols. Allen, Tex.: Christian Classics, 1995.

Tugwell, Simon. *Early Dominicans: Selected Writings*, The Classics of Western Spirituality. New York: Paulist Press, 1982.

Vagaggini, Cipriano. *The Flesh, Instrument of Salvation; a Theology of the Human Body*. Staten Island, NY: Alba House, 1969.

van Hooff, Anton J. L. *From Autothanasia to Suicide: Self-Killing in Classical Antiquity*. London; New York: Routledge, 1990.

Vernon, Mark. "'I Am Not What I Am'—Foucault, Christian Asceticism and a 'Way out' of Sexuality." In *Religion and Culture: Michel Foucault*, edited by Jeremy R. Carrette, 199–209. New York: Routledge, 1999.

Visser, Margaret. *The Geometry of Love: Space, Time, Mystery, and Meaning in an Ordinary Church*. New York: North Point Press, 2000.

Waldstein, Michael. "The Project of a New English Translation of John Paul II's *Theology of the Body* on Its 20th and 25th Anniversary." *Communio* XXXI, no. 2 (2004): 345–51.

Ward, Graham. *Cities of God, Radical Orthodoxy*. London: Routledge, 2000.

Weinstein, Donald, and Rudolph M. Bell. *Saints and Society: The Two Worlds of Western Christendom, 1000–1700*. Chicago: University of Chicago Press, 1982.

West, Christopher. *Theology of the Body Explained: A Commentary on John Paul II's "Gospel of the Body"*. Boston: Pauline Books & Media, 2003.

Wilken, Robert Louis. *The Christians as the Romans Saw Them*. New Haven: Yale University Press, 1984.

Winstead, Karen A. *Chaste Passions: Medieval English Virgin Martyr Legends*. Ithaca: Cornell University Press, 2000.

———. *Virgin Martyrs: Legends of Sainthood in Late Medieval England.* Ithaca: Cornell University Press, 1997.

Wright, N. T. "The Letter to the Romans." In *The New Interpreter's Bible,* vol. 10, 395–770. Nashville: Abingdon Press, 2002).

Wogan–Browne, Jocelyn. *Saints' Lives and Women's Literary Culture c. 1150–1300: Virginity and Its Authorizations.* New York: Oxford University Press, 2001.

Woodward, Kenneth L. *Making Saints: How the Catholic Church Determines Who Becomes a Saint, Who Doesn't, and Why.* New York: Simon and Schuster, 1996.

Wyschogrod, Edith. *Saints and Postmodernism: Revisioning Moral Philosophy, Religion and Postmodernism.* Chicago: University of Chicago Press, 1990.

Yoshikawa, Naoë Kukita. "Veneration of Virgin Martyrs in Margery Kempe's Meditation: Influence of the Sarum Liturgy and Hagiography." In *Writing Religious Women: Female Spiritual and Textual Practices in Late Medieval England,* edited by Denis Renevey and Christiania Whitehead. Toronto: University of Toronto Press, 2000.

Young, Kathleen Z. "The Imperishable Virginity of Saint Maria Goretti." In *Violence against Women: The Bloody Footprints,* edited by Pauline Bart and Eilen Geil Moran. Newbury Park, CA: Sage, 1993.

Young, Robin Darling. "Recent Interpretations of Early Christian Asceticism." *Thomist* 54 (1990): 123–40.

Index